Stories of Childhood

Stories of Childhood
Shifting Agendas of Child Concern

REX STAINTON ROGERS
WENDY STAINTON ROGERS

New York London Toronto Sydney Tokyo Singapore

First published 1992 by
Harvester Wheatsheaf
Campus 400, Maylands Avenue
Hemel Hempstead
Hertfordshire, HP2 7EZ
A division of
Simon & Schuster International Group

Figure 9.1, from *Psychology of Adolescence*, Seventh Edition,
by Luella Cole and Irma Nelson Hall, copyright © 1970
by Holt, Rinehart and Winston Inc., reprinted by permission
of the publisher.

Typeset in 10 on 12pt Times and Optima
by Inforum, Rowlands Castle, Hants.

Printed and bound in Great Britain by
BPCC Wheatons Ltd, Exeter

British Library Cataloguing in Publication Data

A catalogue record for this book is available from
the British Library

ISBN 0-7450-1229-9 (hbk)
ISBN 0-7450-1230-2 (pbk)

1 2 3 4 5   96 95 94 93 92

Contents

Caveat   vii

Acknowledgements   viii

Chapter 1   Looking forward to a story   1

Chapter 2   Deconstructing and reconstructing child knowledge   15

Chapter 3   Deconstructing the alembic myth   37

Chapter 4   Kidstory: Reconsidering histories of childhood   54

Chapter 5   Telling stories of child concern   70

Chapter 6   Modern times and great dictators: A genealogy
             of developmentalism   85

Chapter 7   Being had: Biosociology and the production of
             new children   105

Chapter 8   A minority group: The condition of childhood   123

Chapter 9   Childhood's end – overlords and underlings   141

Chapter 10   Rearing its ugly head: Children and sexuality   162

Chapter 11   On our own doorsteps and beyond our
             own backyards: Concern about concern   188

v

vi   *Contents*

Bibliography   198

Index   215

Caveat

Persons attempting to find a motive in this narrative will be prosecuted; persons attempting to find a moral will be banished; persons attempting to find a plot in it will be shot.

Mark Twain, preface to *Huckleberry Finn*, 1884

Our business is children. Do you believe in children?

Graham Swift, *Waterland* 1984, p. 136.

Acknowledgements

There is more than the standard authorial cliché to our acknowledging here the many otherwise hidden hands and voices who have made this book possible – there is necessity. As a text upon texts it could not be otherwise. In writing a story about stories, there can be little more space for hubris than lies in the claim to have raised plagiarism to the craft of montage. In doing that, we have drawn upon tales that: go back to the beginnings of our biographical myths in our own childhoods; ran through the raconteurs (successful and otherwise) who impinged upon our lives and taught us our crafts; permeated the times of our deconstruction and reconstruction; and continue in the collective badinage of the Beryl Curt Fan Club, the Sarnia Institute, the Barcelona Brigade, and the Mount Effort Foundation. Special thanks and love are due to those young people who most constructed us and childhood in the flux and fragmentation of our lives: Amanda, Bekki and Karina.

Finally, we also acknowledge (as solicitors are wont to discourse):

the effingphone;

the British Psychological Society;

our cats;

the Charity and Second Hand Book Shops from Oxford to Ojai, and the kindness of students, friends and strangers who found books for us;

indulgences;

Stan and Dee, in their various manifestations;

the policy of the University of Reading which denies its staff any system of sabbatical leave;

the pressures in the self-financing units of the Open University which makes the taking of statutory study leave a virtual impossibility;

The Children Act 1989;

Rae Smith's kindness, diligence and infinite patience;

The Department of Health; and

one very sick hard disc and ACS who mended it (a bit).

Without them this book could never have been written in a postmodern condition.

'Thamesis', Long Wittenham, 1992

1

Looking forward to a story

The tale of Nema

Are you sitting comfortably? Then we'll begin One November evening
the police are called to a shopping mall by the security staff, to deal with
someone they found naked in the women's lavatories at closing time.
Wrapped in a blanket and taken to the local police station, 'Nema' (as
she gets called by the policewoman who takes charge of the case – it
means 'nobody'), appears to have totally lost her memory. She makes no
protest when examined by a police doctor, who can find no obvious
injuries or possible identifying marks (scars, tattoos, dental work). The
doctor is puzzled, and cannot put Nema's age more exactly than somewhere between fourteen and twenty, though she does discover that
Nema has borne a child. Dressed in borrowed clothes, Nema sits passively in an interview room while the doctor, the policewoman and the
duty inspector debate what to do. With no positive evidence that she is a
minor, and faced with someone 'behaving abnormally' they decide to
have her admitted to a hospital. Two hours later, Nema is in a psychiatric ward where she rapidly seems to 'come to' and starts talking to the
staff in unaccented English. While her amnesia over her personal life
remains total, she proves to have an excellent memory and a voracious
appetite both for conversation and for books, magazines, television and
radio. Within a week, she seems as normal as anyone could be with a
personal memory that is only seven days old and built out of what was
available within the psychiatric unit. Trial trips into the outside world
reveal that Nema deals extremely competently with ordinary city life –
situations such as shopping, sight-seeing, ordering a meal, using a taxi.
Tested by a clinical psychologist she proves to have an IQ of 148 (on an
adult scale), although once the testing is over, Nema gets into a complex
argument with the psychologist about whether it makes any sense to try
to determine the relative contributions of 'nature' and 'nurture' to

1

measured intelligence! However, problems of a quite unexpected kind soon start to emerge. On her next trip out, Nema wants to take in a movie and a trip to the pub afterwards. She is also beginning to talk about life after her discharge. Sexual relationships, friends, holidays, cars, jobs are starting to occupy her mind.

Interlude: What shall we do with Nema?   In British society (and much the same would be true in any industrialised country) the only way of resolving the dilemmas 'Nema' raises would be to legally create an identity, and most crucial of all, an age for her. Only then could we know what to do about her. But how would that be decided? Medically, her body could reasonably be that of any female between fourteen and twenty (depending on 'hereditary' and 'environmental' factors – which, of course, are unknown). Socially, she seems extremely competent, but a lot would depend on her background (nothing exceptional in a city-reared young person but pretty exceptional if she came from an isolated rural community). There is every sign that she is very bright (although how bright would depend on how old she is – she would be judged more intelligent as a fourteen year old 'school girl' than as a twenty year old university student).

Every clue we try to use turns out to be ambiguous. What about her baby? Nema might be a 'gym-slip mother', or she might have been married for several years. Either way, this would affect who stood as her 'next of kin'. Even if the one thing she could remember was that she was married, it really wouldn't help that much, as she might have married abroad, and in some countries that is possible by the age of fourteen. By the by, in all of this we may have misread her 'sexual identity' altogether. Remember, her knowledge of herself only came from television, papers and from conversations in the psychiatric unit, but prior to her amnesia she might have been a lesbian – for all we know the child was conceived by Artificial Insemination by Donor (AID). Medical and social science, in short, cannot give us an unambiguous answer, and neither can we reason one out from 'common sense'. In the end, we seem to be left with a moral decision – how to do what's right in a situation of uncertainty. Immediately, we come up against a problem – who makes the decision? Do we turn to an 'expert' like a judge or a psychiatrist? Or do we let Nema decide for herself? One solution favoured by moral philosophers would be to ask: who would I want making the decision if I were Nema? The usual answer is *me*, I would want to make that choice. But if Nema chose to be fourteen, would we see that as a sensible choice, or might we find ourselves thinking that anyone who made that choice wasn't rational enough to make it! The notion of 'Nema's choice' also raises awkward questions about actual fourteen year olds. If we were to allow Nema to choose to be an adult when she might 'really' only be fourteen, why not allow other fourteen year olds so to decide? There is also another cloud in this already murky atmosphere – Nema's child. Suppose this infant were to turn up as mysteriously as Nema. We have every reason to think that the life chances of a baby born to a fourteen year old in our society are inferior to those born to a twenty year old. Surely then the decision is not Nema's alone but needs must take into account the welfare of her child?

The tale continued: With a pinch of chaos   With everyone around her in a state of self-engendered alopecia, Nema herself breaks down under the strain. She blurts out that she is in fact a young woman social history student from the twenty-fourth century. Her amnesia was hypnotically induced prior to her transportation back to our time. These facts were never supposed to emerge under the time travel code of non-interference, but so bizarre did she find our world that her mind-block failed. Now she cannot seem to stop herself talking to her psychiatrist. What emerges in an amazing two-hour recording, prior to her mysterious and instantaneous disappearance, goes roughly like this:

Nema's narrative   Although age doesn't have the meaning in her society that it does in ours, Nema is in fact thirteen. Changes in environmental conditions, diet and health care mean that most young people reach full reproductive sexual maturity at around the age of ten. In her world, quite a lot of young people decide to have children in their early teens, as they are by then physically capable and economically and socially independent. The Equal Rights Law of 2030 substituted the notion of competence for what were previously age-related entitlements. For example, to drive a fuel-cell car all anyone has to do is to pass their driving test – there is no minimum age. The same is true over work. Even before they can talk, children learn to operate touch-controlled robotics, and once they can talk they get into using voice-controlled devices. The result is that appliances that are too dangerous for the young in our world (like cookers) are rendered safe for them in Nema's world. Innovations like new public transport systems and 'clever' cars which can sense possible hazards mean that children of three or four can safely go out alone. Technologies that make learning 'fun' and technologies that make the difficult easy (e.g. robots and waldoes for heavy lifting and very fine work like electronics) mean that by around seven most young people can run their lives more or less independently from adults. Of course, their wrist communicators mean they can always call for help if they need it, and enable tabs to be kept on the very young ones. Nobody has to work for longer than around fifteen hours a week to be financially independent, and once someone has the competence to do a job they have the right to do it. Rates of pay are based on a good job done and cannot by law vary by age. There are still skills which take a 'long time' to develop, but this tends to mean that they are acquired by the age of twelve rather than at nine.

Nema's own life story was fairly typical. When young, her mother had a wide network of friends who by seven or eight tended to move from one person's home to another as a 'gang'. They would save money to take trips together staying in hostels and learning about the world as they went along. Clannish and mutually supportive to one's 'gang' rather than to 'olders', the peer group was the normal place to which to turn for affection and care. Over time 'gangs' tended to slowly intermingle and change. Both single sex and mixed gangs existed, and most young people had access to each kind of network. They were places to 'experiment' with interpersonal and sexual relationships (tackling HIV infection was vaguely remembered history at most). There was no 'age of consent' as such; any 'competent' had the right to 'body control' over sex as over anything else. 'Olders' had little to do with the young and little power over them – one result was that physical and sexual abuse across age was virtually unknown. At fourteen, with a lot of both 'homo' and 'hetero' sexual experience behind her (although people didn't tend to make those discriminations), Nema's mother decided she was ready to 'move on', relaxed her ovulation control and became pregnant. She took a residential unit in a family cooperative. Some moved in as couples but Nema's mother had no wish to bond.

Nema was born with the aid of a natal-chine which her mother used to control the birth and deliver the baby. Several members of the 'gang' (including Nema's father as it happened) were around to give encouragement. Although a lot of baby care could be automated, most parents chose to 'do it by hand' in small groups. These groups often attracted 'gangers' and non-parents who also got involved with the infants. By eighteen months, Nema herself was running simple sound-touch machines with other youngsters in the cooperative play area. She tended to go home to her mother to sleep, but also spent time in other units. Her electronic tag meant that both her mother and her other carers always knew where she was. By four Nema had learned to use her interactive terminal to create a 'total personal environment' of furnishings, sound, pictures, and food and drinks dispenser. She could play complex computer-based games with her friends and access libraries of entertainments and information. An interest in electronic music composition brought her first real earnings and by six she was in a 'group'. 'Gang' music was very popular and her income plus her success at 'second go' at the competency test (popularly called the DeTag) meant that by seven she acquired the right to control over her own communicator. Now she could 'switch off' if she chose, enter contracts and be made to pay if she over-spent on her credit card! 'Switch off' parties were 'the thing' and, although olders tended to worry, the major 'dangers' tended to be a temporary deafness from the music and the odd recreational drug hang-over! Nema managed both. Although 'sex play' was common, her first serious sexual involvements came, as they did for most young people, later during the time of moving between gangs. A far greater 'passion' for her at this time was a powerful interest in twentieth century history.

Although public transport was good, getting your own fuel-cell car was an important symbolic event. Nema passed her test at ten and at eleven joined a small group working and driving their way along the old trans-Asia highway through Russia to Japan. Treks like this were often the prelude to 'settling down' and she did indeed use the trip to get pregnant. However, back home, she once again developed 'itchy feet' and so she left her baby with a friend-carer and got work with the Time Travel Institute. Work as a vocation was very much left to 'olders' (anyone past sixteen) but there was no age-bar as such, and so at thir-teen she got involved in the 'twentieth century project'. At this point, the psychiatrist had the presence of mind to suspect that such a 'youth culture' must have a down-side. Was it just being young that caused Nema to say so little about 'olders'? Sadly, just at the moment when he was exploring what Nema meant by saying that her mother had never found a vocation and 'elected out' at 26, Nema disappeared back to the future.

Amen to that

Developed into a short story or a novel, Nema's tale would become a speculative or science fiction story. Not, you may feel, one destined to be a best seller! The characters are cardboard, the situation grossly con-trived. But in the hands of a specialist in the genre – a Doris Lessing, or an Ursula Le Guin – speculative fiction can both entertain us and chal-lenge our taken-for-granted assumptions (see, for example, Haraway, 1991; Katz *et al.* 1977; Lefanu, 1988). We merely set our sights on the latter, by creating a parable which would make the notion of childhood strange and problematic. First we challenged the idea that childhood is a 'thing' that can be known and defined objectively. Within the confines of our story, it cannot and consequently, all our laws, rules and expecta-tions are suddenly rendered problematic. We then constructed an alter-native account of being young, something sufficiently familiar in its technology, social dynamics and culture to be a credible extrapolation of the present. The only development about which we have serious doubts is time travel, but every science fiction is allowed one 'impossible'. Finding Nema's world in any way believable does not demand that you like or approve of it – our own reactions are highly ambiguous. But any glimmering of plausibility that it has for you serves our purpose – to set the stage for rendering other stories about children less able to be 'taken for granted'. Not every story, of course, has a specific gloss overtly attached – something that tells us where to look and what to look for. Few are so patently didactically located. But every story, we want to argue, gains its meaning through a socially sedimented 'contract' for engaging our regard. One does not just read it, but give it a reading. The reader is drawn into a social process between peruser and perused, which involves the direction and manipulation of attention, both within the material text and between the text and meta-textual understandings. Nema's childhood is a 'fiction', but then so (taking examples from western cultural experience) are many of the textualised childhoods we know best: Jesus; St Joan; Katy; Tom Sawyer; George from the Famous Five or Todd from *Neighbours*. Furthermore, while being social fictions, they are also social facts, in the sense of being parts of the fabric from which our understandings of children are woven. In writing Nema as a deconstructive tale, we have deliberately added a key-thread to this tapestry of texts of childhood, something which, if pulled, threatens the stability of the whole cloth. That whole cloth contains not only fictive children but what we may think of as real ones: Victorian 'kids int' mill'; child prostitutes in Bangkok; the child subjects of developmental psychology; the 'children within' uncovered through psychoanalysis; ourselves when young – even our own children!

About such children, it might seem there are real 'facts' that can be established, a 'true knowledge' to be told. This is what we want to challenge. 'Facts', we maintain, are also stories – ones gleaned from our own particular viewpoint and ones that, if believed, help to bring into being the thing we think we see. For example, we may consider 'facts' such as the finding that child prostitutes and some sexually abused children (as does Nema) show 'precocious' sexual development. However, such a 'fact' can only be 'discovered' within certain social regards, in which there is a prescribed appropriate or normal age to be a thing called sexual – it is this which *creates* the reality of 'precocious sexual development', which may then be variously represented, for example: as a personal *pathology* to be treated; a social *problem* to be tackled; or a 'turn on' to be savoured.

The basic thesis of this book then, is very simple. We live in a world which is produced through stories – stories that we are told, stories that we recount and stories that we create. Children are drawn into this web of understandings (and their material consequences) from the moment (whenever our stories tell us that is) they enter the social world. Our stories of childhood largely pre-date and create the locations in the social world for each child, yet each child adds to the story-stock in making their place their own. All this is giving the term 'story' a much broader span than does its day-to-day definition, but it is one which can be found in many recent, post-structuralist treatments of the idea of text (e.g. Shotter and Gergen, 1989). What we are attempting to develop in this book from the initial seed of Nema's story fits very much into such a redefinition.

The polytextualist's tale

Nema's story is a particular kind of narrative device – a thought experiment used to trouble understanding. The more general proposition that all we have to work with are 'Stories of Childhood', a multiplicity of texts on the young, is meant as a radical challenge. Hence, we call the approach we are taking *critical polytextualism*. The term is new, and runs an obvious risk of generating a 'Oh no, not more jargon' reaction. However, the alternative strategy, that of overlaying a claim to a pre-existing title, with an already established agenda, is even more problematic. Like Nema then, critical polytextualism is to start out unknown.

No approach, obviously, emerges *de novo*, there is always a tale to tell about where it came from. For us that tale begins with the emergence of the idea that features of the social world, like children, can be 'knowledged' i.e. can be formally accounted for in a nomic project of discovery. We are talking here of the emergence of the human sciences under the social-economic revolution of industrial capitalism, the era of what is now commonly called modernism (see, for example, Ibañez 1991). The human sciences were grounded upon a post-Enlightenment agenda of human betterment through the application of scientific reason. Within them, the pursuit of uncovering the mysteries of human development became a central feature of that humanistic project, drawing in particular on the pivotal discipline of psychology, the claimed intercept of the knowledging of the biological and of the social. Its product was developmentalism – a set of theories about the way children are socialised, and grow up to be fully fledged members of the adult community. So powerful did this project become, that until very recently, virtually everybody working in any area concerned with children assumed that the findings and the theories of developmentalism were *the* knowledges, and the *only* knowledges worth considering. This concentration of power over knowledge was made possible by the claim of its proponents to operate within a unique discipline for the pursuit of truth – the discipline of science. As one well-regarded developmentalist has written, in advocating the scientific approach to knowledge about the child:

> The intent here is not to criticise the early social philosophers. In fact, contemporary developmentalists (and today's children) are indebted to these men [sic] for helping to modify the ways in which society thought about and treated its young. However, so-called great minds may produce miserable ideas on occasion, and if poorly conceived notions have implications for the way human beings are to be treated, it behooves us to discover these erroneous assumptions before they harm anyone. The scientific method then, is a value that helps to protect the scientific community and society at large from flawed reasoning. The protection comes from the practice of evaluating the merits of various theoretical pronouncements against the objective record, rather than simply relying on the academic, political, or social credibility of the theorist. (Shaffer, 1985, p. 15)

In our own academic apprenticeship as psychologists, this was the venture and the worldview within which both of us were trained, and from which we began our academic careers. But we no longer subscribe to this viewpoint. Something fundamental has changed for us, something that has brought us to reject its epistemological status as 'truth'. In Chapter 3 we will spell out why we think the developmentalist account of socialisation is both so captivating *and* so necessary to challenge. But even before we start, we can illustrate an obvious and immediate problem – that developmentalism simply misses the point that *all* children are 'manufactured' (as Nema was 'manufactured') via a process of representational labour. Like it or not Nema, for all her lack of flesh-and-blood reality as a 'real child', is now in your stock of possible children. If we can manufacture a child, simply by writing a story, in what way is she different from other children in your archive of stories about children? This question is woven throughout the chapters which follow, but it is the core of the case we make here. It is also a question which is only made possible by the worlds of knowledge that came into being under modernism. Critique can only be a predicated craft, and modernism provides a mosaic of predications – for, of course, modernism is not a singularity but a *Zeitgeist* – both it, and the project of the human sciences, have always been pluralised.

The notion of *Zeitgeist* – 'the spirit of an age' – itself, of course, needs to be recognised as a narrative device. We are not claiming that some mysterious causal force entered western culture around 1770. Society did not, as if by magic, suddenly start to create knowledge – knowledge creation had gone on for as long as there was anything to be known. All societies are socially productive, manufacturing both a material social world of concrete products, and manufacturing the persons who live in them. What makes our modern (i.e. western industrialised) world unique, justifying it being seen as a special epoch (i.e modernity), is its pace and focus of innovation – the change of gear that has given to the 1990s the products and identities of 200 years of late capitalism. To take just a few examples: Christmas-card Christmas and computers; penicillin and play-groups; television and theories of socialisation – all are products of the last two centuries, and each has played a part in creating new stories of childhood.

It is, of course, within the diverse productivity of modernism that the roots of disillusion lie. The more a system is based upon change, upon planned obsolescence and unplanned consequences, the less lawful, the less predictable it becomes. In this context, knowledge is no less susceptible to vagaries of 'market forces' than any other commodity. It is not just that whole systems of knowledging the social have shown the same potential to become as defunct as has Pan-Am, the very project itself can be seen to only have the power to address that which has already past with tools fashioned in that past (cf. Gergen, 1973). The optimism of the project of control through knowledge has eventually culminated in a profound climate of doubt. Hence, we are not just writing here about problems emergent in the specific academic area of socialisation, or of a personal loss of faith in our human science roots, but of an intellectual climate of doubt over the continued viability of modernistic thought itself. A number of commentators have analysed this ennui, and the critical perspectives it has collected around itself – which usually get encompassed under the label postmodernism (see Featherstone, 1988, Harvey, 1989, for overviews of the various debates about and challenges to this concept). However construed, this climate of criticism is based upon doubt, in particular about the way in which, under modernism, certain analytics and analyses of the human condition have come to dominate thought. The specific targets of this critique are the very grand theories or meta-narratives that are the hallmark of modernity (cf. Ibañez, 1991, Vattimo, 1988). In place of their promise of consensus, clarification and ultimate control, postmodernism, as a critical position, draws attention to local, particular understandings over whose competing and contradictory claims no grand order can (or indeed should) be imposed.

There are certainly good reasons for thinking that our dilemmatics (cf. Billig *et al.*, 1988) over young people are moving in that direction. This shift is proving painful because it questions claims to certainty and hence warrants to power. The old certainties are gone. In their place we are offered a tenuous, uncomfortable, traction of contradictory ideas and stories, vying one against the other. Thus, whether or not the label 'postmodern' is attached to that doubt is less the issue than that our agendas of child concern – as all other agendas – demand new conceptual frameworks within which to argue them. This need arises precisely because, for most ordinary people (and, to a perhaps surprising extent, in expert circles too) the only intellectual tools available to address childhood are fashioned out of conceptions which were produced within modernism. That is as true of 'critical' perspectives such as Marxism and feminism as it is of orthodox human science itself. All are grounded upon analytics that originally serviced the needs of the architects of knowledge of nineteenth century society.

Of course, it is not possible to make sense of the 'now' without reference to the past it implies – the archived conceptions of earlier epistemologies cannot just be bracketed off as though they never existed. Postmodern ideas about the young are, in certain ways, predicated upon how modernistic society came to know: what children are; what constitutes childhood; and what ought to be done about children. Modernistic approaches too would accept that there can be no taking of a fresh new canvas on which to paint unique new contemporary portrayals and polities as though a history of art did not exist. What the postmodernistic approach adds is that neither can such new portrayals deny the critique of art history. Every new conception is inevitably crafted out of some reading of what we have inherited from this past. This requires a looking backwards, then, as well as a looking forwards. A major task must be to trouble those taken-for-granted ideas to which we are heirs; both to deconstruct and dislocate them and their purposes from their own story of their genesis.

Further, as Rorty (1989) argues, challenge to a dominant order of knowledge is not a matter of individual acts of redescription (even, perhaps, if they are as powerful as those of Wittgenstein, e.g. 1953). Rather, what is required is the incorporation of redescription after redescription into a new collective language out of which language, new (previously 'unthinkable') actions come into being, and old (previously 'taken for granted') actions become undo-able. To put this into 'new language', deconstruction is a precondition of reconstruction (although these terms are deliberately slippery: cf. Armistead, 1974, Parker and Shotter, 1990).

From one voice this new postmodernist analysis has been couched in terms of a specific denial that science offers a transcendent path to truth, above and separate from social life and social process (cf. Brannigan, 1981, Knorr-Cetina, 1981, Kuhn, 1970, Mulkay, 1991). From another, it has emerged out of more general assertions of received (i.e. neo-Marxist) and emergent (e.g. feminist) critiques of knowledge, power and oppression (cf. Armistead, 1974, Kitzinger, 1987). Debts are clearly also owed to the cultural analytics of Berger and Luckmann, Douglass, Foucault and Habermas (see Wuthnow *et al.*, 1984, for a review). Berger and Luckmann (1967) were particularly instrumental in popularising '*the sociology of knowledge*' and in giving a telling descriptive (if not always theoretically rigorous) account of *the social construction of reality*. To Foucault has been due not only part of the critical conceptual vocabulary (most notably notions of *discourse* and *gaze*) but a unique approach to social history which has had a major influence upon understandings of the issues such as disease, sexuality and punishment. Indeed, compared to the Anglo-centrism of, say, 'scientific' psychology, one of the notable features of critical social writing in English has been the obvious openness to inputs from continental (notably French) authors. There has been a revived interest in the writings of the neo-Marxist social theorist Gramsci (e.g. 1971), the proto semiotician Saussure (e.g. 1974) and the linguistic-structuralist psychoanalyst Lacan (e.g. 1977). Most recently, the post-empiricist, post-structuralist flavour of critical thinking has been further stimulated by the postmodernist linguistic philosophy of, for example, Baudrillard (e.g. 1983), Derrida (e.g. 1982), Jameson (e.g. 1984), Lyotard (e.g. 1984) and Rorty (e.g. 1989).

Social constructionism

The weaving of some version of this story has been a common feature of the texts of 'critical' analysts within psychology. Within that discipline, these have been most consistently brought together under the label *social constructionism*. Social constructionism itself is a wide church (cf. Gergen, 1982, Harré, 1983, Shotter, 1984), whose members differ considerably in the degree to which they 'radicalise' their agenda. To the extent that there is a common corpus to the radical agenda, it is probably best summarised in the tasks outlined by Kitzinger (1987):

1. Deconstructing the ideological content of received knowledge.
2. Deconstructing the mystique surrounding social science itself.
3. Recognising and appreciating the reflexivity of its own theory.
4. Offering radically different definitions of the world, which startle, shock, anger or surprise in a way that focuses critical awareness on the taken-for-granted.
5. Engaging in overt and explicit moral and political evaluation of the alternative constructions presented, not passing them off as value free.
(Condensed and modified from the original)

Even in offering this summary, we are aware of problems. The list does not precis social constructionism, but is itself a textual device, a rhetorical agenda, one that can (and should) be read in a variety of ways and itself be subject to reflexive challenge. If there is a 'best way into' social constructionism, it is by acquiring by doing, a discipline of *not* looking at things self-evidently but rather deconstructively as socially constituted reifications, produced by human endeavour, to serve particular ideological or rhetorical purposes. Some concepts of the child and childhood almost seem to invite deconstruction, often because their purely local range of use is pretty self-evident. Their ability to appear both real things *and* cultural products is as good a starting point as any for constructing social construction. It is easy to see, for example, 'dyslexia' as socially constructed via literacy. Where there is no written material in a culture and there are no psychologists, there can be no dyslexia – it simply cannot exist. Similarly, 'school phobia' – if there were no schools, then there could be no 'school phobia'. These examples also establish that the notion of social construction implies very much more than 'all in the mind' or 'conditioned into us'. The ways children are construed not only determine the way we make sense of them *as* children, but also inform and reflect social and economic policies towards children and the institutions that manage children. This point has been argued cogently by Denzin (1977):

> Children, then are political products – they are created, defined, and acted on in political terms . . . Caught . . . without a clear spokesman [sic] for their collective position, children find themselves talked about, legislated over, tested and scrutinized by society's experts: by its social workers, educational psychologists, probation officials, judges, courts, teachers, sociologists, anthropologists, politicians and psychiatrists. (p. 16)

Furthermore, these construals are never static. Indeed, in our contemporary version of modernity, they are in constant flux, subject to legislative changes and more socially mediated agents for change (such as the current concern over 'ritual abuse'). Hoyles, in his justification to the title for his book *Changing Childhood* (1979), expresses this idea thus:

> [It] is meant to *indicate both that childhood changes historically*, which could be seen merely as a passive event, and that it can be changed by people's actions. In other words, it is a political issue and one which, though it seems strange to need to mention it, involves children's actions as well as those of adults. (p. 1)

Our book and its argument draw upon social constructionist, post-structuralist and postmodern critiques of the developmentalist project – we regard 'childhood' as constructed through its telling.

Conte et raconteur: **The moments of critical polytextualism**

In proposing as a radical challenge that there can only be stories and storytellers of childhood, we are, in effect, arguing that, say, 'Mark

Twain' and 'Sigmund Freud' are both best treated as narrators and narratives of the young. To adopt a critical polytextualist approach is to doubt the viability of making distinctions between the human sciences, and the arts and humanities. If the project of the human sciences can be doubted, so too can their claim to a special location for the knowledging of the young. Although individual social constructionists have shown a willingness to cast human development under a narrative gaze (e.g. Gergen and Gergen, 1986), social constructionism *per se* remains very much the property of the human sciences, postmodernism that of the arts and humanities. There is now certainly a movement for cross-talk, for the fostering of intertextuality but it is firmly placed at the level of confederation or commonwealth: 'The present series – Inquiries in Social Construction – is designed to furnish a forum for expression of what many find an exciting dialogue taking place through the social sciences and humanities' (Shotter and Gergen, 1989, p. ix).

We worry that notions of dialogue presuppose and precondition a continuing series of binary divides (a notion that is highly modernistic). Hence, in arguing for a transdisciplinary approach, we have sought a term which dissolves duality. Hence, our adoption of the rubric critical polytextualism. The expression also serves the purpose of giving textuality an explicit rather than tacit centrality. Our focus on the narrative root metaphor is not itself new. Sarbin (1986) for example, has proposed the constitution of a narrative psychology noting that: 'Long before there was a science of psychology, men and women created and told stories about the efforts of human beings to make sense of their problematic worlds . . . story making, story telling and story comprehension are fundamental conceptions for a revived psychology' (p. vii). However, as with social constructionism, we see here a reluctance to let go of the discipline base itself. In our view, narrative is not best seen as a rejuvenating elixir for a senescent psychology, but as a catalyst to speed up the reaction into the new. What is needed, we believe, is 'a general turn against theory and towards narrative' (Rorty, 1989, p. xvi). There is a final rationale for the approach we are taking, and it is one which our topic of childhood powerfully brings home. Both social constructionism (cf. Parker, 1989) and postmodernism (cf. Shusterman, 1988) are open to the criticism of either 'relativising' ethics or dissolving them. While we share with them radical doubt as to whether morality can be foundationed (i.e. we operate as though it must be approached as local and contingent) we also feel that our book *Stories of Childhood* cannot proceed in an ethical limbo. Over this (although we would worry about the label) we would like to import Rorty's idea of the 'liberal ironist', who include among their 'ungroundable desires their own hope that suffering may be diminished, that the humiliation of human beings by other human beings may cease' (1989, p. xv). The young deserve no less than such a desire of those whose cast stories upon them. All we would caution is that such a position cannot be other *than* storied, it can only be held in doubt. Rorty's dream of a 'liberal utopia: one in which ironism . . . is universal' *(ibid.)* needs to taken as a rhetorical device. But his call to see 'other human beings as "one of us" ' (p. xvi) has particular power when applied to young, who are so much (not least under developmentalism) seen as *other*. When Rorty says: 'This is a task not for theory but for genres such as ethnography, the journalist's report, the comic book, the docudrama and, especially the novel' *(ibid.)*, the need to explore the place for an ironic transdiscipline seems manifest. What critical polytextualism attempts to rescue from absolute deconstruction is the notion that, at the moment of telling stories (i.e. being social), we are both seeking in the 'reader' and creating for ourselves, small, local, pockets of plausibility. As Shotter and Gergen rightly observe 'any social practice entails the people involved in it treating both themselves and one another in particular kinds of ways' (1989, p. xi). What we would add is that what practices our stories make credible, and what they make incredible, *matters*. That concern, of course, cannot escape its time and its place, cannot escape doubt. If there are no absolute methods and, hence, no answers, a doubting concern is all the ethic that is possible. It is also all that is needed, the minimal condition for trying.

2

Deconstructing and reconstructing child knowledge

In this chapter we will begin to address the question of how children and childhood have been and are 'knowledged into being'. This is an issue which will concern us throughout the book – in particular in the subsequent four chapters, which will focus upon specific discursive domains within which children and childhood are ontologically and epistemologically constituted: developmentalism; social history; child welfare; and, child science. Here, our concern will be primarily upon problematising conceptualisations of the child and childhood in the ordinary domain of commonsense knowledge. By such ordinary understandings, we refer to those regimes of knowledge-generation common within western, scientised, late-modern culture. What, for that space and place, are children and childhoods as they are perceived and understood in everyday experience? How, in other words, do we discover what children are like, what it is like to be a child, and what 'being a child' means?

Trying to find out about children – The empirical wild goose chase

In this first section we will examine the ways that can be used to 'find out about children', and challenge some of the assumptions that have been made that characteristics of childhood can be empirically established. For this we need to start with the basics.

Accounts of the child

For most of us schooled under modernism, knowledge is not just something to be passively received, but to be sought out. Our expectation,

15

built up over countless school projects, has been to learn by investigation and exploration. So, having bought that story and acquired its craft skills, in any quest to find out about children, probably our first move would be to consult the non-fiction section in a library. What we would find there would not be children, of course, but various texts, containing *accounts of* children: what the writers hold to be known about children. The same, of course, would be true once we move from library study to more active forms of research. When we ask people (whether 'experts' or parents) for information concerning children, once more it would not be children, *per se*, about which we learned, but these people's *accounts of* children. Even if we were to ask the 'real' experts (i.e. children), all they would be able to offer us would be their accounts of being a child or experiencing childhood. Whatever we did, the text or the story would always somehow 'get in the way' when we tried to address the object of our study.

Testing credulity

One of the strongest stories of modernism is that if we want to know about something, what we need to do is to measure it. Guided by just this recipe, psychologists have tried to crack the limitations of 'mere anecdotal evidence' by employing more direct means of investigation, such as using psychometric tests (e.g. to measure the child's IQ). The idea of testing children is now not just accessible to but taken for granted by many in our society – even our politicians! However, the very term 'test' is a give-away. Just like a simple classroom test, the psychologist's IQ test proves to be no more than a highly regularised way of asking questions. The answers cannot tell us anything *directly* about any quality of the child, only about a hypothetical property of the child (e.g. the child's 'intelligence') as constructed by the designer of the test. But whereas the typical school test makes no greater claim than to be assessing last week's work (a situated and contingent evaluation of performance by question and answer) psychological tests are purported to achieve *direct* indicators of fixed and stable properties ('traits') of the child. Even in terms of simple commonsense, they have not – the child still eludes them. Indeed, the futility of the endeavour is shown by the shift from the 11 plus examination to SATs (Standard Attainment Tests). While they use very similar techniques, in the former, it was *the child's* capabilities which were being evaluated; in the latter, it is *the school's*. But, of course, neither tells us anything direct, either about the child, or the school. If anything, they tell us about the ideology within which each test has been conceived.

The production and use of psychometric tests none the less beguiled child psychologists (and their customers) into assuming that they were directly testing what children are like. Yet patently all such tests achieve is to replace one unknown (the child) with a set of other unknowns (the 'traits' out of which the child is assumed to be constituted). As soon as we probe further to find out about what 'intelligence' (or any other trait e.g. of personality) means, we find that they too are 'subjects' about which texts are written (i.e. accounts *of* intelligence, accounts *of* personality). There is nothing but regress here, nothing to prevent the movement further and further away from the original matter of concern – finding out about children. Basically what this means is that there is no device for inquisiting the child, which can tell us what a child is like. Of course we can use things like tape measures to quantify some qualities of the child as *embodied*. A tape measure will tell us that children tend to be shorter than adults (i.e. possess the childhood syndromic sign of dwarfism, as lampooned by Smoller (1985) in 'The Etiology and Treatment of Childhood'). But no psychometric device provides direct knowledge about what a child is 'made of' *psychologically* speaking. There is no more a thing 'intelligence' behind performance on IQ tests than there are things like 'slugs and snails and puppy dog's tails' behind a performance of juvenile masculinity.

Observing children

Another widely accepted approach to knowledge would be the prescription to simply go and *look at* children (as countless wildlife programmes have shown ethologists doing with less naked little apes). This was where child psychology began in the early nineteenth century. However, even in its sophisticated modern forms, this is no more a solution to the search for a 'direct line' to the child than trait testing, because there can be no such thing as a *simple* or *objective* observation. To be able to observe children, we have to use an account of children to tell us where to look and what to look at. At the very least, this is needed to tell us what to include in and what to exclude from our looking – cut off toe-nails, clothes, toys, verbal outputs, products like drawings, a whole bedroom, a network of friends, a game with others, and so on. To be able to see a 'child' requires that we already know what (for our purposes) a child *is*. In any act of observation we have to decide such questions as whether a child's diary is a part of them or not. Furthermore, our *a priori* assumptions about where to look (and not to look) also implies a moral account. To try to look at a child's diary, just as to try to look at a child in the bath, draws observer and child into a moral relationship. There is another serious problem which surrounds finding-out-by-looking:

'I'm looking at the children.'

'Why, what are they doing?'

To observe is to imply that which is observed is engaged in some meaningful 'action' or inaction. More specifically, it implies that the observer is making the claim that they are an instrument for detecting and indexing that doing:

'Getting up to no good.'

or

'Initiating cooperative play.'

This is only to find out what children are doing in a very limited and restricted sense – that which the observer, using a given understanding of children, *says* they are doing. What is revealed are not what children *are* doing, but the observer's accounting vocabularies and working hypotheses. These may well agree from one observer to another because they are common cultural property, but that does not make them real. Precisely the same understandings can be obtained without any *actual* children being there at all! It would work just as well if the dialogue we just looked at was from an animated cartoon or from a book or a radio play, where there would quite patently have been no flesh and blood children, but only the observer's understandings (and the creator's ability to signify them). It may often be useful, of course, to check whether our meanings are consensual social understandings. The children we observe may agree with our interpretation (they may say that they were indeed 'being naughty' or 'starting a game with my friends'). Or they may not, and then we may wish to negotiate meanings (or impose them). But consensual, negotiated or imposed, accounts of action are *only* true or false by virtue of further cultural reference. Looked at in this way, all we can ever discover by observation are the subjects of some kind of representation.

Knowledging children into being

For orthodox developmental psychologists, this elusiveness of the 'real' proves the source of terminal problems in both theory and explanatory power. From a critical polytextualist perspective it is not a problem at all (except as it might be studied in the social history of ideas about the child) but *the way things are*. We discover that which we bring into being, there is nothing else we can do (Woolgar, 1988a). Once the shift is made to an endeavour which seeks merely to discover what we can learn from examining the different stories that are told about children, then the very source of difficulty becomes the subject of study. Thus liberated, we are free to ask what we consider to be more legitimate (and answerable) questions of social epistemology, concerning the nature of child knowledge itself. Mulkay (1991) argues that once the unproductive search for validity is called off, two questions in particular emerge as salient. For every story that knowledges children, we need to ask either (or both): what is the function of the story (i.e. can be *done* with it?); and/or, what ideology is the story peddling (i.e. what can be warranted by it?). It is these two questions we will pursue in the remainder of this chapter's exploration of child knowledge.

Storying childhood

One of the deep paradoxes of finding out about childhood lies in our having been children (and therefore having 'known' childhood at first-hand), and yet having no direct – only represented – access to that experience. Stories are all that we can ever have – stories compounded out of: the stories we re-tell to ourselves and to others (our childhood memories); stories our caregivers and others (like siblings and childhood friends) told to and tell us; and stories woven around the odd artefact we have retained (like family photos, pictures we drew or a battered teddy still sitting in the cupboard). These autobiographical stories have been produced in ways which define and construct for us what it is that is significant about childhood. Thus, in a western culture based in modernism, we may, for example, expect to find personality resemblances to our parents, precisely because our culture tells us stories about the way character is transmitted from one generation to the next. Those conversant within the 'psy' complex (see Ingelby, 1985, Rose, 1985) may well also weave their stories around the factors that twentieth century psychology has made critical (such as the impact of our relationship with our mother, the effects of our potty training, etc.). It is worth remembering that many of these matters are likely to prove absent or mere trivial asides in accounts drawn from history or from other cultures.

We will be concerned here with an examination of those stories of childhood and children from our own (as authors) cultural archive of fictional accounts. Once we began to look for these, we were at first surprised how commonplace and pervasive they are in late modern culture. Compared both to our culture's own historical past and to the demographics of cultures elsewhere in the world, ours is an ageing society – actual flesh-and-blood children make up an atypically small proportion of our population. Yet this by no means implies that our culture lacks interest in stories about children. On the contrary, we frenziedly consume children as commodities, along with everything else. Representations of children, visual as well as textual, permeate our daily lives, providing accounts which pass in and out of young and old alike. We all participate in this discursive flux, within which our mutual identities are constituted. Childhood fictions flourish in areas like advertising and greetings cards, no less than in more developed narrative forms such as novels, movies and television programmes. Some fictions are aimed specifically at children (such as the evergreen but diminishingly 'coloured' tales of Enid Blyton), some at Walt Disney's ubiquitous 'family audience', and some at a distinctly adult consumer, such as Nabokov's *Lolita* (1980). Others (from Godfrey's 1907 analysis of children in Shakespeare's plays to Rustin and Rustin (1987)) have reviewed portrayals of children in fiction, and we do not intend to recapitulate their work here. Rather, we will concentrate more specifically on the ways fictionalised children and childhoods have been used as emblematics for constructing child knowledge.

An author-ity on children

Before, however, we can begin to look at these, we need to make a small foray into some features of postmodern analysis which are critical in this context, particularly the notion of author and text. Within postmodern literary theory, these have been strenuously deconstructed (Barthes, 1977 is generally seen as the key text, but a more readable and extremely amusing treatment is offered by Mulkay, 1989). Put simply, the relationship between text (this term is used for any signifying device, including not only things like advertising slogans and movie scripts, but photographs and paintings) and author is not seen as a one-way process of individual authorial production which is passively received by the reader, but a much more complex nexus of interactions – not just between text, author and observer, but also the whole cultural milieu within which texts are made and read. The text is thus seen as a *cultural* product, with the author and the reader as vehicles for cultural construction. What is salient is how the text is *read* – itself a deeply culturally mediated activity. We do not, in this analysis, passively read text, but *give* it a reading. Another person, in another situation, would inevitably give it a different reading. Sometimes this is conveyed by the concept of the 'worldview' within which an individual or group operates but more generally the idea used is that of 'gaze' (a term originated by Foucault, 1970). Gaze is more local and contingent, and implies the capacity to shift. For example, we can think, say, of the way child abuse might be made sense of differently through a 'medical gaze' compared with how it would be understood through an 'ethical gaze'. As we will see in the next three chapters, considerable difficulties are raised by questions of gaze for those who try to draw up grand stories from studies in the social anthropology and social history of childhood. However, the problem is particularly acute in those stories of childhoods that are an obligatory part of any twentieth century narrative and condition all our dealings with the young.

A gazing game

Probably the best way to convey a sense of what all this entails is to work with a specific example. So we will begin our exploration of the storying of child knowledge with the 'autobiographic' tale 'Child of the Deep' by Joan Lowell (1929) which deals with her childhood and youth as the Captain's daughter aboard a succession of sailing ships in the Pacific around the turn of the century. It is an intriguing yarn, both a challenging account of female identity and an exemplary representation of Romantic childhood (a concept we will deal with later in this chapter). As such, and for the purposes used here, it is reported as told. Questions as to its power as an absolute 'objective record' are inappropriate within a postmodern analysis, and are unnecessary for our purposes. Indeed the author begins her preface with the disposal: 'Hundreds of people have written me asking if my story is really true.' In the sections that follow, we have taken selected incidents from Joan's experiential pastiche in order both to highlight them as features of Romantic childhood and to suggest how they may be apperceived under a different vocabulary and gaze, of a childhood 'lost' to various forms of abuse. We have used the device of adding contemporary headings to the sections we have selected in order to make clear the different reading a more recent gaze brings into being.

Cycles of deprivation? Joan's family background itself sets the stage. Her father, known in the book simply as 'Father', was himself an abandoned child brought up by Jesuits in Australia. In a by-now familiar story, he found running away to sea at the age of ten a preferable alternative to their care. At eighteen as a deckhand on a clipper visiting San Francisco he met a fourteen year old doctor's daughter, Emmaline Trask Lowell, with whom he eloped. Joan was their eleventh and last child (four of whom had died in the span of two years). At eleven months Joan was taken away from her land-bound mother to sea by her father (by then a Captain), determined that she should survive. Unable to thrive on the patent baby food of the day, her life was saved early on by the ship's sailmaker 'Stitches', who procured a milch-goat and became her 'nurse and guardian' for all her sea-board life.

Emotional and physical abuse?   Joan wrote of her father: 'He never in my life fondled me affectionately – never held me and kissed me as fathers of little girls ashore do' (p. 95). His expressions of affection were 'a good hard kick or a hearty punch on the back such as men use to express emotion to each other' (p. 96). In the book Joan also reported a number of incidents in which she was physically punished. As she observed, 'Father believed in the wisdom of a rope's end to my southernmost portion to discipline me' *(ibid.)*. She recounted such matters as part of the ongoing narrative, without attaching to them any special gloss. The text is not an account of experience of privation. As she noted in the introduction 'I learned to hand reef and steer, spit a curve in the wind, take lickings without squawking, cuss for four minutes without repeating a word, and to live life as it came to me and not just talk about it.'

Sexual abuse?   For all that, Joan was both the Captain's daughter, and the subject of a thought-out regime of protection: 'I wore overalls all my life on board the ship. Father dressed me as a boy in fairness to the crew and for my protection. He did everything in his power to keep them and me from becoming conscious of my sex' (p. 26). Nevertheless, she reported that at the age of seven she experienced a sexual assault by a Swedish sailor, Alex Svenson:

> I forgot the candy and turned to run. He made a noise in his throat like a snarling animal and grabbed me up in his arms. His face was against mine. He forced my mouth open and kissed me – horribly! One of his arms nearly crushed my ribs and his big paws patted over my body as I kicked and struggled. With his face against mine I could not make a sound. I managed to get my fingers in his eyes and tried to push them in. Suddenly he dropped me . . . (pp. 58–9)

Quite what Joan's readers in 1929 (lacking our contemporary constructions of sexual abuse) made of this we can only speculate – it is an unusually blunt account for that period, of what would have probably been called at that time 'molestation'. It gains a great deal of plausibility to a modern reader because some of Joan's reactions fit our received wisdom, although everything is not what it, at first, may seem. Subsequent to the assault, she reported that she did not want to be touched by her obviously concerned father, neither would she explain why she was upset. But here the resonance breaks down, for she explains her silence not as a reaction to fear or guilt (as conventional wisdom would now view it), but in terms of her own internalisation of sailors' rules. Not 'squealing' but getting even was the accepted prescription on the boat, and through that, she noted: 'I licked Fear'. Her later revenge on Svenson left him with a broken jaw, confined to the brig and subsequently discharged in disgrace. When Joan says of the incident, 'what followed did more to shape my character and life than anything I can remember' (p. 55) she is referring not to the assault *per se*, or any sexual trauma or psychological sequellae, but to the way following 'the code of the sea' enabled her to win through.

Crossing the line into ritual abuse?   Later in this chapter, we will briefly explore the recently-emergent concept of ritual abuse, not least because of its unreflective definition of 'ritual'. As we shall see in the following quotation, in Joan's story-world, Poseidon not Britannia 'ruled the waves', as she described of her initiation on crossing the equator:

> 'Smack' on my behind went a plank, heaved by the ape-like Slops. It was such a hard wack that I opened my mouth to holler, and no sooner had I done that than Neptune stuck a big gob of lather in the wide aperture of my jaws . . . [F]rom head to foot they soaked me in that lather. The tar in it matted my long thick hair together and stuck my eye-lashes so that I couldn't open my eyes . . . Overboard I went, tied by the same rope that had been on Slops. The salt water has the interesting effect of making tar stick so that it will not come off without turpentine. When they thought I had had enough of a bath, they hauled me out and sprinkled me with some dried copra. (pp. 91–2)

Romance of the sea?   Just as with *Tom Sawyer* (cf. Chapter 9), the ending of this tale of romantic childhood reflects on the dilemma of childhood's end itself. Joan Lowell used two mechanisms: a first, unconsummated romance followed (significantly for those who like psychodynamic readings) by a shipwrecking fire. The latter left Father a broken man but for Joan her swim to safety was the culmination of her shipboard training – the successful test of a 'regular sailor'.

In *Child of the Deep* Joan Lowell presented herself as a 'survivor' – not in the self-conscious and often psychoanalytically informed discourse to be found today in accounts of 'abuse survivors' – but in an older sense, as a full-blown hero of a romantic saga. Stories of the 'romance of the sea' and 'messing about in boats' had for the nineteenth and much of the earlier part of this century somewhat the same symbolic journey dynamics as contemporary road movies though few had young women as their central hero figure. For us it has served a different discursive function. Her story compellingly illustrates how a text, given a contemporary reading, can enable us to explore issues like the politics of 'child abuse' in ways we would miss by only looking at the current academic literature in this field or at proselytising leaflets and reports. However informative in themselves those texts may be, they tell a story powerfully entrapped within the 'taken for granteds' of their own gazes, within them we cannot easily escape the singular reading they demand. By contrast, what Joan's story does for us is suggest there can be (because there once can be seen as having been) more than just a self-serving, reactionary, antithesis to the child concern promoted by the 'child savers' of the nineteenth century (like Barnardo) and child protectionists of today. Through Joan's story it is at least possible to contemplate the possibility that sexual assault may not be *the* worst and most damaging trauma that a child may have to face; that 'surviving' sexual assault *can* be achieved without a panoply of therapeutic intervention; that subjecting a child to a fairly barbaric ritual need not, in itself, be harmful (and indeed may be experienced as a route to 'belonging'); and that a childhood wanting affection and permeated with physical violence may none the less be accounted for (as Joan does) as happy and empowering. In other words, to make these suggestions via the reading of an historically differently located text makes it possible to raise certain possibilities which would otherwise expose us to the accusation that we are condoning sexual abuse, or belittling its impact. The power of the narrative voice, in these contexts, enables us to raise just the form of radical doubt proposed in Chapter 1. The illustration of *Child of the Deep* provides a device to convey this argument, more compellingly than any dry academic analysis could do. It is irrelevant whether the story is a 'true autobiography' of Joan Lowell's childhood, or a 'fictional story' told by Joan Lowell, or somebody else, as an adult (or some intermingling of both). Indeed, from a postmodern analysis, we cannot determine a significant difference between these possibilities. What matters is that at a different time, under different conditions, the story *was* told in the way it was. What matters is that parts of the story are now shocking, because they perturbate our present day 'taken for granted' wisdom about childhood experiences. By shocking, they make us think – they introduce the kind of radical doubt upon which postmodernist analysis more generally, and critical polytextualist analysis more specifically are founded. By so doubting, our thinking can be liberated from the chimerical 'realities' that fetter our perception of the here and now.

Stories of childhood

We will progress then, with the remainder of this chapter, by looking at some of the ways that childhood has been storied; how childhood, in ordinary, everyday, commonsense terms, has been knowledged into being for us by the world of fiction. We will begin with adult authors' stories of the way children become (and are made into) adults and their treatments of the qualities of childhood which differentiate it from adulthood.

Stories of growing up

Literature has a long tradition of cultural melodramatisation about the way children become adults, dating back at least to classical Greece and the tragedy of *Oedipus Rex*. All centre around the interface between nature and nurture (a theme we will develop in Chapter 3), in terms of the contribution each makes to the emergent adult and how they inter- act. In most utopian literature, the bulk of the leavening power is placed in the environment – this is how the young of Skinner's *Walden Two* (1948) are conditioned to become members of a idealised collective. By contrast, in H.G. Well's dystopian *The Time Machine* (1927) it is the dominance of genetics which splits the human race into those who de- velop into the cannibalistic Morlocks, and those who become the effete Eloi. Fiction makers, in other words, cannot but draw upon the cultural resources available to them. They are part of a collectivity in which, reactionary social theorists (like Galton, 1883) accredit great power to nature; revolutionary ones (like Robert Owen, cf. Butt and Clarke, 1973) accredit great power to nurture. It is a collectivity furthermore, in which to philosophise the human condition, requires that the moral quality of both nature and nurture need to be addressed. Indeed, from its very inception, the boundaries between fact and fiction in modernism (although formally established) have, in practice been crossed with im- punity. Rousseau, for example, inserted into the puritan cultural archive the antithetical child who is born with goodness, subsequently corrupted by the environment – and did so by the same route of the didactic novel that Skinner was to adopt over a century and a half later.

Such narratively instantiated children and childhoods have also pro- vided story-tellers over the centuries with the ability to speculate about the dynamics of the nature/nurture mix. In fairy tales and myths, the classic forms are the changeling, the child whose environment is switched at birth and the hybrid, the child of mixed human and non-human (e.g. animal, fairy) parentage. A typical modernistic version of the first location occurs in Twain's *The Prince and the Pauper* (1891) and of the second in Duffy's *Gor Saga* (1983). Explicit moral lessons have been drawn around the representation of the rescued child (a young person of poor stock transformed by the impact of superior environment): Dickens' *Great*

Expectations (1862) and Kingsley's *The Water Babies* (1853) both tap into this vein. The vagaries of genetics are also held to occasionally produce good material out of bad. To identify such individuals and foster their potential by a changed environment was the role assigned to intelligence testing. Hence the representation of the scholarship child and the ideology behind selection for grammar schools: a typification employed in the movie *The Guineapig*. The dynamics of nature and nurture have also been held to produce some down-side effects – the bright child twisted by bad environment, of which Dickens' 'Artful Dodger' in *Oliver Twist* (1837) is a good example.

Much the same story-telling devices enable the hackneyed but still powerful tension of the boy Jesus who transcended his career as trainee carpenter and became recognised as the Son of God. The fundamentals of what we will come on to argue is a socialisation myth – the separability of our inbuilt nature from our enculturation milieu – inhabit stories as culturally and historically diverse as: Romulus and Remus; Moses; *The Wild Boy of Aveyron*; Burroughs' *Tarzan*; and Heinlein's *Stranger in a Strange Land*; and, of course, those of our comic book heroes like Superman. Near the beginning of the movie version of *Superman*, he, as a young (but fully human-appearing) alien, is found as a baby by a couple and adopted by them. What makes the Superman myth particularly instructive is what it must take for granted in order for the story to work: only a child, conveniently abandoned for the purposes of the story, will do. Only a child can fit the requirements of being culturally empty (thus with the potential to absorb culture) while, at the same time, be pre-primed with inbuilt special powers waiting to unfold. Consequently, when these powers become manifest (e.g. as in our first experience as an audience of the young Superman's amazing strength) that too seems 'only to be expected'. As a result, Superman's claims to be 'just human' are called into doubt – a tension requiring him acquiring a mundane alter-ego, the slightly bumbling figure of Clark Kent. Another and more recent mythic theme is the creation of the person who isn't quite a person: the robot, the cyborg, the android and the super-computer. In the movie *2001: A Space Odyssey* the intelligent computer HAL is shown first as a friendly if rather Spock-like (the reference is to *Star Trek* not *Baby Care*!) co-traveller in space, sharing in the social life of the astronauts. HAL then experiences the very human condition of 'going mad' and becoming homicidal, killing first the freeze-sleep crew and then one of the two active astronauts. Finally when the crazed HAL is overcome and being decommissioned by the remaining spacer, he is shown regressing back to a kind of childhood in which he recites, in reverse sequence, his programming right back to the nursery-rhyme stage. Such stories as *Superman* and *2001* reinforce our culturally sedimented understandings of how childhood 'works'. In the next chapter we will examine the idea that in doing so, they have imbued the similar story told by developmental psychology of how childhood 'works': with a plausibility we find very difficult to resist.

Stories of the nature of childhood – the age of innocence?

Possibly the most pervasive quality of childhood which is dealt with in fiction is that of innocence, and its opposites – variously (and paradoxically) sinfulness, knowingness, ignorance, savagery and animality. One feature of modernism is the way it has formalised such binary tensions into useful sites for later critical analysis – for example, in the use of the 'madonna/whore' polarities for understanding representations of women (cf., for example, Walkerdine, 1990). Within the use of such oppositional significations, the juxtaposition of qualities of childhood provide a paradigm case, woven into the western cultural fabrication of the child since at least medieval times. Within Christianity these are evident in the opposing concepts of child as either born spotless and pure, or the child born sullied by 'original sin' (both, according to Shahar, traceable to the writings of St Augustine Hippo; Shahar 1990). These thematics have been used in a number of different ways in fiction, including: romantic stories of childhood innocence; stories of childhood innocence depraved, betrayed and lost; or of the sinful child redeemed, or of innocence saved or secured.

The image of the child as born sullied by original sin, which drew upon Aristotelian notions overlaid with the Judeo-Christian 'Adam and Eve' story, pervaded the Middle Ages, and was strong within puritanism, and later evangelical perceptions of the child. In this children were seen as naturally wicked, and hence needing redemption – a theme which has not lost its power today, as told, for example, in Winterson's *Oranges Are Not the Only Fruit* (1987). The romanticisation of childhood (see Hendrick, 1990, pp. 37–9) was told by the valorising of the opposite pole, as a time of natural purity and innocence began to be storied within the Enlightenment. Probably the foundational telling of this story is Rousseau's *Emile* (1762), but it was widely propagated by such poets as Blake, Coleridge and Wordsworth, persisted through a plethora of Victorian sentimentalist writing into the early twentieth century in such works as Barrie's *Peter Pan* and Ransome's *Swallows and Amazons*, and finds its natural home today in Disney Studios.

By contrast, from the alleged medieval European custom of burying children alive in the foundations of buildings, to the sacrificial virgin iconographised for all time in Stravinsky's ballet *Sacre du Printemps*, stories of childhood innocence corrupted by occult and alien cults and religions abound. It is clear, for example, from accounts of the Witch Hunts in both Britain (e.g. Trail and Mann, 1904) and the United States (e.g. Morison, 1972) that there is strong evidence that children feature both as the victims of witchcraft and as among those punished for witchcraft, often encompassing within their gaze sexualisation of the child as a specific means of contamination. It might be thought that the Enlightenment project of scientific human advancement would have banished notions of witchcraft for all time. But, as with so many of the values of modernism, rationalism produced its own subterranean 'inversion'. Victorian England became deeply interested in spiritualism, while in France the publication of Huysmans' *Là-Bas* (a fictionalised account of author's own experience of 'black [sic] magic') brought magical practice once more to the public attention. It is significant that in *Là-Bas* it is the involvement of a girl-child in a 'black mass' which shocks the hero: 'Then at the back of the Chapel in the shadows a little girl, who had not stirred till that moment, reeled forward and began to howl like a rabid bitch! Overwhelmed with disgust and almost stifled, Durtal longed to escape' (in Haining [ed.] 1975, p. 34). However, probably the best-known example are the stories of the Salem Witch trials in the late seventeenth century:

> To the already vast literature on witchcraft the Reverend Cotton Mather . . . contributed a book on Memorable Providences, describing a case of alleged witchcraft in Boston. . . . The second edition of this 'how to do it' book, filled with data on how the 'possessed' were supposed to behave, got into the hands of a group of young girls in a poor settlement near Salem. More or less as a prank, they accused a half-Indian, half-Negro [sic] family slave of being a witch. . . . The 'afflicted children', finding themselves the objects of attention . . . persisted in their charges for fear of being found out, and started a chain reaction. (Morison, 1972, p. 176)

The intertextuality of this highly sedimented story motif with popular and professional concern is evident today in debates about the 'ritual abuse' of children. Finkelhor *et al.* (1988) suggest that whereas 'true' ritual abuse is extremely rare (i.e. the use of children in Satanic worship, specifically *as* innocents to be corrupted), it is not uncommon to combine elements of ritual permeated with significations of evil, particularly with the *sexual* use of children, either to make the child(ren) too frightened to complain or seek help, or as part of the 'turn on' (and possibly both). Certainly the attributed quality of 'innocence' to the state of childhood makes children thereby targets for those for whom the *corrupting* potential of sex is a key to gaining sexual release. What the notion of 'ritual abuse' does, then, is bring together two powerful emblematics of how childhood innocence may be depraved – by sexuality (by far the most common – a theme we will examine in more detail in Chapter 10), and by evil itself.

We can then ask how, in terms of socially sedimented ideas, does the notion of corruption of childhood innocence operate? One way that effective mythologisation works is through the drawing together of previously disparate strands of social understanding and representation. If we look at the science fiction films of the 1950s and 1960s, for example, a common theme involves the emergence of monstrous 'horrors' (themselves part of the cultural archive – the social mneme Jung mystified into the collective unconscious) which are released, created or summonsed by that which is feared – in recent times, this is often nuclear energy. In this way an old representation (the monster) comes to be reconstructed to serve new discursive anxieties over radiation, fall-out and the bomb. In a somewhat similar way, the rather dusty and dated trappings of the sedimented, archetypal seducer – such as Don Juan or Faust – have now been brushed down and re-fettled as a new villain – the child sexual abuse perpetrator. In the new mythologising, the child replaces the maiden (very occasionally the 'spotless youth'). Where not very long ago (e.g. in the 'good old days' of Dennis Wheatley, Hammer Horror and traditional science fiction) it was the maiden who had to be rescued from the monster, in the newly emergent social myths, that victim has manifestly become a sexually innocent child.

One of the most fascinating recent literary explorations of the child's innocence as the target of corruption, however, concerns not sex but scent. In Süskind's historical horror *Perfume* (1987), the anti-hero (himself a victim of emotional and physical abuse as a child – evidencing the myth of recapitulation) becomes a perfumier. Working with the supposed power of human fragrance, he eventually comes to murder several adolescent girls. It is not sex he is after, but the power of their virginal attar, which he carefully expresses for its euphoriant impact on human mood. When we first read this book we were struck as much by its wealth of accurate detail about perfumery and the extraction methods which provide its raw materials, as we were by its sheer gruesomeness. We recognised its links to culturally current ideas about pheromones, but what we did not know about were its resonances with sedimented mythic themes – not, that is, until we stumbled across a copy of Bloch's *Odoratus Sexualis* (c. 1905). In this he discusses the practice of Shunamitism (after I Kings I: 1–4) i.e. the sleeping by the sick or elderly with (literally not euphemistically) young virgins in order to be revitalised by their scent. Much the same practice seems to have been adopted by Mahatma Gandhi and Mark Twain.

As yet, the reflected myth – that of the devilish, evil child as found in *Daimon, The Exorcist* and the like – has not made the big time as a social fable. Yet despite the persistence of childhood innocence as a motif, and the comparative rarity of tales of florid evil – children are none the less frequently storied as 'naughty' (i.e. a singularly childish form of 'bad'). Literature abounds with tales of 'naughty boys', from Huckleberry Finn to Dennis the Menace, and particularly so in school stories from *Tom Brown's Schooldays* (1856) to the recent television series *Grange Hill*. However, more recently the term 'naughty' has itself been subverted (via in the British case such fictives as *St Trinians*) to apply a distinctly adult form of knowingness to a very 'grown-up' child. The recent emergence of a number of narratives featuring younger 'naughty girls' is, therefore, of considerable cultural analytical interest. Arthur Wise's book of that name (1972) is a good example. In it, Thelma ('just nine') forms a holiday friendship with Elizabeth (also nine years old) which subsequently leads them to extorting money from an adult couple (Berger and Dorothea) for photographs the children took of them copulating. Growing conflicts between the girls results in Thelma murdering Elizabeth (who wants to own up) with a gun stolen from Berger. Thelma engineers adult perceptions so that the blame for taking the photographs falls on the dead Elizabeth, and blame for Elizabeth's death on Berger.

A no more charming heroine occupies Maureen Duffy's *Love Child* (1973). Kit, a sophisticated adolescent of jet-setting parents, spies on her mother and her mother's lover Ajax (literally, by home-made periscope focusing on one hotel room from another!), subsequently contriving to masturbate in their empty bed: 'And I lay there as naked as either of them, playing first one and then the other as I'd seen them. Now, when my mother's lover lay down it would be into a mingling of my sweat with theirs' (p. 147). By dint of forging letters and subtle hints, Kit works Ajax up into a jealous fugue leading to a row between him and her mother at a party from which he drives, drunken, to his death. What unites these otherwise very contrasting books is the delinquent power of their young women lead characters. It is interesting to note how naughtiness has been gender divided. Generally, the assumption was made that 'troublesome boys go in for crime, whereas troublesome girls merely go with boys' (West, 1967, p. 15). These novels (and others like them) draw upon the possibility of female juvenile wickedness which escapes the traditional category of mere 'wayward girl' (see Chapter 9).

An innocent gaze?

Nema, in our thought experiment from Chapter 1, then, can be seen as one of a multitude of children who are told by us and to us in the various modes of communication that make up contemporary discourse. Any given text on a child can gain a particular reading (of, say, sexualisation, of innocence or of brattishness) according to how we locate its maker (cf. the discussion of Lewis Carroll in Chapter 10). The same text would be read differently, according to whether it was made by a paedophile, a besotted parent or an advertiser. How we read any text depends a great deal on whom we think wrote it, and for what purpose. Take, for example, the following passage, in which some adults come upon this scene:

> There two children, a boy and a girl six or seven, had hung their light summer tunics on the vine-like flags and they were seriously engaged in an attempt to have sex together. It did not look like an attempt that would prove immediately successful, but it was one into which they were putting great effort.

This results in one of the observers reflecting on a memory of childhood brother-sister sex play: 'But every so often they climbed into the old car up on blocks behind the chicken coop next door and they touched each other where it felt best to touch'. And the other to moralise thus over childhood sex: 'Mostly they learn sex from each other . . . We don't find coupling bad unless it involves pain or is not invited'.

What are we to make of these passages? Once the author is located as Marge Piercy (*Woman at the Edge of Time*, 1979, pp. 138–9), the plausibility of a voyeuristic placement recedes in the face of her self-description as 'active primarily in the woman's movement' and by the imprimatur of 'The Women's Press' whose remit is: 'to present exciting and provocative feminist images of the future'. But how would we have read them if they were instead extracts taken from an underground paedophile magazine? Through its positioning of men as the 'dangerous sex' (both to children and to adults) feminism has problematised any male author who reflects upon children and sexuality. In turn, through being placed in the same kind of sanitised location that has been given to women in such roles as children's nurse or primary school teacher, a female author is now in a fundamentally different position from a male author when evangelising for children's rights (particularly sexual rights). From a postmodern location, this resurfacing (now cloaked in feminist discourse) of a quintessentially nineteenth century Mariolatrous representation of women – as the selfless protectors of virtue, and hence, of the selfless protectors of children – deserves to be confronted. This is not just a matter of challenging both this singular positioning of women (as, to be fair, many feminists themselves do) and the simplistic equating of author and text. It is also more fundamentally concerned with a deeper argument about the need to deconstruct modernist notions of a structuralist morality of imputed intention (see also Chapter 11). To consider whether a particular text is 'good' or 'bad', 'true' or 'false', is to ask the wrong question.

Playing with the child

An alternative technique for generating reflection and debate is to explore presentations of 'the unchild'. This is a common device to provoke us to think again about our preconceptions – it has been used to good effect in (e.g. 'Look Who's Talking', a movie portrayal of the talking baby). Indeed, there are a proliferation of postcard pictures of children dressed up as adults, which variously shock, bemuse or charm, according to the gaze employed (see Ward and Ward, 1991). The portraying and telling of children-who-are-not-normal-children provide us with counter-normative locations for the child. By troubling our stereotypical assumptions, they enable us to reconsider those stereotypes anew. They include, for example, the political child; the working child; the sexual child; and so on. Emblematic of political 'unchildren' (cf. their appearance in the emancipatory writings of Hoyles: 1979, 1988) are the two adolescent charismatic leaders of the Children's Crusade of 1218, Stephen of Cloyes and Nicholas (for a historical novel treatment of this episode see Rhodes, 1979). The message of such 'unchildrening' does not require any 'reading', for it is made quite explicit for us – 'children', says Hoyles (1979, p. 211), 'engage in political action'. This contention carries no rider that the particular politics of the Children's Crusade has any claim on our support (indeed it resulted in a debacle of massive child suffering and death). It merely serves to draw our attention to the observation that there existed, in medieval times, large numbers of children who set out across Europe to engage in political action, in a way we would find totally incredible today. Once their historical facticity is established, the bounds of what is credible get stretched. This observation does not tell us that children have to be political, but that they *can* be. It implies that when we observe that children in Britain in the twentieth century tend not to be political, this is not to do with incapacity but something else. It may be that (like many adults) they simply choose not to be, or it may be that we prevent them from being political, or it may even be a bit of both. But once we know some children, somewhere, sometime, were (or are) political, we must stop seeing children as inevitably and naturally apolitical. The same holds true for the working child, and the sexualised child. What Marge Piercy's text (above) does is suggest to us that maybe children *can* be sexual – not that they should be, or must be, but that at least they have the potential to be. Once we agree at least to contemplate such 'unchilding', then representations like Piercy's copulating 6–7 year olds can draw us into a child's sexualised identity potential, without getting bogged down in issues of the endorsement or otherwise of the particular permitting discourse in which they are located. This potentiality should only become compromised if it can be shown that the sexual locations opened up by it are constrained in ways which imply exploitative motives (e.g. when they all portray young boys with adult men). Hence, our attention should not be on the author but on readings of the text (i.e. the kinds of sexual identities it promotes). Likewise the term 'potential' allows us to recognise the difference between desexualisation as a form of depowerment, and the *elective* construction of identities, which can include an identity as celibate. Children, like adults, can be as depowered by a compulsory sexualised or politicised identity as they can be by compulsory desexualisation and depoliticisation.

Children's stories

None the less, it is striking just how often that, for girl-children in particular, it is the introduction to sexuality which is seen to mark the end of innocence – and hence, the end of childhood. Possibly the most deeply sedimented fable carrying this message is *Little Red Riding Hood*, a story told and retold from Grimm to the movie version of Angela Carter's *The Company of Wolves*. Viewed through a psychoanalytic gaze (e.g. Fromm, 1951) it is a cautionary tale about the threat of male sexuality, and an expression, according to Fromm, 'of deep antagonism against men and sex' (p. 241). Such 'tales of warning' (see, for example, Soriano, 1969) abound particularly in stories *for* children. Writing stories specifically for children to read (or to be read to them) is an activity Ariès (1973) traces back to Charles Perrault's *Contes du temps passe* published in 1697, although telling stories to children unquestionably pre-dated this. Cautionary tales for children were used to warn them of dangers. Delarue (1951) noted the ubiquity of tales stressing the need to avoid wandering off alone, and the dangers particularly of water and the wild beasts who roamed in woods and forests, especially wolves (a genuine danger in historical times). Often they had unhappy endings, with children being carried off or killed – not really surprising, given their educative function and little different from contemporary warnings 'not to take sweets from strangers'. As Soriano notes, ordinary parents discovered long before educationalists and psychologists the usefulness of using stories, games and rhymes to help children acquire the essential knowledge of their culture. As, of course, children do in their own oral culture (see Opie and Opie, 1959). Within a modern gaze it is sometimes salutary to recognise just how far such stories went, including helping children to make sense of what we would now call 'child abuse' (e.g. Hansel and Gretel) and indeed, 'sexual abuse' – Robert (1969) cites Grimm's *The Bear Skin* as an example, in which a little girl learns to hide under a bear skin to avoid the sexual advances of her father. Another deeply sedimented tale is that of childhood as an heroic journey to adulthood, in which the hero must solve riddles, slay monsters or pass over hostile terrain, in order to achieve a goal (often marrying the princess, but often simply surviving). Robert *(ibid.)* suggests:

> From the most improbable fabulations a very real fact emerges: the necessity for the individual to pass from one state to another, from one age to another, and to be formed through painful metamorphoses which terminate only with his [sic] accession to true maturity. In the archaic conception which lives on in the tale, the passing from childhood to adolescence, then to manhood. (p. 47)

The moral educative function of such stories is often incorporated by weaving in a sub-text within which the hero can only solve the puzzle or complete the task because of a prior altruistic action. Alternatively, the message may be given that the youth can only be saved by the intercession of a wise elder. More broadly, stories for children often shock, surprise (and hence amuse) in ways which require children to reassess their preconceptions, and make sense of their world more inventively (a device not unlike the ones we are using in this book!). The extent to which children are devourers of stories gives some force to the argument about their importance in constructing the child's world, and mediating the child into cultural competence. They compellingly serve the didactic function of presenting to children not just the received wisdom of a culture: 'this is the way the world is' and 'this is how an okay sort of person behaves', but also of conditioning a more general acceptance of a narrative existence (see Rogers, 1974b). It is in that broader sense that it becomes plausible to suggest that reality for the child is (as is the reality of childhood for us) storied into being.

Stories by children

Thus far, one voice has been largely missing from our deliberations, that of children themselves. This is not accidental, it very much reflects a general dismissing of such texts in our culture. At least for British readers, the most famous 'child autobiography' of the last decade has been *The Secret Diary of Adrian Mole Aged 13¾*, the fictional work of an established, adult, female author (Townsend, 1983)! From the North American experience, we have an even more inter-textual tale *The Secret Diary of Laura Palmer* (written by Jennifer Lynch, 1990). Jennifer Lynch is the daughter of David Lynch within whose postmodern soap opera *Twin Peaks* the possibility of such a diary is seeded. The childhood of the 'late' Laura Palmer is indeed hyper-real. Of course, the 'secret diaries' of actual young people are (at least supposed to be) 'secret' – few, one suspects, would actually wish to share their experience with us. But, it is also the case that within the stories of human powers that we tell, explaining one's experience, telling one's story – particularly in the approved form of written text rather than the oral account – tend to be built into our definitions of the adult (and by default built *out* of our models of children). Within conventional schooling the function of the self-referential essay is not to yield a product *per se*, an outpouring of subjectivity, but an apprentice-piece, a text for correction, a means to the fostering of better competence later. The oral accounts of children have, until very recently, held a very dubious status in modern cultures even amongst ethnographers – a situation whose recent reappraisal owes more to changes in legal practice concerning the acceptability of children's evidence in court (see Spencer and Flin, 1990), than to any sudden shift in cultural respect for children's accounts in general. It is indicative, in this regard, that those children who seem to have spontaneously generated material that corresponds to adult biographical and autobiographical myths are accorded *ad personam* 'exceptional' status (e.g. Anne Frank, Mark Twain's daughter Susy) and are allowed to talk to the adult world of great events and 'great men'. Alternatively, where children's writing emerges out of the experience of schooling – as, say, in the work reported in Kohl's *36 Children* (1971) – the 'exceptional' status has a tendency to transfer to the teacher:

> His achievement was to gain the confidence of his children and to demonstrate that the world was more open to them than their ghetto surroundings might suggest. Their innate [sic] exuberance and liveliness come through in the series of writings and drawings which form a major part of this book. As Herbert Kohl makes clear, the process of educating necessitated profound changes in his own sense of himself as a teacher and a person. Few books on education give such an inward view of what it is like to face an impossible teaching situation and, in some measure to come through.' (From the cover text to the Penguin Edition)

Further, such work by teenagers often gets discounted from the category 'stories by children'; they are seen to belong to a fuzzy category where individuals can be absorbed into (because they can 'pass' within) the adult (cf. Chapter 9). By contrast, what the adult gaze accepts as experiential accounts by 'true' children are, by definition, not only conventionally 'childish', they show the predictable maturational sequencing. This is as true of their drawings (Rogers, 1969) as it is of their verbal outputs (see Lively and Bromley, 1973). As trainees in the highly stratified cultural craft of creative expression as adults define that, it could not be otherwise. However, the inference conventionally placed upon it, of an inner deficit, is no fairer than would be such a conclusion placed upon us trying to communicate in 'bar Spanish' by a monolingual Spaniard. We do survive in Spain, just as did Joan in the hardly child-friendly world of sailing ships.

3

Deconstructing the alembic myth

The troubled origins of developmentalism

We would argue that the overall form of current academic and professional interest in and concern about the child, derives from early modernity, and hence predominantly reflects modernistic concerns for the controlled evolution of society (including its youngest members) informed by an ideology of scientism. This imposed a social Darwinian framework for understanding which sought to make sense of what humankind can become (socialised, civilised, and moralised), given what they start out with (their base animality). 'Character', wrote Dr Barnardo, revealing where he stood in the debate 'is better than ancestry' (Rose, 1987, p. 17). In consequence, the dominant story told to account for childhood was constituted out of attempts to intermesh two sets of knowledges – those about the effects of nature, and those about the effects of nurture. Each of these sets of ideas occupy the domain of a distinct branch of knowledge – nature from within the domain of the biological sciences, and nurture from within the domain of the social sciences.

The study of the person (psychology) was one of the later human sciences to crystallise (see Rose, 1985). Furthermore, when it achieved independent academic status, it did so predominantly as a bio-social science, with the specific agenda of reconciling and integrating these two sets of ideas – nature with nurture (along with other dualities critical to nineteenth century thought: psyche and soma; subjectivity and objectivity). Developmental psychology – the study of the psychology of childhood – was one of the first branches of psychology to be established, precisely because childhood was seen as the prime location to investigate how nurture impinged on nature – how, in other words, we, as people, become socialised, civilised and encultured. Thus developmentalism – the set of ideas about the child and childhood systematised and promulgated by developmental psychology – is what dominates and weaves through our current orthodox western understandings of the young (see Morss, 1990). Its power to do so, we believe, comes from two (albeit interlinked) sources. The first is its use of metaphorical devices to link into the tenets of natural science, thus capitalising both upon the immediate plausibility of the analogies drawn, and upon science itself as mandate for its truth value. The second is its resonance with common-sense knowledge, deeply and enduringly sedimented in western thought, perpetuated not only through the passing on of traditional wisdom within the popular discourse of everyday life, but also within the stories and gnomics of our culture.

Science as metaphor

The provisioning of the bio-social science knowledge of psychology took place in an atmosphere where the natural sciences had already achieved very compelling accounts of the inorganic world. It is hardly surprising, therefore, to find that psychological reasoning drew heavily upon ways of thinking already found fruitful in those contexts. In the specific case of socialisation, psychological theorising drew upon metaphors of con-joining nurture and nature (in particular, chemical ones) from natural science. Socialisation was portrayed as a process akin to the creation of a compound out of base elements. In the way, say, salt (sodium chloride) is constituted out of the elements sodium and chlorine, and thereby acquires chemical characteristics of its own, distinctively different from both; socialisation was portrayed as a developmental process, fed by heredity and environment, the outcome of which is a socialised individual compounded out of both.

This kind of metaphorical device had a powerful effect upon understandings of the kind of processes involved in socialisation. Yet once the tacit psycho-chemistry is made explicit, we can begin to see the problems it created for psychologists. Unlike the chemist (but like the alchemist) psychologists have never had any clear idea of how their metaphorical process actually operates – how the melding together of nature and nurture actually happens. Since what they are dealing with is a metaphor for a process (and not a model of a process itself), psychologists can only speculate in extremely vague terms about the way it may operate, let alone how it might fail, be reversed, break down or whatever. Unfortunately, this has not prevented them doing so at great length, and in some arenas with far-reaching impact upon the way people lead their lives.

Similarly, the biological bases of heredity and the cultural medium of environment cannot be equated with constitutive elements in a chemical

equation – even ones as diverse as sodium and chlorine which are com-
poundable (in molecular theory) because they are similar in make-up
(sharing conjoinable electron shells). Nor are they like already compound substances such as of oil and water which can be further admixed
through known electro-physical mechanisms into distinguishably different forms (water-in-oil and oil-in-water emulsions). Nature and nurture, like the process assumed to concoct them together, are abstractions
– hypothetical constructs. Moreover, their interplay takes theoretical
and moral resolutions.

The warrant of common sense

As with many concepts used in bio-social sciences like psychology, a lot
of the apparent plausibility of the pursuit of socialisation also comes
from its employing reasoning that is very little removed from the common sense of society (i.e. popular understandings). We are all familiar
with such ideas as 'as the twig is bent, so shall the tree grow', and that
'blood will out.' Popular understandings themselves, of course, are not
static givens, however much they may seem that way to the society that
employs them. Rather, they reflect the passage of peoples and societies
through time, and are successively modified and sometimes transformed
by changing models of the world as developed by an over-class of knowledge mongers. None the less, they do reflect the qualities of traditional
knowledge in that their authorisation derives from epistemological continuity, as 'time-tested' (see Whorton, 1982).

Socialisation stories, then, were able to gain and maintain credibility
because they resonated with a long tradition of cultural melodramatisation about human nature and human nurture, aspects of which we
outlined in Chapter 2. In other words, our culturally sedimented understandings of how childhood 'works' imbue the similar story told by
developmental psychology with a plausibility that is very difficult to
resist. However, the latter has presented itself not as merely intertextual
but as a superior kind of knowledge, one warranted by the addition of a
magic new ingredient – science.

The alembic myth

We would argue, however, that the process of socialisation as promoted
under developmentalism *is* no more than a story. However, it has become a story with such compelling plausibility it has overwhelmingly
acquired the seeming status of incontrovertible truth – this is the way

things *really are*. Thus it has come to be treated as an objective analysis of human enculturation in childhood and its boundedness by the biology of the child. Yet, once this story is stripped of its adhering commonsensicality and its trappings of scientific reasoning validation, it becomes possible to be recast as an alembic myth. The alembic, the old swan-necked retort which nearly always appears in images of alchemy, serves as a useful emblem of its Faustian arrogance and futility. Yet the homunculus the alchemists vainly sought to manufacture in their laboratories haunts us still – we remain entrapped by the idea that little people can be made by the magic (science fiction) admixture of nature and nurture. The fictive stories discussed in Chapter 2 form plausible narratives because, however speculative their science, however creaky their plots, they employ the constructive elements of our dominant discourse on human and, in particular child development: the bio-social compound (see Figure 3.1).

This supposes a child to be grown out of an alchemical transformation of two kinds of substance: a semi preprogrammed, vital, material frame (nature) and an impinging and pro-active cultural medium (nurture). Each is accorded some leavening power, each some ability to engender

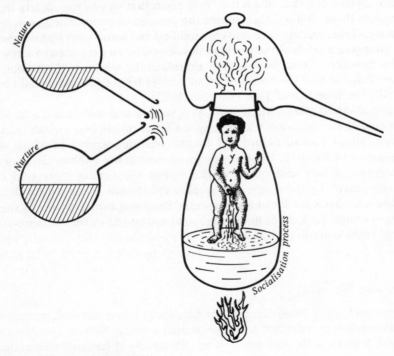

Figure 3.1 *The alembic myth*

personhood (albeit in proportions that take considerable variability from one story to another). Each may also be accorded a qualitatively variable productive role (a better or a worse material frame; a better or a worse cultural medium) in a child's developing personhood. Finally, each may also take on a moral condition as a source, in the way we account for an individual's goodness or badness as a person.

If the alembic myth were to be found only in the world of fiction, there might not be a problem – what else should be there but mythic and other narrative devices? Certainly we might want to be concerned about its prescriptive power as parable, and its potential to construct a social reality from its mythic fabric. But its status as myth in the fictive domain at least offers no direct mandate for the formulating, for example, of law or public policy. Where the alembic myth is much more dangerous, we believe, is when it permeates our science as much as our art with a false sense of established (indeed, of growing) knowledge.

Only very recently has the developmentalist hegemony come under critical scrutiny. Where it has, the results have often been devastating. Morss (1990) for example, concludes as follows:

> I have argued in this book that developmental psychology is built on foundations that are rotten. Not only its more classic formulations, but also in its present day versions adhere to outdated notions of a biological-philosophical nature . . . It may be that the discipline is *constituted* by the appeal to evolutionist logic and the related doctrines and could have no independent existence. If so, developmental psychology might be seen as a mere hangover from the 19th Century: A blind alley in the outward progress of the social and life sciences. (p. 227)

The root of our own concern also goes right back to foundational concepts. Our focus here will be on the three constituents out of which the bio-social compound of the alembic myth is wrought: a biological material frame, an environmental cultural medium, and their transformation into a child. Problems arise as soon as we start to ask questions about what these terms mean, and how they (and not other ideas) have come to serve as the tools we use to answer questions about becoming human. What is their place, in other words, in developmentalism viewed as what Wittgenstein (e.g. 1953) dubbed a *language game*? Clearly, we can only consider their place as products of the very things we seek to understand. In so far as we can give a meaning to the term *culture* (or at least a use for the word) it must inevitably include language itself and the very linguistic artefacts out of which the model is constructed. These constituent terms thus cannot be regarded as 'things' or 'processes' in themselves, but as working ideas in language games – language games which change over time, and, crucially, serve functions that are often far from any role they may play as hypothetical constructs in the pursuit of pure knowledge (cf. Jordanova, 1989,

Riley, 1983, Rose *et al.*, 1984). Our questioning of their status is therefore not merely one further irritation in an ongoing process of worrying (to which working ideas are always subjected). It leads to something more – a much more fundamental troubling of the credibility of the paradigm itself. This is not merely a dispute about what words 'mean'. This is a much more radical critique within which the meanings attributed to the terms used by developmentalist theorisation, once troubled, cast doubt upon its very claims to be a theory at all. We are not interested in trying to improve developmentalism by correcting its errors. What we are arguing (as is Morss, 1990) is that the whole enterprise of developmentalism needs to be abandoned altogether! Working ideas and their terminology are seldom abandoned because they have been worried to the conceptual equivalent of death – indeed working ideas seem to thrive on the kind of attention a degree of worry implies. What leads to abandonment is a much more cataclysmic conceptual fracturing which becomes acknowledged as a paradigm shift (see Kuhn, 1970). In this process, long-established working ideas lose their ability not only to credibly explain but both to grip and to signify, to persuade that the issues they raise are worth, or even capable of, pursuit. We argue that theories of child development based on the alembic myth are in just this way ripe for being troubled out of utility and credibility.

In this section we draw mainly upon a specific developmental psychological text, Scott (1968). Even though in some ways rather dated, we have chosen it as our exemplar because it illustrates so beautifully a whole genre of narratives articulating the alembic myth as bio-social discourse, which continue to permeate the thinking of the vast majority of child care professionals today (Alderton, 1992). We will approach this deconstruction by giving a critical reading of each of its three constituents in turn: material frame; cultural medium; and transformation.

Troubling the material frame

In developmentalist writing the material frame is portrayed in terms of three distinct concepts: our biology, our body, and our genetics. For all their semantic intertextuality in both popular and academic narratives, these concepts are not only far from equivalent, they signify concepts so diverse as to admit no strict commonality.

The notion of 'biology' is an extremely vague and abstract set of ideas about those attributes of humanness which arise because people are animate (rather than inanimate), and which people share with other living things (though primarily other animals). These include morphology (e.g. having a heart, lungs, liver) and physiological processes (e.g.

breathing, digesting food). This assumed mutuality with the rest of the animal world enables developmentalists like Scott to assert 'human development is in many ways quite similar to that of dogs' (Scott, 1968, p. 41). As textualised, 'biology' takes on the power of an abstract causal model, offering theories about the sources of our actions – as in the common phrase 'the biological bases of behaviour'. However, once writers like Scott begin to make concrete the possibilities, causal modelling soon drifts into trivialisation and truism. Here, for instance, is Scott on the adolescent growth spurt: 'learned habits for sitting down or going through doors are based on a much smaller physical size, so that the adolescent appears and feels awkward until he [sic] is able to readjust' (*ibid.* p. 121). By contrast, 'body' tends to refer to the state and powers of a specific thing or parts thereof (e.g. our neurological substrate). The concept of body is much more problematic than is often supposed; Berger and Luckmann, for example, make the point that: 'On the one hand, man [sic] *is* a body On the other hand, man *has* a body . . . In other words, man's experience of himself always hovers in a balance between being and having a body, a balance which must be redressed again and again' (1967, p. 68).

Hence, while of the three constituents of the material frame, body appears to have the greatest concreteness (given, for example, that we can point to parts of the body, we can weigh and measure its dimensions, and that we can picture it in a diversity of different ways, from X-rays to portraits), it too is a production of a particular gaze. What enables the Berger and Luckmann example is mundane body/mind dualism, whereby that which is physical – the body we are – is rendered different from that which is mental – that which has a body – not by classifications that mirror 'what is' but by constructions in embodiment language games. We *are* nauseous but we *have* diarrhoea. Except for that dualism, of course, the moralisation of body as embodiment is lost. If we are merely bodies, natural objects, then as Sedgwick notes '[t]he fracture of a septuagenarian's femur has, within the world of nature, no more significance than the snapping of an autumn leaf from its twig' (Sedgwick, 1982, p. 30). In the bio-social compound model, to exist a body must have a history of prior existences – as bodies move through time, they are in a continual state of transformation by the cultural medium. Hence, of course, the attraction of (indeed, the necessity for) arbitrary definitions of first true embodiment, points when bodies become persons with a psychology – such as the moment of birth. This strategy is often enabled by notions that prior to birth we are not persons maturing in the womb but mere mechanisms responding to stimuli:

> It is therefore possible to conclude that the effects of changes in the prenatal environment are largely physiological rather than psychological

in nature. From the biological viewpoint, fetal behavior has chiefly a physiological adaptive function. Movements promote circulation, prevent the formation of adhesions to the surrounding membranes, and help develop and strengthen bones and muscles. (Scott, 1968, p. 59)

The third concept constituting the material frame is the notion of genetics or heredity, which are also hypothetical constructs – speculative original causes of some later condition. As such heredity is thought of not just as a material thing (genetic material) but also in terms of its powers to act as a blueprint for the construction of the biological components of organisms. If that were all heredity implied, then assumed interplays between it and the body and biology might not be such a problem. At least within such a conceptual system, all that is being assumed is the capability of complex molecules to store and transmit information about physiological processes. However, this is generally not how heredity is treated in psychology. Not only is genetic material held to have the power to specify how things are to be made (e.g. to lead to a person having blue eyes or tall stature). It is also seen as capable of specifying behaviour (the domain of behavioural genetics), and even to specify predispositions to believe, e.g. to be religious (cf. the writings of the sociobiologist Wilson, 1975).

That such sociobiological notions have permeated into developmentalism is illustrated by the way genotypes (indeed persons) are seen as having an existence prior to the reproductive process by which they, themselves, were made:

> Heredity thus operates very much like a lottery, but one in which the results are biased in favor of the gambler rather than against him [sic]. There is always an element of risk, but an individual has a good chance to draw a favourable combination of genes from the gene pool. (Scott, 1968, p. 49)

Thus not only are each of its three constituents themselves deeply problematic, once their claims to 'reality' are exposed to critical decomposition, the very concept of material frame itself is thereby revealed as highly slippery, permitting it at different moments of gaze to take on the form of an object, a form of information, a force, a cause and a consequence.

Troubling the cultural medium

The concept of culture or environment is deeply ambiguous, ranging from cultural heritage to the literal nourishment an organism feeds and grows upon. When both ordinary people and developmentalists talk of 'the environment' they often elide between such grossly different readings of culture. Scott, for instance, happily talks in one place about 'the egg as an environment' (p. 49) and in another about 'a complex environment of books, pictures and museums' (p. 151). Thus, for example, the 'environmental' contribution to intelligence generally implies little more than that part of intelligence which is not 'genetic'. Being brain-damaged during birth, and acquiring a fluency in completing IQ tests by practising a lot, are *both* treated equally as environmental effects upon measured intelligence, although – apart from both arising from events during childhood – these 'environmental' impacts have no other equivalence. They are linked only because they can both be regarded as causes of an effect, an effect itself brought into being by the bio-social gaze, measured intelligence.

While scientism purports to assume a reality in which causes precede effects, science, in practice operates by constructing effects which then require causes (in the case of bio-social compounding, material and cultural ones). However, the cultural causes that result are not homogeneous but a mélange of material, societal and even self-generated impacts. This variability is obscured by a vocabulary which implies universality: 'Having decided to have children, normal parents can help to provide a favourable early environment for their future off-spring, starting with the prenatal environment and extending their efforts to the early post natal years' (Scott, 1968, p. 151). Even the restricted term 'early environment' slips all too easily from prescribing eating the right food and not smoking in pregnancy, to cuddling and the telling of bed-time stories. The moral gloss to the developmentalists' notion of environment is patent. 'Normal parents' are of course, PLU (people like us).

Troubling transformation

Developmentalists also tell a tale of how causes in nature and nurture operate in interaction. So long as it is restricted to describing events in a biosphere, the notion of interplay between material frame and environment is relatively unproblematic. The sedimented plausibility of common-sense agrarian metaphors, using some kind of seedbed analogy, normally serves in the teaching of the bio-social myth. We are primed for it by the naive science that begins in early schooling: 'In a moist loam (i.e. good environment) our chosen seeds grow well; in a dry sand (i.e. bad environment) they grow badly.' Indeed, so sedimented is this form of example that it has served as a metaphor for the human condition for around 2000 years (Matthew 13:3–8). Just as exemplary is the assumption that wheat seed-grain always produce wheat and rye seed-grain always rye (genetics), and that some varieties of wheat produce better overall yields than others (i.e. superior or inferior strains).

Finally, when we are told that environment and heredity can interact, there is another homely example – heathers do best in a lime-free soil, brassicas thrive on lime.

However, we are not generally encouraged to pursue how problematic this makes talk of a 'good environment' in the abstract, or indeed in the area of child development. Both plant and animal biochemistry address processes whereby chemicals pass from the environment into the organism, once there, being transformed by and in turn transforming the organism according to rules chemically written into its genes. But even these mechanisms of material life itself permit no moral order. The genes of heathers are 'bad news' in a lime-rich soil (or the soil is 'bad news' for them) but 'good news' in a lime-free soil. But, it needs to be asked, good or bad news for whom – the selfish gene or the missing gardener? Thus the metaphor used by developmentalists disguises their moral investment and carefully ignores the fact that they themselves are normally concerned with vastly more than, and other than, the child as mere object in a biosphere, a seedling in a seed bed. Their interests are much more likely to be focused upon abstract essences in the material endowment of the child (e.g. dispositions, traits, even motives) and with culture in an agentic role (e.g. the impact of parental values, the peer group, the mass media and so on). Here developmentalists are operating in an area where there is no consensual – let alone empirically substantiated – account of the seed bed. Their attempts to 'fill in the gaps' are often amazingly naive:

> All our present information indicates that the best environment at one stage in development is not necessarily the best at another. The benefits of a rich and varied environment are manifold when a child begins to learn about his [sic] physical environment, but a complex environment of books, pictures and museums obviously has little meaning to a child who is only six months old. (Scott, 1968, p. 151)

The very notion of bio-social compounding itself becomes problematised to the level of disintegration when we start to recognise that the environment can consist of things like books and museums! Does it make any sense to ask how much of our knowledge of genetics is caused by our genetics, and how much by our access to education about genetics, let alone to try to answer that question in terms of our existing (or likely) knowledges of the biological or the social?

Biology as a discipline is not designed to address questions about how biological knowledges are represented in the social world of books and museums. The social disciplines are not designed to address questions about the genetics of knowledge. The two respective theory languages are, in that respect, immiscible. The language-games that work for representing the biological and those for representing the social lack the needed translation rules. Beyond a certain point, all we encounter are the very tensions upon which they are grounded – the metaphoric bipolarities of modernity itself: body/mind; personal/social; objective/subjective; noumenal/ phenomenological. Yet, so strong is the pull of the underlying myth, that the developmental literature abounds with notions like 'under-socialisation' (too little enculturation) contrasted with 'over-socialisation' (too much enculturation); deprived/understimulating environments, de-socialisation/re-socialisation (brainwashing, conversion), and so on.

Old wine in new bottles

This critique illustrates how the bio-social alembic myth is grounded in unreflected-upon notions of causality. Somehow, its proponents argue, the effect we observe in the child must be caused by something; and those causes can only lie in nature, nurture and their compounding. These accounts are not only opaque to the possibility of causes being constructed by effects; they are also naively unsensitised to the constructed character of their effects *per se*. What are regarded as effects could equally well be construed as social concerns. Doing so makes it possible to acknowledge that they are not the timeless, culture-free phenomena that the mechanical language of bio-social science connotes. Rather they emerge as 'things-brought-in-being-in-a-gaze' (and thereby contestable both concerning their unity and their definition.)

Loose interactionism

Developmentalism has, over the past twenty years, taken a number of knocks from within that have helped to erode confidence in its methods and its concepts. A good example is Rosenthal and Jacobson's (1968) very influential *Pygmalion in the Classroom* study, in which teachers were given misinformation about the children they were teaching. Some children, they were told, had high intellectual growth potential ('rapid bloomers' – note the horticultural metaphor again); others had no such potential. In fact, these allocations were arbitrary. Yet when later tested, the spurious high-potential children were assessed as having significantly higher gains in reading achievement and IQ. This study raised the uncomfortable questions: What precisely is it that tests test? What kind of science is it whose measures can act as self-fulfilling prophecies? Meanwhile, the work of the only knighted psychologist, Britain's Sir

Cyril Burt, on the inheritance of IQ via studying twins was beginning to attract attention as substantially fraudulent. (As we go to press the British Psychological Society seems to be back-tracking on its previous condemnation of Burt. In the immortal words of Mandy Rice-Davis, 'Well they would, wouldn't they?') The broader venture of seeking to separate the impact of nature and nurture via IQ data was attacked as both specious and racist (see, for example, Taylor, 1980, for a review).

Hence, whereas early developmentalists (such as Galton and Watson) were able to adopt a hard form of strict biological or social causalism (as suited their ideological agendas), more recently theorists in this field, embarrassed by the excesses of their collective past, have felt the need to devise a softer, warmer, more liberal-humanistic version of the alembic myth. At first, this showed itself in a tendency to back-pedal over some of the more florid claims of the past, an attempt to discard strict causalism and import mechanisms which clearly involve, but do not specify the roles of, both organism and context. 'Learning' is one such loose interactional concept. A good example of this shift is provided in Nash's first edition of *Developmental Psychology: A psychobiological approach*: 'It should not be claimed that all deviant [sic] behaviors have a genetic basis. In a later Chapter homosexuality will be discussed as a form of behavior once believed to be genetically determined, but now seemingly learned to a large degree' (Nash, 1970, pp. 41–2). However, we would argue that such waterings-down of hard causalism (and attempts to resist them) have not so much solved the problem as reduced developmentalism to a highly public game of 'pass the hot potato'. This has happened whenever a developmental concept has become recognised as politically located, be it racial differences, gender differences or sexual orientation. Once, however, the possibility is allowed that developmentalism is intrinsically political then instead of a timeless, universal 'telling it how it is', the practice of the discipline becomes seen as inevitably symbiotic with its social location. Thus Nash's theoretical reconstitution of homosexuality is coeval with the decision of the American Psychiatric Association in 1974 to abandon the idea that homosexuality is a mental illness. Increasingly, then, developmentalism can be detected as reconstructing its language and refocusing its gaze, as what is politically correct shifts from one concern to another. This shift directs the focus of theorisation predominantly onto the third moment of the alembic myth – the transformation process. In a sense this makes it all the more alchemical, for the main 'cause' of socialisation thus becomes invested within the magic process which somehow combines the legacy of the material frame with the impact of culture, to produce qualities neither ingredient possesses of itself.

Probably the best known proponent of this new loose interactionism approach in terms of child development is Martin Richards. Contrasting his writing between his 1974 and 1986 texts evidences this shift well. Whereas his earlier theorisation was concerned predominantly with the 'essential tension between the biological and the social' (Richards, 1974, p. 1), his more recent formulations import a more abstract social psychological transducer: '. . . the development of children cannot be understood outside the social context in which it occurs' (Richards, 1986, p. 1).

This substitution reflects not merely a shift of preferred focus (from one to the other side of the transduction of biological and social), but a tacit recognition that they are two different concerns, addressing two different questions, exploring two different objects (cf. Henriques *et al.*, 1984). So long as both were there, the failure to resolve the nature/nurture tension was manifest. Once viewed as separate, it goes away. When loose interactionists were still, within their earlier conception, concerned with a process of mutually active interpenetration (transformation) between material and medium, they were only able to see them as separable, and hence open to study, by setting the focus upon the child as: 'A biological organism with biological propensities and organisation who becomes social through his [sic] encounters with social adults' (Richards, 1974, p. 1). The solution to this worrisome pull created by 'looking outwards from psychology, both towards biology, and sociology' (1974, p. 1), was attempted in 1986 by muting the biology and presenting the work of 'a group of social scientists' (p. 1). To model loose interactionism, the apparent precision of the older, robust (masculinised) metaphor of chemistry got discarded in favour of a new, homely (feminised) metaphor of cake making, although it is still clear that it is felt that there is something there to be 'cooked up': 'Social context is, at a variety of levels, intrinsic to the developmental process itself; rather than the icing on the cake it is as much part of its structure as the flour or the eggs that may be used to make it' (Richards, 1986, p. 1).

The cake-making metaphor also enjoyed considerable popularity with other politically correct theorists like Rose, Lewontin, and Kamin (1984), similarly concerned with finding an 'integrated understanding of the relationship between the biological and the social' (p. 10) by viewing their contributions as interactive:

> Think, for example, of baking a cake: the taste of the product is the result of a complex interaction of components – such as butter, sugar and flour – exposed for various periods to elevated temperatures; it is not dissociable into such-or-such a percent of flour, such-or-such of butter, etc., although each and every component (and their development over time at a raised temperature) has its contribution to make to the final product. (*ibid.*, p. 11)

The shift to loose interactionism not only managed to salvage developmentalism but rejuvenated it. For instance it has led to a considerable body of cross-disciplinary research into the 'children of social worlds' (to borrow the title of Richards and Light's, 1986, reader). In fact, it looks much less like a revival than a whole new show! Gone are the psycho-biological markers of their 1974 book index, like: bushmen [sic], crying, discipline and rhesus monkeys. In have come instead their markers as New Men: Beauvoir (Simone de), discourse, culture and reification.

Such tinkering, however, does not actually solve the problem. The myth remains no more than a myth. All that the shift from chemistry to cooking has done is acknowledge there is much more complexity involved than hard causalism allows. It does not address the challenge that social *productivity* imposes. This has been illustrated well by Martin (1989). Commenting on the Rose, Lewontin, and Kamin (1984) description, she has pointed out:

> The example would be much more enlightening if they had added that the cake was chocolate, baked by a 64-year-old widow on the occasion of her only daughter's departure for an extended residence abroad. Adding these complexities, we would be hard pressed to say how much the bittersweet taste of the finished cake was due to the chocolate and how much was due to the social significance of the occasion. (Martin, 1989, p. 12)

The alembic myth, however revamped to accommodate 'right on' sensibilities remains just one among many metaphorical devices to tell a story of 'development'. In order to tell its tale, it takes as 'givens' all manner of concepts which are, in themselves, culturally and historically constituted, including both the notion of 'child' and that of 'development'. This case has been eloquently argued by Walkerdine (1984):

> [T]he very lynchpin of developmental psychology, the 'developing child', is an object premised on the location of certain capacities within 'the child' and thereby within the domain of psychology. [However] developmental psychology is premised on a set of claims to truth which are historically specific, and which are not the only or necessary ways to understand children . . . [P]articular pedagogies and forms of schooling, are not mere applications of a scientific apparatus, but should be understood as centrally and strategically implicated in the possibility of a developmental psychology itself. (Walkerdine, in Henriques *et al.*, 1984, p. 154)

What child? What development?

Under modernism, just as developmentalism was able to dominate psychology, our everyday understandings of children and childhood have been more broadly monopolised by a knowledge industry manufactured by the practitioner and academic entrepreneurs working in the fields of education, anthropology, sociology and social work, and particularly those that Ingleby (1985), following Foucault, has termed the 'psy' complex of medicine, psychiatry and psychology (see Parton, 1991 for a more detailed analysis of their hegemony over knowledge about the child and the family). Their knowledge-manufacture legitimated a particular set of discourses upon the child, representing them as fundamental, invariable truths about the nature of children as true for the children of today as for the children of a century ago; for the children of Newcastle as the children of New York or New Delhi.

The alternative, critical position is that the child and childhood are intrinsically problematic notions. The problematic of the child is well enough summarised by Jenks (1982) to need no further elaboration at this point:

> Simply stated, the child is familiar to us and yet strange, he [sic] inhabits our world and yet seems to answer to another, he is essentially of ourselves and yet appears to display a different order of being: his serious purpose and our intentions towards him are meant to resolve this paradox by transforming him into an adult, like ourselves. This points to the necessity and the contingency of the relationship between the child and the adult, both in theory and in commonsense. The difference between the two positions indicates the identity of each . . . Typically, however, the overwhelming irony of this kind of formulation is its failure to acknowledge that very paradox. The child side of the relationship is, within theory, recovered negatively . . . It is as if the basic ontological questions, 'What is a child?', 'How is the child possible as such?' were, so to speak, answered in advance of the theorising and then dismissed. (pp. 9–10)

A critical polytextualist approach to 'development'

Under the modernistic project then, it has been naively 'taken for granted' children who have been tracked and plotted as they 'develop' through the 'socialisation process' into an adulthood which is itself taken for granted in the prevailing social order. Furthermore, precisely how they develop has also been modelled upon unexamined analogues of growth and/or change. Like the 'nature' and 'nurture' notions in the alembic myth, the very concept of 'development' simply does not stand up to rigorous inspection. Far from offering (as is often assumed) an explanation for the changes children undergo between birth and adulthood, it merely reclothes this transition from a rag-bag of carelessly borrowed garments and accessories: 'What modern developmentalists measure, investigate, even perceive in their subject-matter is, therefore, still defined by . . . outdated biological concepts. What developmentalists discover may be determined in advance' (Morss, 1990, p. xiii).

We are not the first authors to suggest that the ill-cast efforts of developmentalists are sustained not by power of evidence but power of rhetoric. Specifically, developmentalism has drawn upon notions of a good story drawn from culturally sedimented raconteurial practices. Gergen and Gergen (1986) in applying the narrative metaphor to developmental theorising observe that:

> There is, after all, no logical means by which accounts of development may be derived from the observation of infants moving through space and time. Such observation may furnish the opportunity for theoretical accounts; it does not, however, furnish the conceptual categories nor their particular form of relationship. If observation plays only a delimited role in the determination of developmental theory, one's attention turns to other sources. Among the most salient are the cultural forms relevant to discourses about events across time. As we have seen, such discourse is primarily narrative in structure. (p. 31)

In seeking a challenging approach to the distance teaching of development, we ourselves have also promoted a narrative analytic (Stainton Rogers and Stainton Rogers, 1986). The variety of narrative forms used by developmentalists, we felt, would be best put across by recasting them as a set of Chaucerian Tales:

1. *Development as steady increases* (The Accountant's Tale) in which development is presented as a regularly increasing growth of assets – the development of body weight and cognitive abilities like intelligence are often represented in this way.
2. *Development as topological changes* (The Comparative Anatomist's Tale). Here development is portrayed as consisting of transformation of proportion, as in the ratio of head to body size from foetus to adult, or in the supposed elevation of reason over impulse over the same time span.
3. *Development as a series of crucial events* (The Historian's Tale). Under this story our attention is drawn to milestones or benchmarks in development, as in first and second dentition; sitting up, crawling and walking; acquiring breast-buds, hair growing in armpits, menarche, etc.
4. *Development as branching out* (The Organisational Manager's Tale). The crucial feature in this portrayal is that development is like a tree, in which the child's faculties unfold from the simple to the complex, from the general to the differentiated, as in simple emotions like fear and anger becoming differentiated into more subtle emotions like embarrassment.
5. *Development as transformation* (The Entomologist's Tale). Through this gaze we are invited to view development as a series of meta-

morphoses, each a further quantum leap away from immaturity towards adulthood. To achieve a new stage in reasoning or identity represents a qualitative jump, a state of difference to what was before.
6. *Development as planning* (The Systems Analyst's Tale). With this scheme of development, the child can be viewed as passing along a decisional tree in which, say choosing the piano over the violin, leads to a further choices, to specialise in blues rather than Bartok, which present further choice points, say, to joining a rock group rather than a blues band.
7. *Development as chain reaction* (The Domino Theorist's Tale). This model of development is commonly used in 'slippery slope' accounts of precocious sexuality, of drug use and of general delinquency, where one thing is seen to lead inevitably to another.
8. *Development as a sequence of challenges* (The Pilgrim's Progress Tale). Under this account, development is rather like a game of *Dungeons and Dragons*. The child, as hero, is on a life-journey towards some goal of maturity (such as authentic personhood). On their way, they must meet and resolve a series of challenges. The risk of failure at any of these hurdles is real but for those that successfully pass the course, a full self-realisation awaits.

Viewed in this manner, the question that needs to be addressed to those who talk of 'a development process' (within or outwith 'social worlds') is – *which* story of development? Given its varied meaning and assumptions, it makes little sense to treat 'development' as though it were a singular concept, let alone an *explanation*. Patently, as one would expect of a narrative device, it can link in a plausible way diverse things for different authors with varying agendas and in a manifold of narrational circumstances. What makes any one such story convincing is also a narrative quality which pre-exists the telling of that tale. Developmentalists, as competent members of their culture, know in advance what kinds of narratives to spin.

> We would not accept a developmental account in which the child showed decline until the age of six and then demonstrated miraculous recovery at the age of seven. Or, a developmental story in which odd years were progressive while even years were regressive would be equally untenable – not because such accounts are manifestly false but because the narrative forms are not constituents of current intelligibility norms. (Gergen and Gergen, 1986, pp. 38–9)

4

Kidstory: Reconsidering histories of childhood

Recently a number of feminist authors (see, for example, Wells, 1982) have promoted *her*story in opposition to 'his-story', determined to bring to our attention the many influential and important women which conventional history ignored and obscured. Even more than women, the young have been excluded from traditional historical analysis, a point not lost to recent historians themselves: 'Of all social groups which formed societies of the past, children, seldom seen and rarely heard in the documents, remain for historians the most elusive, the most obscure' (Herlihy, 1978, p. 109). In particular they have been concealed in the analysis of early history, and thus made virtually invisible within the stories told of pre-modern times (Godfrey, 1907, is a notable exception as we shall later come on to see). Up until comparatively recently, it was only when mainstream historians reached the period of the Enlightenment philanthropic gaze upon the child (from around roughly 1740) that they gave much attention to children at all, and then children have been predominantly portrayed as the objects of the concern of 'great men' like Thomas Coram (see Stainton Rogers, 1988). Excluded within the domestic sphere they shared with women, the only children afforded any substantial interest in classical history were the few child-monarchs who gained the status of quasi-adulthood. Lately, however, an argument has developed about the historical child and the historical condition of childhood. The most cited stimulus is the work of Ariés (1973) who asserted that the reason for the obscurity of children within traditional historical sources is, quite simply, that prior to the sixteenth century, childhood as a separate life-stage did not exist, i.e. that childhood is a recent invention. Within this thesis, considerable effort has been expounded in discovering how and why the social reality of 'childhood' was constructed, and the conditions which led to childhood becoming a life-world separate from that of adults.

In this chapter we have not set out to summarise this history. Instead, we want to bring a critical polytextualist approach to address three questions: the extent to which the historical condition of children and the way they were understood in the past *can* be established from the records, by formal rules of historical evidence; whether childhood (and the history of childhood) really is a new invention; and whether the historical changes in children's lives and the way they were constructed and treated over time *can* be located under a simple story of progress.

Childstory: The historical knowledging of childhood

Although usually presented as belonging to the post-structural challenge, the narrative deconstructive analytic of history is of considerably older vintage. In their comic work *1066, And All That* (1960), Sellar and Yeatman had already announced the end of history, and exposed the key narrative devices of received history: the exaltation of the author; the valorisation of the author's cultural location; and, its developmental, triumphantist agenda. We think the following brief extract, via its ironisation, both illustrates the workings of narrative in history-telling and introduces a necessary sense of caution over what can (and more importantly, cannot) be achieved in historical analysis:

> The English resisted the Danes heroically under Alfred, never fighting except against heavy odds, 'til at the memorable Peace of Wedmore Alfred compelled the Danes, who were now (of course) beaten, to stop being Danes and become English and therefore C of E and get properly married. For this purpose they were made to go back and start again at Thanet, after which they were called in future Thanes instead of Danes and were on our side and in the right and very romantic. (p. 19)

Historical analysis can only ever produce highly distorted and partial stories of what the past was like. The main (but not the only) reason is that such analysis is limited by the kinds of evidence available.

Artefacts

There is a genre of history book (kinder, perhaps, not to give examples) in which we are informed about the social life of proto-humans as a supposed mirror on our own – in which humankind (often, more particularly, *man*kind) is, by nature, aggressive and sexually promiscuous, evolved from hunters and warriors. This view is necessarily distorted by the limitations of the artefacts upon which historical analysis can be based. Fossil and archeological remains, even cave paintings, while they can intimate about hunting and warmongering, have no capacity to convey what individuals shouted or grunted at each other (let alone what they meant). They cannot preserve one-night stands or fisher-person's tales or the cave-person equivalents of kitchen sink dramas. The historians of childhood in ancient times are no better off. While they have been able to infer something from the 'toys' purportedly made *for* children, they can intimate nothing of the *objets trouves* that children themselves may (or may not) have *made into* toys. Indeed, for most of the children of history, the only thing they did that left evidence about their lives was to die (for that may leave a trace, such as a skeleton)! Other objects, like clothes, leave some clues, but none of these things can tell us very much at all about the games proto-children may have played, or the extent to which proto-childhoods were treated as separate from adulthood.

Only words?

So far as language is concerned, historians have fared little better in their attempts to trace historical understandings of 'the child' and 'child-hood' by examining the use of these words:

> When Anna Freud after a half decade of psychoanalytical work with children can recite what she calls 'a long series of trials and errors' . . . one might think the rest of us would be ready for a longer view of what child-rearing has been about – indeed what the very words 'child' and 'child-hood' have meant over the centuries. (Coles, 1979)

What we can tell is that the word 'child' in English (as in other European languages, cf. Plumb, 1975) is richly polysemic, and only knowledge of the historical and textual context in which it occurs allows us to locate its referent (Boswell, 1991). Try this for an etymological amusement:

> My child[1] (not my child[2]) is with child[3]. Will s/he go to school and so become a child[4], I wonder? Come to that, as an infant will it be a child[5] or a boy? Strangely, as a youth it could only be a child[6] if a boy. When it is an adolescent, it will both be a child[7] and yet not be a child[8]. Perhaps it will work as a child[9]? In any event it is likely to be a child[10] of its time. If you find playing with words irritating blame my 'child[11] within'.
> 1. Any relation.
> 2. Offspring of any age.
> 3. Foetus.
> 4. Pupil.
> 5. Girl.
> 6. Noble youth.
> 7. Legal minor.
> 8. Someone below puberty.

9. House servant.
10. Product.
11. That part of my child experience I retain as an adult.

However, unless one is merely concerned with the history of word usage (and clearly, the social historians of childhood are not) questions need to be raised about how word-evidence is being utilised to construct the child as historical object. No writer in this area, so far as we are aware, adopts the strong version of the Sapir-Whorf hypothesis (i.e. that language literally constructs thought). Instead, except where it is true by definition (i.e. in law where it may say 'By a child is meant . . .') the analytic of examining the changes over time in the ways words are used is *itself* subject to a particular contemporary world-view about knowledge intended to be taken for granted by the reader, for example: 'The suggestion that the emergence of childhood as a special period of life developed in the early seventeenth century is *underlined* by changes in European vocabulary which occurred at the same time' (Franklin, 1986, p. 9) (our emphasis).

The use in the text of the word 'underlined' necessarily draws the reader into a specifically twentieth century discourse, which is informed by practices like 'underlining' text or 'highlighting' it (e.g. with a fluorescent marker pen). Word use, the metaphor implies, matters enough as collateral evidence to deserve emphasis. Remove the metaphor, and all that is left is contingency: as childhoods were undergoing change, at the same time changes were also occurring in language about children. Once we attempt to unpick the 'taken for granteds' within the arguments used by historians (in this case, those that focus on word use for evidence) we see that their analysis can tell us little of any great insight about the history of the way the notions of 'child' and 'childhood' were conceived or written or spoken about. What we discover instead has more to tell us about the history of word use itself (i.e. linguistics), and the narrative devices (e.g. the metaphorical referents) utilised by historians.

Iconoclasm

Considerable dispute also surrounds the use of images as an analytic in social historical investigations of childhood. In contention is the extent to which images of children-past (or their absence) can inform us about what it was like to be a child, or indeed, what constituted 'childhood' in historical times. Schorsch, for example, claims to document:

> Some of the more provocative changes in the life of the child from the Middle Ages to the nineteenth century. Its first aim is to bring forward some fascinating information about the nature and nurture of children, known

perhaps to scholars but generally unfamiliar to the 'common reader', its second aim is to explain how the changing attitudes towards children over centuries of time have been reflected in the visual arts. (Schorsch, 1979, pp. 12–13)

Claims such as these, however, are contested by other historians, such as Clark (1969) who ponders on 'how hard it is to equate art and society' (p. 24). For example, earlier Clark noted that following the fall of the Roman empire, 'man [sic] has almost vanished' from European art. He observes how, in the Irish gospel books a 'scribe has thought it best to write Imago Hominis – the *image* of a man' (our emphasis). Yet all that Clark feels able to infer from this absence of images of mankind is that, during that time, something happened to the portrayal of men. Clark does see any necessity or justification to argue that this is evidence that men, *per se*, were unimportant over the historical period in question! Yet this is exactly the kind of conclusion that the lack of representations of children in the Middle Ages has drawn from Schorsch. Even so, her analysis is highly contradictory. One moment she asserts that because there were so few pictures made of children, 'children were generally ignored' at that time. Later, she claims that 'medieval communities dealt with their children as they dealt with their animals' because that is the way they were portrayed. And yet a little further on still in her book, we are asked to believe the antithetical proposition – that the lack of family portraits can be attributed to the fact that 'pictures of them would have been unwanted reminders of too many painful memories.' Clearly, she wants it all ways. Indeed, the operating modern psycho-ideological gaze of many historians working from visual images of the child has itself been deconstructed by right-wing historians of the family such as Mount (1982). Not only does he redirect our gaze to, for example, find the modern family in the fourteenth century Venetian Marriage Capital (p. 116), he also draws the conclusion: '[i]s it possible that the changes we are examining have nothing to do with the history of childhood but a great deal to do with the history of art?' (p. 143). Such an analysis is very damaging to another major plank in the visual history story, the claim that the portrayal of children as 'little adults' in some early (and not so early) art reflects a failure of adult apperception, which evidences a conception of children *as* no more than smaller versions of adults. For example: 'Prior to the Renaissance children were typically depicted in contemporary art as small adults, and this reflected their role in society' (Franklin, 1986. p. 8).

However, in our iconoclasm, we need to be careful we do not 'throw out the baby with the bathwater' (one wonders what a social future historian might make of our use of such a metaphor). In many instances, visual representations from the past offer a major (albeit class- and gender-biased) source of evidence concerning matters like: the clothing of children (e.g. head binding, swaddling, gender reflection); ante-natal and nursery practices; and, the position of children in social space (e.g. in the home, in social events). Over these matters, the historical visual record does show changes, although no more perhaps than the record of the last hundred years and certainly of less variety than one could bring home from a world trip with a camera. Why then does the historical visual gaze fascinate us? One answer is that because, unlike the broader human tapestry we can locate in the wider contemporary world, we *own it.* The illusion is that because the visual historical record is European (and more recently also North American) it is 'ours'. Embedded within this lies a pernicious 'taken for granted' form of social 'genetics'. While the ideological content of a deterministic view of biological genetics is well aired precisely because it is simply politicised as a right-wing discourse (cf. Gould, 1981, Kamin, 1974, Rose *et al.*, 1984), the world view behind our own entrapment with 'our social evolution' (ours by cultural inheritance and ours therefore to bequeath to others) is part of a much more consensual liberal-humanistic myth (cf. Kitzinger, 1989, Mount, 1982). Hence, paradoxically, while a gaze upon the relative and the specific in the child and childhood has the potential (as Hoyles, 1979 points out) of engendering a radicalising deconstruction, in the hands of most historians it has been used for the reverse purpose – as an extension of the developmental gaze of the storytellers of progress. Further, in the visual mode, the notion of 'progress' in the western artistic representation of children is seen as co-woven with their social constitution in 'our' culture.

Texts and voices

While images of childhood, either as literal illustrations or recoded into interpretative language, are woven into historical stories of childhood – it is always, ultimately, in text that these narratives are cast – or rather, texts, because, both in tacit form and literally in the form of quotations, the overall story is always a compounding of voices. It is the borrowed voices of folk ballads, proverbs, literate parents, the famous and the experts, the diarists, and the travellers which are used to evidence the story along. Typical of one use of quotation is where Tomalin (1981) cites an extract from a letter written by an 'unknown Venetian ambassador to Henry VII, 1497': 'The want of affection in the English is strongly manifested towards their children; for after having kept them at home till they arrive at the age of 7 or 9 years at the utmost, they put them out, both, males and females, to hard service in the houses of other people'. Tomalin weaves this fragment of text into the case she is making that in previous times the emotional bonds between parents and children were less strong than they are today (nicely forgetting the large numbers of seven year olds currently sent to boarding school). The effect of this kind of interpellated voice can be to draw us into an empirical discourse – is there supporting evidence for this assertion? How general was this practice – was it true just of the nobility, or for all classes? Was it an urban effect? Was it new or had it gone on for a long time? And so on. Out of such reactions is social historical research made, and out of it may well come studies into things like apprenticeship contracts or the diaries of parents and of children (Pollock, 1983).

But such research, in and of itself, can only add to the archive of historical material. It cannot resolve the problematic of the historian's *voice*, in the case of Tomalin the attribution of 'lack of affection' and the apparent jointless abutting of a nineteenth century translation of a fifteenth century text into a twentieth century narrative. The term *voice* (Gleeson, 1991) is a useful shorthand for reminding us that what is said (or written) is just that. What is made of it in retelling (i.e. in accounting for it) is something quite different. (Such a position is usually referenced to post-structuralist and postmodernist work, but as in all history, there are alternative attributions and we would suggest Thurber's (1953) *The Macbeth Murder Mystery* as an alternative source worth exploring). We could, for example, account for the sixteenth century couplet 'Thus a child six summers old is not worth much when all is told' highly concretely as clearly evidencing the lack of value placed on children at that time (Schorsch, 1979, does). However, this may be as odd a reading as would be a concrete treatment of W.C. Fields' supposed response to 'How do you like children?' – 'Boiled!'. Certainly, the couplet Schorsch uses as evidence would not sit easily in the same text as Thomas More's contemporaneous assertion: 'Brutal and unworthy to be called father is he who does not weep himself at the tears of his children' (quoted in Tomalin 1981). But what then is More voicing? The context was a letter he wrote to his children, but we know nothing of what reading they gave that sentence, and can only speculate about the alternative readings his contemporaries might have put upon it. A sixteenth century version of 'Dad getting on the moral high ground ' perhaps, or alternatively 'Old Tom's been at the child psychology book again I see'.

Furthermore, with text – perhaps more than anywhere else – our present gaze is restricted by the fact that it was mostly the writings of an élite sub-group of the literate and the powerful, those with the time, the hubris and resources to set down their ideas, from which inferences about childhoods past have been drawn. Those with the power to produce enduring texts were, for the most part, by gender and/or by status, those whose contact with children was severely limited, and whose interest in childhood highly particularised. Thus even though documents have the capacity to encode information about a far wider range of child-knowledge than artefacts or images, what they have actually handed down to historians reflects just the particular areas of concern of those specifically located individuals who wrote them. The consequence of past investments of epistemological power (e.g. within a male élite, itself cut off from contact with children), is to render virtually everything about past children's lives undiscernible. Once more, the analytic endeavours in this field have arguably told us much more about the history of textual production and re-production (*text*story, perhaps!), than about the history of childhood.

Literary children

Similar difficulties beset the analysis of children in the history of fiction, with the added problem that such children are fictive products to begin with (although, as Boswell (1991) notes, they are still worth examining, since they reflect what passed as credible in the times they were written). Here once again we learn more about the construction of the history of expression (here literature), than of the history of children's experience. McKeon (1988) writing of 'The Origins of the English Novel', for example, does not even index children. They do appear in the text but only as apprentices in 'Stories of Virtue' and under the rubric 'Parables of the Younger Son'. At best then, we may get a glimpse of a novel's 'operating rules', at the saliency in the genre of children as objects of interest at all. These 'rules' may indeed reflect the discursive concerns of a culture, and where they permit the treatment of child-salient locations (such as school) they can add to more direct historical evidence. But the move from that to a grand narrative about how those concerns and locations have impacted upon the experience of living children requires an act of historical story-telling of heroic proportions – an invention of invention! Moreover, an invention that cannot escape from the contemporary location in which the narrative is being constructed.

If what we do now is address this problem reflexively, it is evident that in writing this book we, its authors, have obviously 'read around'. We looked for material which we thought would mirror the interests of its readers and our own concerns as story-tellers. An obvious start was what is often claimed to be the only surviving novel from the ancient world, Petronius' fragmentary *The Satyricon*. In reading (a translation of) *The Satyricon*, we found that it does indeed have a little to say about children. We come across, for example, a monologue on parents more concerned with pushing their children into learning lucrative job skills than with solid education and children (read boys) who react to such schooling with rebellion. A voice no doubt, but how is it to be taken? That nothing changes? That analogous material conditions reproduce analogous social realities? Or that we can always find continuity if we go looking for it?

As it so happens, *The Satyricon* also touches upon childhood sexuality (cf. Chapter 10). In the *Preliminary Adventures* of the tale we find a description of Quartilla's party (orgy would be too much of a cliché), at which a servant girl Pannychis, aged about 7, is 'married' to Giton, a young man of about 16. When the male narrator, Encolpius, protests at this 'wanton performance', Quartilla argues that it will do no more than reflect her own experience:

> 'Why,' said Quartilla, 'is she any younger than I was when I first went through it? May my Juno turn on me if I can remember at all when I was a maid. When I was a child I had my games with boys of the same age, and when I grew bigger I used to romp with bigger boys, and so on, stage by stage, till I've come to where I am today. And that's how the proverb came, I'm sure, that she will bear the bull who bore the calf.' (pp. 59–60, trans. J. Lindsay, 1960)

Encolpius goes on to note that Pannychis and Giton show no reluctance to being so bedded together, and his own protest is soon replaced by a shared spying upon the couple with Quartilla who shows 'lascivious enjoyment'.

Whatever Petronius' contemporary readers made of this, their understandings could not have included a 'child abuse' discourse of the kind we have recently constructed – ours, by contrast, can. What is more, within our late twentieth century gaze, it is a discourse that has its own contemporary tension with another discourse that stresses a child's 'right' to the kind of experience Quartilla reports. Perhaps even, the tension can be resolved – Pannychis is abused because adult power was employed, Quartilla not abused because her account sounds elective? Petronius as the 'real' voyeur? But what emerges here is not an historical enlightenment but a contemporary one. The very suggestion that we are dealing here with pornography (and the work certainly bears similarities to much eighteenth and nineteenth century erotica) reveals the problem of the reader's location. Arguably, no more comprehensive study of the child in fiction could offer us otherwise than a compounding of such problems.

English children in the olden time

Given all we have written of the effect of the gaze the writer brings to such texts, it is fascinating to see what an historian from the late

Victorian/early Edwardian period makes of much the same material as has been drawn upon by later authors – particularly when that historian is a woman. In 1907, Elizabeth Godfrey (probably better known for her writings on home and social life under the Stuarts) published a history of British childhood entitled *English Children in the Olden Time*. For all its (to present sensibilities) florid style, this is serious work in which, for example, she gleans every scrap of information to build up a story of pre-Conquest child life, a skill she also brings to her chapter on *Children in Shakespeare's plays*. She is also good on schooling, particularly on weaving a story about early co-education and its relative sexual equality of instruction. Her detail (e.g. the comments of John Lydgate on his childhood naughtiness in a fourteenth century monastery school) is well worth extracting from its moralising contextualisation. The same can be said for her material on toys. Like later writers, Godfrey has clear views about the social construction of childhood, although, of course she does not call it such. For example, she is aware of the construction of the child as hero for children: 'To write stories of the doings of little boys and girls for the entertainment of little boys and girls hardly occurred to any one before the middle of the seventeenth century' (p. 49). Prior to which, as she covers in considerable detail, tales for children were of an altogether more gothic quality, on the impact of which she speculates in a charmingly pre-Freudian way:

> After supping on such horrors, one can picture the frightened rush of little ones to bed, and one hopes there was an elder boy valiant enough to protect his little sisters with his wooden sword along the ill-lit, vaulted passages between the great hall and the women's quarters where the children slept. The custom of sleeping two or three to a bed, which obtained till well on into the eighteenth century, must have been a great comfort on these occasions. (p. 61)

However, Godfrey, while not discussing aspects of childhood sexuality *de rigueur* in modern text, does introduce us to the early seventeenth century couple Kenelm Digby and Venetia Stanley who seem to have been 'making love' (i.e. courting) from earliest childhood and of whom she quotes an unidentified source as saying:

> the very first time that ever they had sight of one another, they grew so fond of each other's company that all who saw them said assuredly something above their tender capacity breathed this sweet affection into their hearts. They would mingle serious kisses among their innocent sports. (p. 300)

It is also clear that she is far from taking a negative view of child marriages, like that of Mary Blacknall (aged 12) and Ralph Verney (aged 16), noting: 'The astonishing thing is that these child marriages should so often have turned out so well; perhaps because the young people were brought up together with a view to adapting themselves to one another' (p. 88). 'So with the changing centuries the children change', begins her last chapter, in which she argues that there has been very little development over time of adult knowledge of children – 'we have travelled so far and learnt so little'. Godfrey argues strongly for the critical value of reflecting on childhoods past, reasoning that: 'We must not imagine when we read of the marriage of a little maiden of twelve that she was the nursery child we look for at that age; probably she was much what a girl of eighteen, just leaving school, would be now' (p. 329). The modern child is, for her, the result of processes which 'have tended to prolong the age of childhood'; and of 'keeping boy or girl much longer in a state of pupilage'. In perhaps the most interesting claim in the whole book, she comes very close on her penultimate page to a constructionist position: 'Perhaps, too, the pre-occupation of the adult with childhood in itself, as if it were something more than a mere phase leading to manhood [sic], but almost as if children were a race apart, has helped to this result' (pp. 299–300).

History as narrative

Traditional historical analysis (like positivistic sciences) employs a judicial meta-story – the weighing of evidence in order to come up with a verdict (i.e. is childhood a new invention? Let's look at the evidence and decide). However, the problem is that this approach can only choose between alternatives – it cannot accommodate uncertainty and polysemy. Unless we are to assume that an heterogeneity of accounting language-games is yet another recent cultural invention, it must be acknowledged that these existed in past times as they do today. Yet what is so often read from historical analysis is an homogenised, simplified narrative, which does not reflect the rich diversity of vastly different understandings being debated and gossiped about at the time. Moreover, the narrative we are offered, while it purports to be built out of scholarly interpretation of the available evidence, often reflects much more about the endeavour of scholarship itself (and the preconceptions and ideological leanings of the scholars concerned) than it gives us a 'safe verdict' over what happened, or what people thought, or how they saw things. Whether based upon text, pictures, artefacts or fiction, all we have (as in other domains of knowledge production) are advocations, told to make a particular case.

Challenging the myths of histories of childhood

In much of the history of childhood, we thus find ourselves drawn into stories about stories, and the pursuit of the singular, linear theme may be no more than a product of the construction of medium itself (i.e. the demand that it should convey a single message or a meaning). Rather as in the Popperian view of scientific method, this demand may result in the situation where a new evidential history may falsify an old hypothesis, but never prove the new one. Yet, as we have seen, the empirical base for hypothesis-testing is itself often dubious. It becomes part of a self-serving apparatus, with which to promote a particular viewpoint. However, although the constructing, deconstructing and reconstructing of social histories of childhood can never give us 'Truth', it can be a useful way to discovering the operation of myth.

The invention of the invention of childhood

Although the formalisation of particular discourses about childhood can be (roughly) historically located, this does not amount to the 'invention of childhood' (as claimed by, for example, Ariés 1973 and Schorsch 1979) in the sixteenth century. As we have noted, different accounts of childhood are likely to co-exist wherever a society has the time to recount them: 'Before I got married I had six theories about bringing up children; now I have six children and no theories' – Wilmot, Earl of Rochester (1647–80). Neither, on the one hand, a loose use of child-words and a minimal treatment of children in text; nor, on the other, a 'little adult' or other stylistic device for their visual representation, constitutes plausible evidence for an inability to apperceive childhood. From Roman times Europe has employed a phase sequence to describe a passage through childhood, roughly in modern language: neonate; infant; toddler; pre-school; child; youth. True, these conditions were defined by doing (e.g. a child might be a servant) rather than by psychologised inner essences (such as a state of concrete operational thought). But such reconstitutions (and there have been several) do not permit us to identify any singular historical or cultural point of 'invention'.

Hunecke (1985) suggests that the 'invention' thesis is undermined by the observation that the abandonment of children – one of the main pieces of evidence used to support it – actually increased at the point at which Ariés suggests Europe began to 'discover' childhood. Different readings can indeed be applied to texts interpreted as indicating a lack of concern for children, but there are ample examples of affectionate and indulgent treatment towards children being advised, back into very early history. Boswell (1991) notes: 'Documenting parental affection is somewhat like documenting the existence of parents – i.e. impossible precisely because nearly all documents are apposite' (p. 37) and cites a convincing counter-case from Euripides: 'The best of mortals, and those who are not, love children; they may differ in means, the haves and have-nots, but all love children' (*Hercules Furens*, 634–6, cited in Boswell, p. 37). Boswell goes on to say that throughout early times, across western culture, from religious literature to secular poetry, parental love is evoked as the ultimate standard in selflessness and devotion, assuming central metaphoric status in theology and ethics. He also makes the point that while there are few pictures of people eliminating bodily waste, nobody has tried to argue that defecating is a modern invention! But ultimately the 'invention' story will not pass, not just because there is so much contrary evidence, but because it assumes that in times before, there was only one 'story of childhood' around. Clearly there was not. What certainly is the case is that different stories were dominant in different periods.

Reassessing the tale of progress

Whether current society can be called child-centred is itself a matter of dispute (cf. Chapter 11). However, here we are concerned with the stronger claim of a dominant contemporary myth, that history over children consists of a civilising journey from infanticide, cruelty and neglect to a time of love, care and attention (cf. de Mause, 1976, Kempe and Kempe, 1978). In an article entitled 'Our forebears made childhood a nightmare' de Mause (1975) argued that the history of child concern shows a shift from an 'infanticidal' mode in pre-medieval times to a 'helping mode' today. Yet from a critical polytextualist analysis, the shift can be read just as plausibly as not one of moral but of technological and economic progress. The transition is not from child-killing to child-cherishing, but from infanticide-tolerance to foeticide-tolerance. Now that we have the technological skills and know-how to safely (for the mother) dispose of unwanted children before they are born, and the economic resources to make this technology generally available, we do not have to face the distasteful business of disposing of live children after they are born. Where even today that technology is not available, infanticide may still be tolerated. Among very poor women in Brazil, sometimes allowing a sickly baby to die (as a culturally sanctioned act, and not merely as a consequence of 'neglect') is seen as just as 'inevitable' or 'for the best' as a woman in a richer country deciding to have an abortion (Scheper Hughes, 1987). Indeed, in much the same way in the

West, where technology fails (e.g. to discover Downs' Syndrome), it is not unknown for medical staff to allow a baby to die, although that decision may be legally challenged. Similarly, de Mause labelled medieval times as operating within an 'abandonment' mode. In his erudite and well-argued book, Boswell (1991) argues that this is a gross misreading of history. In Roman society and prior to the late Middle Ages, Boswell asserts that systems of abandonment were devised primarily for two reasons. In rich families, this was to tackle the socio-legal arrangements which determined the transfer of property, land and wealth between generations. Inheritance in those times operated according to partible principles, by which a man's possessions were divided, at his death, among his (usually male) heirs. Thus property-owning men, from early Roman times right into the Middle Ages (when systems of primogeniture were developed) had strong motivations to limit the number of heirs raised in their household. However, according to Boswell, they were not (as Ariés and his followers have suggested) left to die of starvation or to be devoured by wild beasts, but abandoned via highly systematised procedures (e.g. in specified places, with food, and at specified times) with the unambiguous intention to transfer them, with relative safety, to other families. The disposal of children by the poor, and by those who fell on hard times (e.g. during famines) was largely a matter of survival. With a few notable exceptions (Boswell cites Constantine, the first Christian Emperor of Rome in AD 331), neither the state nor the Church saw themselves as in any way responsible for enabling families to rear their children. If parents were too poor, or lost the means, to feed and look after their children, the solution was not seen to be to provide them with the wherewithal to do so, but to provide alternative forms of nurture for the children outside the family. As the Middle Ages progressed, poor parents were encouraged, instead, to pass responsibility for their children to the Church (e.g. via oblation).

In pre-modern times, a child born with any form of 'imperfection' – indeed, any deviance from 'normality' (e.g. birth as a twin) – was construed as a sign of parental misbehaviour, such as conceiving the child at proscribed times (e.g. on a Sunday or during Lent), outside of marriage, or within an adulterous or incestuous relationship. Not surprisingly, parents were motivated therefore to dispose of such children, by killing them, abandoning them, or later, by giving them into the service of the Church. Indeed, this reached a point where those running the monasteries became thoroughly disillusioned. Boswell cites the twelfth century Abbot of Andres complaining that he was 'horrified and shocked by the crowd of deformities' in his monastery, 'among whom were the lame, the malformed, the one-eyed, the squinting, the blind, the crippled' (*ibid.*, p. 299). However, it is a moot point whether we have become more 'caring' towards such children, given the large numbers of 'imperfect' foetuses who are aborted, the still common practice of placing such children into substitute care, or the abandoning of them to the medically sanctioned practice of allowing babies with severe disabilities to 'fail to thrive'.

In western culture the idea that parents have a right to do what they like with their children derives historically from the ancient Roman notion of *patria potestas*, in which the freeborn father had absolute power over his children. He could kill them, abandon or expose them, or dispose of them by selling or pawning them to pay off debts, or buy food. However, this right extended to the whole of his family, including his wife and slaves – it was not just a matter of children. Children were thus part of a whole social organisation of oligarchy. In early Christianity, the warrant changed somewhat, from that of parental 'right' to use their children as they wished, to a parental duty to break the child's wilfulness, and redeem them from original sin. Thus deeply sedimented was the notion that parents were entitled – indeed expected – to chastise their children, to rid them of evil.

The question is, to what extent do these historical assumptions of a parental right to physically punish their children evidence a less 'caring' mode of child concern in the past? Firstly, we would contend that this is certainly not a view that has been relegated to the past. Nothing in the new Children Act 1989 has reversed this principle. All that has happened is that some control is now imposed upon the degree of physical chastisement (this topic is expanded in Chapter 11). Secondly, while it is true that recent legislative changes have replaced the notion of 'parental rights' by one of 'parental responsibility', we can ask whether this really does indicate a shift to more child-centred concern. In practice, it falls very far short of challenging parental rights (see Eekelaar and Dingwall, 1990, Masson, 1990b for more detailed critiques).

By reconsidering these four aspects of the case for progress in child concern, we have seen that, predominantly, structural arrangements in the past indeed reflected concern *about* rather than *for* the child. Deciding 'what to do' about a particular child was determined far more by the needs, wishes and preoccupations of adults than specific considerations about the safety, welfare, rights or aspirations of the child concerned. There was a discourse (although it was not the only discourse around) that represented children as 'commodities' – to be invested in, bought, sold, disposed of or acquired (an analysis proffered by Tanner, (1987), with specific reference to adoption).

Wherever life has got rough for an adult segment of society, it has usually got rougher on their children. Such anarchic pockets of economic deprivation, poor health and social breakdown have been regular features of European history. They have also been met with interventionist strategies from the earliest times. Medieval life may well have been more haphazard, less modulated, than our own, and harsher on all who lived in it. But there is no evidence that children were subject to any more neglect and cruelty, relatively, than other weaker members of society.

5

Telling stories of child concern

In this chapter we shift from a critique of the history of childhood to a complementary exploration of the history of child concern. Again we do not intend to present a chronology of events (like the founding of orphanages or the origins of social work) but concentrate upon the production, justification and use, over time, of different ideas about and concepts of children's needs, rights, safety and welfare; and what should be done about them, and by whom. From these narratives, we shall begin to tease apart the legacy of interwoven assumptions and 'taken for granted' notions about children, archived from our past, upon which our current systems of child welfare have been based.

The background to concern

For humans, species survival is cultural survival. A goodly proportion of our young must not only live to the point where they can reproduce themselves as bodies, but must also want and be able to culturally reproduce – to socialise another generation into an ongoing shared reality which transcends any particular individual embodying that reality. We do not know how we managed it – how the young of our forebears were so socially constructed. But we are the living proof that they did. As Berger (1977) puts it: 'Children are our hostages to history. Consequently, to be a parent means (however dimly and on whatever level of intellectual sophistication) to have a stake in the continuity of the social order' (p. xvi).

Disaster scenarios (e.g. nuclear war and its aftermath) apart, species survival is not generally on our day-to-day agendas of child concern. We care most about the young that are proximal to us, and for them, our concerns run much wider than issues of mere survival. In societies like

70

ours that are media dominated, this can be quantified in the way 'The news' formulates the survival of children *en masse* in some distant famine as meriting no more (perhaps less) coverage than a single case of a British child kidnapped or dying for want of a donor kidney in our home country. We may spend vastly more on a birthday present for a child of our 'own' than we put in children's charity boxes over the year. That we do the latter at all, reflects a relatively recent discourse on the young – one which stresses the rights and entitlements of all the world's children. We are, of course, talking generalisations. Accepting that, however, is not to say that the usually received accounts of such phenomena – ethnocentric or 'blood is thicker than water' motives – should be allowed to pass without comment. The so-called psychological distance from us is also a substantive distance. Quite simply, in most societies one cannot necessarily do for (or to) one's neighbours' children that which you do for (or to) your own. The social rules or nomic order do not permit it. We are, in simple terms, used to a social order which locates proximal and distal children differently. In many cases, these placements reflect differences in conditions of engagement. The parental giver of birthday presents can look forward to appreciation, even reciprocation, and can locate the role of the birthday in a larger story of ongoing family dynamics. It is much harder to take the 'bit part' or even a role behind the scenes in someone else's play – a social reality, of course, that certain charities seek to respond to in their schemes for the long-term quasi-fostering of specific individual children in the Third World.

The professionalisation of child knowledge stories

Once we move to consider child concern in the public sphere we can see that the notion of gaze is critical to understanding many of the unique features of contemporary child management and child welfare. Most generally, the professionalised gaze was what enabled the emergence of the 'experts upon the child' who are a familiar feature of our own social landscape. It is all too easy to overlook the fact that child psychiatrists, social workers and developmental psychologists are not an integral part of a complex society *per se*. They are a feature unique to modernity – roles in a play which first appeared on the stage of western society less than 200 years ago, whose plot depends upon the acceptance of constraints to the parts allocated to children (and indeed to parents) which an earlier age would not have countenanced. Although child concern can be regarded as informed by a number of heterogeneous voices two stories have tended to dominate the construction of accounts of its social history: the *march of civilisation* tale and the *conspiracy theory* tale. These have, respectively, more than a passing inter-textuality with the two grand narratives of traditional sociology: structural functionalism and critical Marxism.

The march of civilisation tale

This portrays a triumphal pattern of progress, in which we can witness an ever evolving and improving concern for child welfare, grounded upon the benefits of the science as an objective source of knowledge about the needs of children. This is the story of child concern favoured by the majority of professionals themselves, and promulgates a gaze which reaches all in society – including children. In the United Kingdom an early moral hero in this story is Dr Barnardo. The tale of 'Carrots', and the origin of the motto, *'No destitute child ever refused'*, is almost as familiar a parable in early schooling as is the story of Baby Jesus. As the discourse has become more and more sophisticated, so has its heroic pantheon. A typical mid-twentieth century exemplar, tapping into an alternative tradition of myth-making is Janusz Korczak (cf. Lifton, 1988), who died with his orphan children in Treblinka. Both Barnardo and Korczak were doctors, but each professional and practitioner group could argue its own heroes. However, in philanthropy as in so many nineteenth century constructions, the age of the entrepreneur has been replaced by that of the bureaucrat. If we still have child concern champions today, they tend to cut an altogether less heroic figure. They are either tokenistic representatives of highly professionalised organisations or media identities pre-constructed before their forays into child concern. The present, the structural-functional analysis would argue, belongs to the largely anonymous army of child care workers in statutory and voluntary agencies including organisations like Amnesty and Oxfam whose broader activities must inevitably address the child. Two recent books which document this approach, both associated with the 1989 United Nations Convention on the rights of the child, pursue this discourse under the titles: *Stolen Childhood* (Vittachi, 1989) and *Broken Promise* (Allsebrook and Swift, 1989).

The conspiracy theory tale

This tells a story of the growth of professional hegemony, highlighting the abuse and mistreatment of children by professionals, and the dubious value of so-called benefits like universal education. Probably it is

Ivan Illich (1973) who is the best-known story-teller from this perspective, although there are a number of others more recently (e.g. Howitt, 1991). In this tale, established philanthropists are, predictably, debunked and presented as tools of the system and oppressors of the poor and the weak. What has given this story a considerable boost in subjective credibility is the recent focus of concern onto child abuse. This has resulted in a marked growth in willingness to accept children's evidence and the accounts, by adults, of their childhood experiences of abuse. As a result, it is by no means unusual nowadays to find this sort of 'hatchet job' on a major figure in the child care field:

> The Bettelheim I knew who, while publicly condemning violence, physically abused children. And the Orthogenic School I knew was an Orwellian world where mail was censored and conversations monitored . . . My knowledge comes from first-hand experience. I spent a decade at his school, against my will . . . To be sure, the blows he struck, though often painful and humiliating, did not physically injure people. But I often saw Mr Bettelheim drag children across the floor by their hair and hit them . . . We had no privacy, Mr Bettelheim often walked into bathrooms where teen girls were undressed. (Pekow, *The Guardian*, 1 August 1990)

What gives this account plausibility is its inter-textuality. Very similar narratives are an all too common feature of autobiographical accounts of abuse in institutional care (e.g. Doyle, 1989). Perhaps the most powerful collection of such narratives is to be found in *Lost Children of the Empire* (Bean and Melville, 1989). This book tells the story of Britain's child migrants – a story, incidentally, that does a lot more than deconstruct the Barnardo legend. Among other things it hammers home the sheer scale of this diaspora: an estimated 150,000 British children were sent to the colonies between 1618 and 1967!

For our present purposes, such arguments between alternative accounts of the workings of paedology are of less concern than that which unites them – a recognition of the power attributed to formalised child knowledge, its experts and its practitioners. In all industrialised countries, agencies and agents for the welfare of children operate through a specific and highly complex body of civil and criminal law which in theory (though practice is patchy) renders every minor under some kind of state wardship (cf. Freeman, 1989). This legislation covers such domains as education, health, physical and moral welfare. By both exclusion and specific design, they also delineate the segregation, to greater or lesser degrees, of children from the life world and experiences of adults: from work, from voting, from legal liability, from sexual activity. In order to penetrate its 'march of progress' gloss, we need to explore the origins of our current systems.

The discovery of child concern

If we look at the stories of child concern the modern era has handed down to us, a critical gaze renders them stories, which we can begin to explore in terms of the realities they seek to construct.

Conquering heroes

Perhaps the best known child saver in Britain is Barnardo. Here is one treatment of his story:

> In the beginning an unknown medical student in the East End of London brought the children of the slums into his home. Thomas Barnardo rounded up [sic] boys sleeping in the streets to house and to teach them; within ten years he had raised sufficient funds to build homes, a hospital, a separate village [sic] for girls and to provide industrial and domestic training for his charges. By the twentieth century his name had become synonymous with orphan homes; a network of Barnardo homes covered the UK and his personal influence on the upbringing of destitute children spread as far as Japan, China, India, Argentina and North America. (Rose, 1987, p. 15)

Just as stories of child development operate so as to both justify and explain our own adult condition as a necessary progress from a less mature, less evolved past, so the constructed histories of child concern too tell of a march of progress. Rose, for example, continues:

> Despite pious hopes, some rescued children found institutional life oppressive. . . . As late as the 1960s, the work had a missionary purpose and a missionary zeal . . . Today the old possessiveness is gone, Barnardo's cares for children in a modern and professional manner. (pp. 15–16)

Such narratives are typical of the story of child concern as told by those located within the moral agenda of reform, as true in the nineteenth century as it is today. However, child concern has never been a singular endeavour. Rather like 'America', child mistreatment has always been there (it took neither a Barnardo nor a Columbus to bring them into existence) and has been subject to periodic rediscovery. Barnardo was in his time one such explorer. Tales of discovery, are themselves, powerful narrative forms, and also have the common feature of remaking history from scratch. Each exposé of child mistreatment not only casts the phenomenon anew, it also provides a new root for a history, changing (often muting) the past and helping to generate a pressing and present condition of crisis.

The discovery of the 'battered child'

Much of our present concern for the 'abused child' (to judge from contemporary texts) stems from the '(re)discovery' of physical mistreatment by Henry Kempe in 1962 which he storied into new being under the rubric 'the battered child syndrome'. Akin to the fashion business, the discovery process thrives on its ability to be successful. Rediscoveries that failed to ignite a sense of crisis, like fashions that failed to take off, are seldom culturally memorable. What sticks in collective consciousness then, are successful rediscoveries. An important ingredient in that success is not just the story but how it is told. The Barnardo operation was very skilled at public relations. So too, sadly, have been a succession of children whose deaths have come to epitomise how the existing system is failing: they get an enquiry named after them, like Maria Colwell, Jasmine Beckford or Kimberley Carlile. However, personalising the victim is not the only route to societal attention. Much of Kempe's marketing skill lay in finding the right brand name ('the battered child') for his product.

The Cleveland crisis

Of course, discovery is not just an active process of construction; sometimes it is the multiple disaster that sets the label and the concern 'naturally' follows. So it was for the village of Abervan whose school was engulfed by a sliding slag-heap. So too, events in child protection in Cleveland in 1987, which rendered the term 'Cleveland' synonymous with (according to one's gaze): a sense that more than the usual tip of the iceberg of sexual abuse had been exposed; that the normally hidden errors (see, for example, Howitt 1991) of child protection work had been exposed; or an excuse for statutory child snatching. Cleveland, the metaphor, has been widely and variously storied: as a judicial report (Butler-Sloss, 1988); from a feminist perspective (e.g. Campbell, 1988); and, as a cautionary tale (e.g. Bell, 1988). From a narrative perspective, these alternative stories are the material not for sifting fact from fiction but for a cultural analysis of the cultural tectonics of the storying of child concern. For, as Ferguson (1992) notes: 'In effect, "Cleveland" was rendered a symbol of the powerful ambivalences surrounding child abuse: over whose construction of "abuse" holds truth, and over the power of class, gender and national and local cultures in the determination of appropriate policies and practices' (p. 147). In other words, 'Cleveland' also became a root of discovery of child concern, but one that was, from its very beginnings, multipli-storied. Like any new origin from which child concern becomes retold, it had the effect of rendering that which went before it diminished in magnitude and compressed in time. This Einsteinian-like relativity effect, in which the location of the observer determines the observations made, is not so much a problem to be faced in any accounting of the construction of child concern, as it is an inevitable feature of both that accounting and that construction. The only way the observer can escape from the effects of location (and even this escape cannot be absolute, only relative) is by striving to avoid narrative singularisation.

Ferguson had the good fortune to be so multipli-located, since he was working in the Cleveland area, researching on child protection work in the locality around the beginning of the century, when 'The Cleveland scandal' broke. Of course, it is not possible to reconstruct how he would have told that history had it merely remained a history. All that can be said is, that with two positions from which to tell a tale, the Cleveland area in 1880–1914 emerges from his research as a place well-policed by child protection services – and needing to be (the 'growth' in child abuse is just one observer-effect operating in current discovery stories). Contrary to one common myth promulgated with those stories, Ferguson found that sexual abuse 'was discovered, classified and worked with' at the time (p. 162). More generally, his work attests to the way the legislative constructions of child concern have very special features as narratives. For they are narratives with particularly powerful conduct implications – the statutory duties and responsibilities that they bring into being.

Telling legislation

The period Ferguson studied is of interest because it covers the period which sees the coming into being of several important pieces of legislation. These were The Prevention of Cruelty to Children Act of 1889 with its amending Acts of 1894 and 1904, and the Custody of Children Act of 1891 (the so-called Barnardo Act) which gave considerable new powers to the voluntary child rescue organisations like Barnardo's and the NSPCC. Then there was the Children Act of 1908 which firmly established the duties of local authorities in regard to the young. This rapid transformation of the legal constitution of child concern and shifting of responsibilities from voluntary to statutory bodies found its reflection in major changes in child protection practice. It saw, for example, the emergence and then the disappearance of the NSPCC children's shelters. After these massive social-tectonic events, a geography of child protection was left whose major landscape features were still in evidence at the time of 'Cleveland 2' in 1987.

By 1989, a whole new, integrated story of child concern was drafted, debated and put on the statute book – the England and Wales Children Act 1989. The details of how this was brought into being are related by Parton (1991). Not least of interest is the way that, given the politicisation that underpins much of the recent child concern discovery, the mandarins of Whitehall (actually, mostly at the less salubrious Elephant and Castle) worked 'behind the scenes' to yield an Act which attracted all-party support in Parliament. In turn, there is no doubt that the dynamics brought to the surface by the Cleveland affair, helped both to shape the Act and create the sense of crisis that brought it into rapid being.

The Children Act textualises out of being a whole era of prior child legislation and along with it their attendant constructions of concern about cruelty to children. In their place, it offers a new, integrated system of concern about the child. Only time will tell the effect of these changes on the way children's welfare is storied in society as a whole but many of the concepts upon which ordinary understandings have operated for generations (e.g. parental rights; custody, care and control after divorce) have literally been written out of operation. However, the claim of the Act to rewrite the whole position of child in law, also renders it open to the very processes of located perception and observer-effects discussed earlier. It has, for example, been promoted as a Children's Charter just as the innovations of nearly a century ago were in their times. A particular feature of the Act often highlighted is its 'new' attention to listening to the child's wishes – although this ignores (or more likely, is ignorant of the fact that) just such a provision was incorporated into the 1891 Custody of Children Act.

Current discourses of child concern

In the post-industrial world, institutions like the law and social policy have undergone many changes in a relatively short period. Indeed it has been claimed by Williams (1992) that in Britain currently, social policy is very much now entrapped within postmodernism, as indexed by increasing fragmentation of provision, rapid change and consequent uncertainty about the future. This has led to a proliferation of large numbers of small-scale, local, fragile groups working on short-term funding. She suggests that what has happened under Thatcherism in the United Kingdom is a reaction against the purported universalism of the post-war welfare state, in which there has been wholesale closure of institutions, without any systematic replacements other than the half-hearted and underfunded 'care in the community'. This can be seen in relation to children in the recent moves away from residential care in 'Children's Homes' to almost universal use of foster care, in the patchy, uncoordinated availability of after-care or therapy for children who have been identified as 'abused', and in the enormous differences between the way one local authority and another seeks to investigate allegations of child mistreatment (see, for example, Parton, 1991).

Such diversity in praxis is mirrored by equal diversity in opinions about and understandings of 'the problems' and how they should be tackled. Again, according to Williams, the nature of public and professional debate is postmodern, in that the guiding consensual meta-narratives and universal values of the past have been rejected, replaced by a proliferation of alternative, competing viewpoints, often reflecting 'identity politics' in which individuals and small groups vie with each other for ideological supremacy. In the area of children, we see vociferous debates between those most concerned to offer children the 'right' to be protected, and those seeking to advance their full emancipation and 'rights' to autonomy. Any attempt to systematise these has to take the form of a simplifying story, justified only for its ability to create a passing order – a structure to be used like any cultural labelling (e.g. classical, romantic, modern) as a tentative analytic, open to evidential and theoretical evaluation. Other critical writers have sought to systematise in this way by a focus on the representations of the child employed. Hendrick (1990) for example, offers: the romantic child; the evangelical child; the factory child; the delinquent child; the schooled child; the psycho-medical child; the welfare child; the psychological child; the family child; and the public child. The one we have adopted, focusing on understanding and praxis, allows an airing of most of the elements in contemporary dispute and draws them together in voices which seem to make themselves heard in social debate.

Traditionalism

Applied primarily descriptively, not judgementally, this refers to an approach not so much to children in general as to proximal children (i.e. the children of our people, our caste, our tribe, our family). It draws upon strongly established, rich and complex cultural patterns. One's young and being young are framed within a continuous past which delineates a specific identity (e.g. as a Romany) which often includes a codified concept (often specifically religious) of good child-rearing practice and established mores (again often with religious roots) for coping with such challenges as orphanhood. The precise content of traditional understandings of the child and of child-rearing are greatly diverse if one takes a global perspective. Culture by culture they vary in received terms along such dimensions as strict to indulgent, childhoods to young personhoods, and state of sin to state of innocence. However, when in tension with other stories of childhood (as occurs wherever traditional stories meet other institutionally evolved stories), traditional accounts of the child are a conservative force – a challenge to progress – whatever their substantive content. They roughly approximate to what Mead (1972) calls a post-figurative condition, in which: 'The past of the adults is the future of each new generation; their lives provide the ground plan' (p. 31). In contrast, a co-figurative condition is where 'old and young alike would assume that it was "natural" for the behaviour of each new generation to differ from that of the preceding generation' (p. 60). The very perpetuation of a traditional culture through its young has been anathema to many powerful religious, nationalist and colonial movements throughout history. At numerous points this has resulted in genocide or programmes of cultural extinction in which the young have been subject to re-education (e.g. through adoption or missionary schools). Even in the recent history of the western democracies, we have seen policies like the imposition of fixed location schooling on the young of wandering peoples. In a typical post-industrial culture, traditional accounts of children can be mapped onto the following groupings:

- Those immigrants from culturally and economically non-indigenous cultures who resist assimilation and seek to construct their young by their own lights.
- Members of historically established sects, particularly religious collectives such as the Amish in North America.
- Indigenous conservatives (e.g. religious fundamentalists) who seek to protect their children from a dominant culture seen as lost to progress, and to seek to socialise the young in what they perceive as eternal values.
- As a nostalgic reaction. Here a traditional childhood is offered as an antithesis to a disparaged modern condition.

Such traditionalism is frequently voiced (if not followed in practice) by right-wing politicians trying to be folksy in pursuit of the moral majority vote – Theresa Gorman's (1991) invectives against what she calls the ills of 'ersatz families' (i.e. single parent families and those where divorce has led to step-parenting) is a good example. It is also offered as counter-revolutionary to progressive education in the prospectus of many a private school. In policy terms, these diverse strands of traditionalism tend, in practice, to come together around concerns about parental rights, discipline, religious education and protecting the innocence of children from corrupting mass culture.

Welfarist protectionism

Like traditionalism, this is a complex of voices. As we have seen, it first emerged in the eighteenth and nineteenth centuries, from within philanthropic and reformatory gazes upon the child. Its intellectual roots, however, lie in a number of challenges to received understandings of children which began to emerge through philosophical treatments of the young (e.g. Locke and Rousseau) and educational innovation (e.g. Montessori). Welfarist protectionism variously sought to improve the educational, environmental, legal, life-opportunity, moral, and physical condition of the young through an uneasy alliance between statutory and voluntary action. In so doing it constructed working understandings of the needs of the young – for example, in defining the needs of children (Kellmer Pringle 1980), and the standards of 'good enough parenting' (CCETSW, 1978) and devised appropriate policy stances for meeting them. The changing legal position of under-class children from family vassals to national assets held in conditional wardship by their caretakers is often presented as the agenda achieved by welfarist protectionism. In so doing, it created large scale monitorial agencies (e.g. child care workers, school medical services). These institutional care systems were devised for those whose families were seen to fail and/or to have failed their children, with a focus upon the prevention and alleviation of cruelty and neglect. Welfarist protectionism was well-established long before a formal discipline of child psychology emerged as a powerful intellectual voice, and many of its long-lasting practices (e.g. adoption with total severance from the natural family, the orphanage as total institution) are now increasingly seen as inimical to the subjective well-being of young people. Its contemporary dialect reflects a sensitivity to such past mistakes and a greater willingness to work with families. It also incorporates attempts to address the experiental well-being of young people missing in earlier expressions. None the less the majority of the clients of welfarist protectionism remain drawn from the perceived inadequate under-class, and the focal concern of the professional gaze remains upon statutorily-defined and practice-delineated cruelty and neglect:

> Traditionally the field of child welfare was established to provide social services that supplement or substitute for parental care and supervision. Many families cannot manage by themselves, and their needs reflect problems not directly child-related – such as poor housing, poverty and adult mental illness. Therefore, child welfare also includes services that attempt to remedy the consequences of inadequate social institutions. Either way, one is providing a deficit service . . . designed for special groups rather than for all children. Thus the field of child welfare is oriented toward pathology and deprivation. (Jenkins, 1975, p. 4)

This creates an understanding which not only influences its practitioners but also society at large. The needs of children (as reflected in, say, the advertising of the older-established children's charities) are often seen in simple class or economic terms, in blatant handicaps or florid cruelty and neglect. The established bureaucratic location of welfarist protectionism may well account for the emergence elsewhere of a concern for less overt, more diffusely located and more problematic aspects of children's well-being such as corporal punishment and sexual abuse. It is noteworthy that virtually all concern about these 'problems' have been directed to families, not to the boarding schools used by the rich and powerful, where both are at least as endemic, and certainly more pervasively culturally sanctioned. Where welfarist protectionism leads us, in the present, is to a situation where the child's 'right' to protection is viewed as paramount. In order to protect a child from, for example, coercion to deny sexual assault, professional intervention is justified in riding roughshod not only over the civil rights of parents, but those of children.

Child emancipation

Welfarist protectionism typically takes a structural-functionalist view of society in which cruelty and neglect of children are viewed as correct-able diseases prevalent only in relatively small parts of the social body. The radical notion that childhood *per se* is a condition of oppression has little cachet within its walls. Such a notion is alien to both its remit and its ways of operating. This is not, of course, to suggest that some individuals working within institutionalised child welfare might not have access to notions of children's rights (and be working at revolution from within). They often are, after all, frequently members of socialist and feminist movements which have a committed if not widespread following in the recent history of the post-industrial world. However, we believe that in general the child-emancipatory understanding and policy stance to child concern, operates by modelling it (with greater or lesser awareness of doing so) upon other liberatory movements.

Of course, radical credentials are not a requirement for the extension of the social democratic construct of 'entitlement as a citizen' to include children. The discourse of the special condition of the child can easily be conjoined with a plea for protected space in which children can grow to a mature ability to exercise their rights when adults. However, in the full-blown 'rights dialect' of child emancipation, the child is seen as suffering from an oversight within 'social chartism'.

Other groups have their rights delineated and organisationally de-fended (women, workers, the physically challenged) – why not children?

Hence, the press to develop bills of children's rights, children's advocates and ombudsmen [sic], children's refuges, etc. The objective is no mere safe 'reservation' but something much more like a growing acknowledgement of the developing personhood of the child:

> Any discussion of children's rights and the welfare of the child has to recognise the tension that exists between those who argue for legislation to protect children better from the adult world, and those who see the best protection for children being in recognising children as independent beings and treating them as adults, i.e. not discriminating against them, whenever possible . . . I argue that the older the child becomes, and the less physically dependent, the greater the importance of treating the child as one would any other person. (Roche, 1989, p. 135)

In its radical dialect, an emancipatory discourse is often achieved by using conspiracy theory concepts developed for other groups – women under the yoke of patriarchy, colonial peoples under the yoke of imperial power, citizens under the yoke of the free market. Here the solution is often seen to be to direct action challenges to the power-bases (men, parents as colonisers, the economic system) which enable the abuse and misuse of children.

> Since the 1970s women have been setting up self-help groups, crisis lines (often run from women's own homes) and education initiatives in the fight against child sexual abuse. Self-help and grassroots political activity were often the only alternatives in the face of widespread professional indifference, disbelief and victim-blaming. (Kitzinger, 1989, p. 254)

What all dialects of child emancipation share is the perspective that the rights of any child can be abused, and that the condition of oppression need not be simply physical. At one level this can result in an internationalist gaze – a concern for 'all the world's children', for their physical and mental health, for their access to education, for their removal from the workplace and so on. Within a national space, the gaze can operate wherever access to children is not grossly class-divided (e.g. in paediatrics, in education, and, potentially, in law). It is evident in the growing systems of children's ombudsmen (see, for example, Flekkøy, 1991) and organisations like the Children's Legal Centre in England, and the Centre for the Child in Israel, and more specialist organisations, such as NAYPIC directed towards promoting the rights of children 'in care'. Yet for all its concerns for listening to the child rather than imposing a needs-driven solution from above, in practice, the child emancipation discourse runs the risk of becoming single ideology-driven (the 'it all boils down to' approach, often with 'power' playing the part of villain). Tensions between its dialects can emerge wherever abstract rights do not actually impinge fairly or evenly in a social structure which itself is neither fair nor equable.

The critical polytextualist's alternative

Currently then, we operate on and within a structurally and historically constituted plurality of discursive practices about and upon child concern. A critical polytextualist analysis of these discourses seeks to address them as socially constructed (and also lived in) stories, and to pursue child concern within the recognition that it is belongs to and cannot be separated from the social-tectonics of social thinking in general. It offers not an understanding of child concern *per se* so much as a concern about concern (which we specifically tackle in Chapter 11). What we need to address are not just the stories told in the extant discourses, but, as importantly, to unpick their ideological motivations (whose interests are they promoting?) and to examine their practical consequences. In other words, we must not only examine (as we have in this chapter) the stories each one tells of children's needs, rights, etc., but what conduct they enable and what ideologies they warrant. We believe it is crucial to be able to highlight and discuss the child-oppressive potentials of each, without being immediately accused either of merely attacking the well-meaningness of those who argue for them, or of failing to acknowledge the dangers of our challenge. It has to become possible to challenge traditionalism, without being held to be racist. It has to become possible to worry about the down-side costs of protectionism, without being implicated as apologists for the paedophile lobby. It has to become possible to worry about the pressures upon children of dumping unpalatable decisions upon them, without being condemned as ageist. Our approach cannot – and would not seek to – offer a singular actionable morality towards the young, precisely because it seeks to address the very plurality of such moralities. However, this itself requires the imposing of distance and contrast upon the received stories and hence, like (in this respect) any critical treatment, it will come to a reconstruction in complementarity to that which it deconstructs. That reconstruction enables a moral gaze upon the young (albeit a self-doubting one) and hence an approach to policy.

All that having been said, we would not deny that, in a culture where multiple understandings of child well-being co-exist, there can still be general moral consensus about paradigm cases. The act of throwing boiling water at a child can stand condemned, despite there being widely differing understandings of that event (e.g. whether the perpetrator is seen as possessed, an inadequate parent stressed beyond breaking point, or as a member of a dominant group making recourse to terror through physical power to maintain authority over the oppressed). Nevertheless, even here, these differing understandings will lead to divergent calls about what action to take in respect of the child, the adult and the collectivity at large. However, critical polytextualism advances the expectation that over a very large range of actions concerning children there may be no consensus at all. We would argue that this lack of consensus is not just confined to how children are understood, but extends to the way conflicting understandings of children are themselves inextricably linked into divergent world-views. The doubts which afflict contemporary child-care in the post-industrial world (which can make action decisions so problematic) are not the mere experience of pulls between differing understandings of the child as situated, but between different moral universes. As a cultural analysis, critical polytextualisation also brings into focus considerations which are often diffuse or absent in other gazes upon the young. Hence, for example, the need to take into account a treatment of children (and increasingly so with growing maturity) as agents in-their-own-right within the social context. This is to go much further than a legalistic concept of children's rights. It is not just a plea that they should be seen as persons, that their voice should be heard but an assertion of their own self-constructive powers of personhood (that they are persons). Simply, the child cannot be construed as just a commodity, the object of policy, a part of a family or just a vehicle of cultural perpetuation. To model the child as construct*ed* but not as construct*ive* diminishes what the model can say. It permits us to see the young person as having their identity constructed by outside forces but not the young person constructing their identity out of the culturally available. That such stories include understandings in which self-construction is denied is just one of the many complexities which the critical polytextualisation gaze permits. The constructs within critical polytextualisation which enable it to allow many stories, and to doubt that more than a situated truth can be established for any, gives the approach its very particular status as a moral account. It says, in effect: be in doubt; know when you are using a self-justifying story; be aware that telling stories is also preaching parables; accept that your actions are problematic but also that non-engagement in the social is not possible.

6

Modern times and great dictators:
A genealogy of developmentalism

In this chapter we will explore the history of academic theorising about the young child science, as it has been formalised within the dominant culture of modern western industrialised society. Unlike the history of the child and childhood *per se*, child science offers clear and extensive primary sources – texts of child development, which belong within a clearly identifiable temporal and geographical location. So too, do the agendas (if not all the targets) of the discourses of child theorising we will examine. This gives a certain shape to the material – a clearly restricted placement in time and space to both author and audience. To explore where those stories 'came from', must inevitably leave much of the broader global tale untold. There is, of course, a theorising of the child outwith the thema of modernism and its discontents. However, as Boyden (1990) notes, any critique of the 'globalisation of childhood' (i.e. the exportation of western ideologies of child concern) is also an acknowledgement of the power-knowledge synarchy unique to those ideologies. The challenge to that hegemony must come, therefore, from within – from analysis of how it brings an evangelical project of bettering childhoods into being. We will tell this chapter as a story woven not so much out of the theories themselves, but of the men (predominantly) who formulated them, the gods and demi-gods, *lares* and *penates*, whose names have come to signify the ideas and arguments themselves. The questions of why theoretical evolution should be so personified, and why women's names and ideas have (so far) been largely excluded from the endeavour we will leave for another time and another book.

The garden of Eden

Even if we reject claims that childhood was invented in the sixteenth century, we can still identify that as the point at which (in Europe at least) the first books of formal theorisation about childhood were produced. Somewhere around that point a massive growth in literary activity began – a new world of books, letters and authors (Williams, 1965). The now-familiar condition of almost frenzied textual disputation over everything (including the child) started in that sixteenth century textual explosion. With regard to childhood those 'origins' arose as medical, religious and philosophical tracts upon the child. The textual codification of a medicine of childhood (paediatrics), at least for English-speaking writers, is usually traced back to Thomas Phaire's *The Boke of Chyldren* (1554; quoted in Tomalin, 1981), which achieved a very-modern sounding run of seven editions. Obviously, the religious textual accounting of children has no such easy anchor, since these pre-date modernism, and its warrant to rationality and science. Prior to that point, issues of the child, the state of the child's soul, and its handling in the medieval religious educational establishments, were in the West part of an ongoing and apparently unassailable Catholic hegemony.

Founding fathers

Hence, it is to the break with that tradition – the Reformation – to which writers usually turn to locate roots for our current theoretics of childhood. This reformationist gaze upon the child (usually called by US writers *Puritanism*, although it reflects much which was common to Protestant Europe) produced as its 'bible' of child management *The New England Primer*. This short didactic text (first published in 1687, but with editions running well into the nineteenth century) sold over six million copies, an extraordinary figure given North America's population over that period. The Puritan gaze saw children as born evil and prone to sin, without moral knowledge, but with a capacity to learn (cf. Thomas, 1985). In (as we would now term it) its treatment of the neonate endowment, it clearly had considerable resonances with the gloomy Hobbesian analysis of 'human nature' (e.g. Hobbes, 1588–1679), which was later to echo in Freudian and ethological voices on childhood. However, in its emphasis upon an epistemological *tabula rasa* we hear the voice of that other 'founding father of childhood', Locke (1632–1704), an often-cited progenitor of the behaviouristic gaze upon the child. Locke serves too as an anchor in the domain of children's rights, when he argued for a parental custodianship until development brought about freedom and rationality – a kind of competence analysis.

Nearly a century separates Locke from the final, most-quoted originator of a root account of childhood, Rousseau (1955). It is a century in which the dominant gaze upon the child (as on all else) shifted from religion to humanism, as part of the Enlightenment and the post-Enlightenment humanistic project. Rousseau occupies a fulcrum position in texts of childhood because he is both a fountainhead and a contemporary (for an analysis of Rousseau in the freeschooling/deschooling debate see Barrow, 1978). To Rousseau are currently attributed major contributions to: humanistic developmentalism; cognitive developmentalism; child-centred education and socialisation. Rousseau is also a crucial hook upon which writers hang their texts because of the means by which he accounted. *Emile* is in the form of a novel. The result is that we come to look not at an abstract theory, but at the personalised events of a fictive biography. In the history of stories of childhood, Rousseau is contemporaneous with many, including a number of women, who were writing (often from much more direct personal experience) of the passage of their children's lives (e.g. Dietrich Tiedemann, Hester Thrale, Fanny Burney, Mary Wollstonecraft). In some cases at least (e.g. Wollstonecraft), these biographies became reflexive in the lives of their subjects, when older children were encouraged to reflect upon their earlier selves and earlier experiences as significant, perhaps causal, events in the shaping of the present self. It was not until well into the nineteenth century that advances in photography made a similar recapitulation easily possible in the visual mode. It is worth bearing in mind in considering the modern condition of childhood and its theorists how far those theories were generated by and taken up by people who had themselves experienced such reflexive childhoods.

Most early 'baby biographies' (Tiedemann is an exception) arose *outside* of the scientific gaze of modernism i.e. they tended not to be conducted by scientists or for scientific purposes. Yet when developmentalists looked for bedrock studies on which to ground accounts, they tended to use 'baby biographies' woven within bio-medical analysis and conjecture, so they could be told within a story of the 'march of science'. A favoured candidate is Darwin's 1877 publication of his reworked notes from 1840, *A Biographical Sketch of an Infant*, itself a response to Taine's account of earlier that same year. These (and a rash of books on the same subject e.g. Preyer's *Die Seele des Kindes*, 1882) established a genre which was to be increasingly taken over by the emerging discipline of developmentalism.

Many names are offered as the pioneer figures for a discipline which (as part of the broader empire of psychology) was becoming increasingly dominated by US and British researchers (and, subsequently, historians of child psychology, of course!) Hence, while work progressed right across continental Europe, the names that have come to be cited are those either of British or US developmentalists, or those few continentals who gained a place in that English-language story (such as Binet).

Sully (e.g. 1895), based in London, gained a high citation index (as we now measure academic merit in the market place of universities) both as a major researcher and collator of findings. He was an early user of the Galtonian problematic nature-nurture tension. Meanwhile, at Clark University in the United States, Hall (who believed that children recapitulate the developmental history of the human species – which is why, he said, little boys play with bows and arrows!) began a child study movement in 1891 which was aimed at providing a complete developmental description of the child from birth to adolescence. Both Sully and Hall were extremely good story-tellers around quite weak and problematic data (a position Hall had the good grace to admit in his 1923 Biography). What they lacked, the books tend to tell us, far more than better methods however, was a good theory (cf. Lomax, 1978).

The erection of the pantheon

Freud as 'God the Father'

It is difficult to think of a better starting candidate for such a task than Freud! Freud was the first of the 'Gods' – a 'god' not only of developmentalism but also of personality theory and psychotherapy. Few figures of the last hundred years have attracted so much citation, criticism, adulation and re-analysis (not all of it psycho-). The main bones of the story concerning the theory (psychodynamics), the intellectual movement around it, and the man himself are too well known to merit detailed reiteration. Space is, however, worth devoting to slightly less well hashed-over aspects of Freud's acquisition of his omnipotent place in the temple of the Gods. Well before the invention of psychoanalysis (1895), Freud had worked as a neurologist, a physiologist and pharmacologist. If things had been different, Freud might have finished up in the annals of science for his work on the aphasias, on the genitals of eels, or on cocaine. The great leap, which left all behind it, was Freud's (not altogether explicit) reconstruction of psychiatry into a language game. Within psychoanalysis, he became a collector of accounts, of retrospections and re-retrospections on autobiography – reflections that were drawn not from the nomic, public voice of remembering, but from the anomic, private voices of hypnotic phenomena, dreams and free-associations. In so doing, he came close to becoming a 'founding father' of theorisation on child sexual abuse since in his early work with his women patients he documented a high frequency of stories of 'seduction' in childhood – often by close relations (and usually, but not always, by men): 'Then he made what he thought was a momentous "discovery": What he had heard from these women were not genuine memories; they were, Freud said fabricated stories, or made up fictions' (Masson, 1990a, p. 25).

Freud's subsequent reinterpretation of these accounts as psychic *constructions* made psychoanalysis possible as a hermeneutic craft. In doing so it also transformed a potential radical theory of the 'child as victim' of sexual assault into a recasting of the 'child as original sinner'. Consequently, although sexual assaults upon children had been documented as early as 1857 by the French paediatrician Tardieu, Freud's decision to recast his patients' disclosures as childhood fantasies about sex, served to reinforce the then contemporary view that it was *the child* who was the moral agent in sexual 'misbehaviour' (e.g. masturbation). Freud created out of such transformations a powerfully compelling meta-narrative. It was so encompassing, so riven by inner tensions, so ambiguous, so akin to an hermetic text, that it has acquired the status of a modern Nostradamus. What else can explain his utilisation by theologians, Marxists, feminists, even psychologists? Freudian theory manages this in part by the highly 'unscientific' validational endorsement of personal affirmation. As Thomas (1985) notes:

> Despite the shortcomings of Freudian theory when judged against common scientific criteria . . . much of the theory makes a kind of existential sense to me. I believe in the unconscious, in repression, in our use of defence mechanisms, and in many other concepts the theory includes. (p. 232)

This extraordinarily liturgical reaction is by no means unusual. Indeed, for some, becoming a Freudian has been by a process of virtually Pauline conversion (hardly a statement one could make of other theories in developmentalism). In the 'talking cure' of psychodynamics, one needs to take on the world-view in order to be able to take the medicine. And as all psychoanalysts also have to be analysed, the presence in culture of overtly 'born-again' Freudians should not, perhaps, surprise us. But there is more than that going on. Freud both tapped into and transformed a significant vein in the cultural discourse mine. He one-sidedly highlighted diverse tensions in his culture (e.g. the savage child over the innocent child, the impulsive over the rational, the hidden face over the public face) and set others in perpetual tension (the biological and the social, the act and the wish, the real and the fantasy), moulding the whole into a powerful mythology. By reworking meanings, recasting words, he constructed a new accounting-language, one in which we now all share as part of our cultural competence (Moscovici, 1984). If there had been no Freud, then we would have no Woody Allen – almost a justification in itself!

Freud's accounting-language (although often not his ideological world-view) has been very much taken up by child protection workers (most notably in social work, but also in other professions) and transmuted into a practice-language. Rose (1990) says of this 'new psychology' of the years between the two world wars:

> The new psychological social workers combined with the psychologists of the clinic in writing narratives of love gone wrong, combining a number of recurrent motifs of family dramas that made childhood maladjustments understandable in terms of the emotions, desires and disappointments of the adults who surrounded them. . . . Abnormality had its roots in the interplay between the desires of parents and the desires of their children, in the medium of love itself. (p. 155)

The colonisation by practitioners of psychodynamic theory, and its appropriation as a technology of social regulation, was grounded upon the attribution to it (as Freud himself wished) of the status of a human-science knowledge. However, as we have argued already, its warrant of credibility comes not from empirical validation (cf. Thomas, 1985) but from affirmation. We, Rex and Wendy, also (in one meaning of the term) 'believe' – we believe in 'the unconscious' as we 'believe' in 'false consciousness'; 'flying saucers'; 'Oz'; and 'bad vibrations'. We believe, for not to be able to enter into the narratives that employ such discursive elements would amount to us being socially disadvantaged across several biographical locations that were, or still are, significant to us.

None of these understandings have an objective, external referent which constitutes them as truth – their meanings come from rules of usage within the language-games in which they are located. Nevertheless, it would be (indeed is) a very strange kind of psychology which held that because they are so constituted, they cannot be admitted into its gaze. Apart from anything else, they are, by conventional meaning, capable of being causes *because* their presence or absence as elements in a discourse yields different effects. If they did not, there could not be a Freudian reality different (in terms of how we act within it) to an non-Freudian reality (such as a Marxist reality or a feminist reality). As it is for us, so too is it, of course, for the child, whose accounting skills, as attributes of a developing person, depend on the ability to voice, to her/himself and to others, the language-games upon which communicability depends. One's id is socially constructed, no less than one's super-ego (cf. Lacan, 1977).

The communicability potential of the Freudian story lies in the construction, by Freud, of the unconscious as a 'wild man' – florid, feckless and feral (as nineteenth century conservative politics saw their mad, their bad and their colonised). Freudian personality dynamics were neatly parodied by Bannister (1966) when he characterised the model as a battlefield between a sex-crazed monkey and a maiden aunt, presided over by a rather nervous bank clerk. As Ingleby (1987) notes: 'we need not seek the origins of Freud's beliefs in his discoveries, his private political views, or his personal state of mind; they are very much a part of his time and of ours as well' (p. 201). By sexualising the child, and by locating this sexuality within an 'anarchy' (i.e. a regime of drives without direction), the repression of the child was rationalised and legitimated – it made the hegemony of parental management (particularly over sex) just as needful, sensible and justified as the hegemony (particularly over sexuality) of men over women, or the coloniser over the colonised. All are warranted by the clever story that 'we are only doing this for your own good' and the even stronger (if less overt) justification of gover-nance itself: 'we need to control you (and particularly your sexuality), because you (and it) are too dangerous (to yourself and to others) to leave to your own devices'. Thus Freud's developmentalism, as Ingleby reminds us, must be recognised as predicated upon a *metatheoretical* conflict model, flavoured by Freud's (or 'Freud as a man of his time's') *ideological* cosmology.

The credit belongs, probably, to Wilhelm Reich for first recognising that this loose-coupled agenda could be dislocated. What Reich identi-fied, from his 1927 monograph *The Function of the Orgasm* onwards, was that the Freudian metatheory could take other ideological readings. Reich offered a simple inversion – that the child's sexuality was not bad but good. The result was a very different reading of socialisation. Now the child's spontaneous eroticism was seen to *suffer* the repressions of the authoritarian family. The result was the neurotic, anorgasmic and sadistic adult. This sexual repression laid the ground for social repres-sion. Reich was not content to theorise the sexual repression of young people, he set out to change it. This he attempted both through sexual counselling and through the promotion of contraception. The establish-ment, however, was not impressed by Reich's advocacy of the (hetero)sexual rights of young people. The outcome was utterly predict-able. Not only did Reich's work bring down the approbation of the psychoanalytic establishment on his head, it also brought down the whole apparatus of state repression. However, the dislocative pos-sibilities Reich recognised were soon to be taken up by all kinds of groups in society (from surrealists to Anglican Bishops) that found in Freud's metatheoretical account a new grounding for their own invest-ment in an irrationalist account of the human condition.

For social critics too, the metatheory detached from its conservative ideology offered an 'explanation of the compulsions and delusions that make people more at home in an oppressive society than they would be in a free one' (Ingleby, 1987, p. 203). And so, despite the thoroughly bourgeois and patriarchal quality of Freud's theorising, radicals – first, neo-Marxists, and then feminists – have adopted psychoanalytic theorising to explain resistance to social change. For Ingleby, what they discovered was that: 'A society run on fairy tales requires, that, in certain fundamental respects, its members should not grow up, particularly the less privileged ones' (p. 203). What Freudian theory provided was a story to theorise the child which should ultimately be seen in terms of what it storied into being about the goal of development – the adult. The Freudian adult is both the neuroticised, fixated, repressed product of conflicted development, *and* the producer of the child that cannot *but* grow up into a clone of its repressors. In Freudian theory development is a reproductive and at the same time inherently repressive process. The orthodox Freudian representation of both the child and the adult proved highly unpalatable to many later psycho-dynamic theorists, particularly after its North Americanisation.

Their liberal-humanistic sensibilities resulted in first revision (e.g. the development of ego-psychology), then expansion of the Freudian 'Pilgrim's Progress' to the whole of the life-span (e.g. Erikson 1963) and finally, into the development of whole new systems of humanistic theorising (e.g. Rogers' client-centred model). Where Freud had located within the adult both child and adult, the newer systems sought to separate the child from the adult. To the former were re-accorded the pre-Freudian qualities of innocence, to the latter were re-accorded responsibility. (There was, of course, a counter-discourse, that negated all responsibility – this is nicely ironised in Rhinehart's *The Dice Man*, 1972.) At least, so it was for the therapist and the successfully therapised. For the patient, the story was still told of ruinous childhoods leading to ruined adults (Carl Rogers, to be fair at least tried to avoid that causal trap, but at the cost of an almost total rejection of external sources of distress, cf. Masson, 1990a). The new ostensible 'user-friendliness' of this revised metatheory helped to create a wider market for both child psychotherapy and work with adults. However, neither group can be said to have gained the recognition of personhood the theories valorised. For the child, the price of the re-instituted innocence was de-eroticisation. Sexualisation of the child became the sign of a Garden of Eden ruination, a sure and certain marker that innocence, indeed childhood itself, had been stolen. For the adult, the cost of earlier ruination was a ruined personality – yet because the adult now had re-instituted responsibility, that damage might account for but not justify present conduct. The result was a location in which there was fault without hope of self-reconstruction. Only by external intervention could the sinner be saved. Thus the patient was translated back into a pre-modern, traditional Christian location of a soul adrift in a sea of troubles, awaiting priestly redemption (for an over-view of some of the more bizarre of these cults of psychobabble see Rosen, 1978). It can now be seen that what Freud did to the child, post-Freudian therapy did to the ruined adult – invested them with a 'wild man within': hence the caricature of therapy as that in which 'the bland teach the unbland to be bland' (Masson, 1990a, p. 245). The talking cures of psychotherapy sought to regulate the middle classes, as the social workers did the working classes – by positioning them as both blameful and incompetent. In other words, they treated them as 'children'!

'Acolyettes'

Given the gendering of professional locations (and the warrant of female immunity from sexual involvement), we should not be surprised that many of the followers best-known for developing Freudian ideas in relation to childhood have been women – including his daughter, Anna, Melanie Klein and Alice Miller. In the case of Miller (e.g. 1985), absence of any direct contact with the analysand proved no deterrent to analysis! Along with such figures as de Mause and Erikson (1963), Miller sub-scribed to the psychohistorical approach – the distal application of psychoanalysis. This particular form of storying into being 'second child-hoods' has been critically evaluated by Stannard (1980) who concludes:

> Traditional criticisms concerning vulgarity, reductionism, trivialisation, and the like all remain valid observations of the psychohistorical enter-prise. But the most important and fundamental reason for the rejection of that enterprise is now clear: psychohistory does not work and cannot work. The time has come to face the fact that, behind all its rhetorical posturing, the psychoanalytic approach to history is – irremediably – one of logical perversity, scientific unsoundness and cultural naïveté. (p. 156)

Miller's work is indeed a wonderland for those seeking instant 'insight' into the 'child within' of Henry Miller, Baudelaire, Adolf Hitler, Freud himself, Flaubert, Rumpelstiltskin, Franz Kafka, Samuel Beckett, and (making a cameo appearance fresh from *Amadeus*) Mozart. Miller's anal-ysis of Virginia Woolf exemplifies the bases for Stannard's evaluation:

> The discovery of one's own inner rooms in the dream corresponds to the discovery of the self, which is no longer the instrument of the other person and only now really becomes free. Very often chronic insomnia or frigidity disappears at this point. Although Woolf's biographer reports that she 'felt that George [her half-brother] had spoilt her life before it had fairly begun,' the link between this fact and her 'mysterious' psychosis remains a riddle to him. Woolf's husband, Leonard, the owner of the Hogarth Press, was the famous publisher of Freud's works in England. Perhaps this acquaintance

with Freud could have saved the life of his wife, the gifted writer, if Freud had not abandoned his seduction theory. (Miller, 1985, p. 128)

Saint Jean de Geneve

It is, perhaps, not that large a leap from the study of eel's gonads to the investigation of molluscs! But it is a jump which takes us from Sigmund Freud's early *curriculum vitae* to that of Jean Piaget. Unlike Freud, Piaget did not create a grand cultural myth, but he is credited with having been the greatest single stimulator of research in the whole of child psychology (a criterion of excellence much valued in the rhetoric of science). Yet outside of psychology and education, Piaget is almost unknown. Certainly, one cannot talk of the Piagetian novel or poem in the way one can a Freudian one. Piagetian ideas do not address vast areas of childhood experience, like child abuse, racism or a hundred and one other issues which might at first sight seem the appropriate grist for a developmental psychology theory mill (by contrast, there are Freudian and other psychodynamic stories aplenty for all of these). The nearest one could come lies in the work of Elkind (e.g. 1979), whose more astute excursions into issues of the child and society are not so much an extension of Piaget's theory as a new theory in its own right.

Early in his career Piaget abandoned two grand theoretical locations: first a commitment to psychoanalysis; and then research work in Binet's Paris laboratory on tests of intelligence. He deserted these endeavours in order to concentrate upon a (partially religiously-inspired) quest to reveal the unfolding of logical reasoning in the child. Piaget did not so much thereby generate a child psychology as a developmental theory of knowledge (a genetic epistemology, cf. Furth, 1969). In so doing he may well have compromised any possibility (if this were his aim) of founding an empirical developmental psychology, for: 'We cannot use a proposition simultaneously as a conceptual yardstick for the construction of observational methods and as a hypothesis to be tested with those very methods' (Brandstädter, 1990). However, there is considerable doubt as to whether this was his objective. Recent research into Piaget's early involvement in Protestant Youth movements has led to the suggestion that he had a far grander sub-text in mind – the scientific study of values (Vidal, 1987). Hence, we may be better to see him as promulgating:

A view of mental and historical development that is the same in different domains . . . a movement from egocentrism, concreteness, heteronomy, authority and transcendence, to objectivity, abstractness, autonomy, contractual reciprocity, and immanence. This movement is progress: from the child and the primitive to the adult and the modern; from undemocratic to democratic regimes; from dogmatic religions to liberal Protestantism. Piaget's developmental research thus resulted in a scientific axiology that reformulated and realised his youthful project of basing morality on science; it granted scientific and philosophical superiority to menaced liberal Protestant values. (p. 288)

Intellectually, Piaget belonged to the predominantly continental movement known as structuralism. His structuralism of the evolving knowledge of children (or cognitive developmental psychology) consists of a programme of tasks, puzzles or challenges (performances) from which the structure (schemes) of the child's thinking can supposedly be inferred. However, unlike psychometricians (from whom, particularly Binet, he learned the interrogative craft) Piaget saw the character of ability not as a continuously growing essence, but as a series of transformational leaps, that must sequentially follow one another just as the molluscs he once studied must metamorphose from embryo, through a larval stage, into their adult form. In this way, Piaget's structuralism renders the child not merely lesser (quantitatively inferior in understanding) but a lesser *alien* (qualitatively inferior in *kind* of understanding). Like Rousseau's, Piaget's theory has been employed to justify 'child-centred' educational regimes (the provision of the right intellectual 'diet' to meet the just evolving cognitive 'nutritional' needs – Piagetians are prone to using nutritional and other biological metaphors to 'explain' their concepts, see Phillips, 1975). However, the theory is intrinsically 'adultist' and educationally élitist, stressing as it does a pre-wired metamorphosis of knowledge through early stages to the final emergence of logical-mathematical reasoning only reliably found in those educated in the western mode to around university entrance level. Needless to say, Piaget has come in for a great deal of stick from Marxist critics, who have pointed out the individualism, the ethnocentrism and class-centrism of his notion of knowledge, and its exclusion of knowledge games other than Aristotelian logic (e.g. dialectical reasoning) (Buck-Morss, 1987, Buss, 1979, Riegal, 1979).

Buck-Morss has been an especially thorough and persistent critic, noting how Piaget's child, like Freud's, is constructed out of a goal for adulthood. For Piaget, that goal is the individual as a citizen in a liberal-bourgeois democracy. The inferiority of the child which Piaget biologises, is, of course, also structural (a position Piaget's own formal-operational logic prevents him apperceiving). The child, unlike the adult, is not the origin of the laws that oppress her or him. Just how a choice of logic is an ideological act is revealed in the following summary of her critique, which also hints at the range of her argument:

> Fairy tales provide an image in which nonidenticals are fused, and in this imagining that reconstructs reality there exists a utopian promise. But the

other pole of that promise is critical thinking that demythifies reality: here nonidenticals converge only when as concepts (children and oppressed, tricksters and heroes, masters and slaves) they are held apart. Fundamental to both fantasy and critical negation (as well as to humor) is the linguistic representation of the nonidentity between thought and reality. The abstract formalism of Piaget's cognitive structures reflects the abstract formalism of the social structure. (Buck-Morss, 1987, pp. 271–2)

At the much more mundane level of Piaget's empirical claims, it now also seems clear that typical Piagetian tasks are problematic for children, particularly younger children, for reasons other than a lack of the schemes supposedly required to solve them. For example, there may be problems of remembering or being able to relate to the task requirements (Bryant, 1977, Donaldson, 1979). Certainly, when recast into more 'user friendly' terms performance can be markedly improved (e.g. Donaldson, 1979, Field, 1981).

However, it is in the area of the social construction of knowledge that Piagetian work has always been thinnest and most vulnerable. Piagetian assumptions that skill in social perspective (e.g. 'seeing' the world of the other, as in empathy) had more than a metaphorical link to skill in geometric perspective, have largely fallen apart (Gelman, 1978). More broadly, Piagetian theory has suffered the same fate as other structuralisms in the hands of post-structuralism. Piaget is seen to have imposed a real or true meaning upon texts (task performances) that possess no such essence. The interrogations can be seen as language games (Wason, 1977) and the tasks as 'trick questions': *Edith is fairer than Susan; Edith is darker than Lily; who is the darkest of the three?* (Piaget, 1950), requiring not an individually activated inner structure to solve them, so much as access to an already sedimented, socially constituted heuristic. If one sees the mongering of knowledge as a form of imperialism then the farthest thrown colonies might be expected to show a form of time-lag, hanging on to practices no longer current at the hub. Just as social work seems to have clung to a Freudian discourse (e.g. Bowlby and maternal deprivation) long after it ceased to be fashion in mainstream developmentalism, so Piagetian notions linger in education and underpin Britain's 'new' national testing of educational competence at set ages.

Conditional Gods

One of the obvious, and yet often overlooked, features of psychology as it has evolved in the twentieth century is its North American-ness. Once psychology hit the burgeoning campuses of the United States, it grew with an impetus no other nation could rival. It could be said that psychology is *the* 'American' discipline – a home base for figures who, from William James to Arthur Jensen, have constructed a powerful reflexivity between the culture and its psychology. Perhaps precisely because the rewards are greater and the downside costs less, it has been the United States not the (newly defunct) USSR in which psychologists have most dabbled in and been part of the social fabric. From the CIA to airport book stalls (stacked with *psychobabble*), psychology seems ubiquitous. Yet, around the years of the first World War, US psychology was far from secure. As our earlier quote from Hall indicated, its methods were far from meeting their early promises. Two events not only stopped the rot but gave psychology a new status as a means of social management and social policing. One of these, psychometrics, is dealt with in our next section. The other, the discovery of behaviourism, is covered here.

Behaviourism heralded forth not so much a God as a discordia of demi-gods. However, much as on Olympus, some were more equal than others and two stand out: J.B. Watson and B.F. Skinner. Watson was the great theoretical entrepreneur: the coiner in 1919 of the term behaviourism, who cobbled together the work of people like Pavlov and Thorndike into a scientific crusade. Psychology was to be the objective science of behaviour and its change. A child, little Albert B., became the unconsenting icon of the new approach. It may well be of significance that Albert had an atypical, bio-medical background. He was the son of a hospital wet nurse who, presumably, saw volunteering her offspring as a 'real contribution to scientific knowledge'. Little Albert, initially tested and found to be unafraid of a range of animals, was allowed to play with a white rat (as students of racism in psychology will know, the colour does matter – *Even the Rat was White*, Guthrie, 1976). Watson then banged a steel rod (or gong – the experiment is varyingly drawn and told, forming a story which is as apocryphal and parabolical as it is real, see Harris, 1979). This elicited 'fearful behaviour' from (a scientific euphemism for scared the bejesus out of) Little Albert. A few repetitions of the experience and the sight of the animal alone produced the same effect, which generalised to a range of other hairy and animal objects. Albert had been 'conditioned' (or abused as we might say now, as it is doubtful if a modern Ethics Committee would permit the study – not least because Watson made no attempt to desensitise Little Albert afterwards). Behaviourism – that was to haunt dystopias for decades to come (e.g. Huxley's *Brave New World*, Orwell's *1984*) – had been born. Watson (1925) was evangelical over the powers of behaviourism not to explain childhood but to make it:

> Give me a dozen healthy infants, well formed, and my own specified world
> to bring them up in and I'll guarantee to take any one at random and train

him [sic] to become any type of specialist I might select – doctor, lawyer, artist, merchant, chief, and yes, even beggar-man and thief. (p. 82)

A claim which makes Francis Xavier sound positively temperate! For a while Watson seemed everywhere in US psychology. His more specific (if equally odd) ideas on day-to-day child rearing and many other issues were channelled widely into popular culture. Sadly for Watson, his knack for the dramatic was to be his undoing. Subsequently, he applied behaviourism to the study of the sexual responses of himself and his young research assistant (the same Rosalie Rayner who had worked-over Little Albert with him) – a pioneering piece of sexology which got him fired! He was, however, to find work in the slightly more 'open-minded' world of advertising and market research (a not uncommon sideways move for psychologists and a source of 'moonlight' income for others, cf. Packard 1957). Rosalie Rayner Watson was to go on to write the amazing *'I am the mother of a behaviorist's sons'* in *Parent's Magazine* of December 1930.

Yet for all Watson's claims, the powers of most of the procedures he described for behavioural management were decidedly limited. Indeed, some – like Pavlov's original dog studies – required a highly controlled environment to work at all (and for Pavlov, it also required the 'right dog' – Pavlov's accounts of doggie personality and conditionability were to form the basis of Eysenck's work on extraversion-introversion and neuroticism in which Eysenck (e.g. 1976) equates temptation with cortical under-arousal and treats the conscience as a 'classically-conditioned reflex'). Their constraint was that they required imposition on the 'organism' (read: rat, dog, person) from without (and often a quite specific regime of imposition at that).

Skinner's major claim to fame is that he developed a behaviourism of the organism's own actions – its operants. In its simple form, Skinner offers us a 'common sense' learning theory – learning straightforwardly means that the consequences of an act determine its future likelihood. What makes Skinner's a radical behaviourism is its thoroughgoing emphasis on constructing a story which is restricted to actions and their contingencies. As an account of child-rearing, Skinner offered an easily acquired language for intervention. A child acts or operates, and as a consequence something starts to happen or stops happening. All that the word 'learning' means is that consequences affect future action, and that holds for animals as well as humans. It works for the trainer as well as the trained, of course, hence, the well-known joke in which a rat says: 'Have I got that psychologist well-trained! Every time I press the lever s/he gives me a food pellet!' Skinner spent much time working upon the empirical rules ('laws') of the contingencies between action and outcome. It is by no means always necessary or even most effective for outcome to invariably follow action. Animal trainers (and no doubt parents) have long used 'Skinnerian' techniques, particularly *shaping* – reinforcing successively better approximations to a desired action – to foster specific skilled actions (jumping through a hoop, pronouncing a difficult word). More complex skills can be built up through *chaining* – the linking together of many operants into a global competence.

Watsonian behaviourism having established the value of the child icon Little Albert in peddling its wares, Skinner was determined to go one better. He choose as his experimental subject his own daughter, Little Debbie, who became the subject of Skinner's preoccupation with a science of behavioural engineering. However, Little Debbie was to escape not only the abuse of Watsonian conditioning but also (though the apparent benefits were contested) a full-blown operant learning regime. Skinner's stroke of genius was the invention of a self-contained, air-conditioned, sound dampened, 'baby box'. This 'heir conditioner' (Skinner's own words) was not so much the training environment it might sound, rather it was Skinner's solution to 'easing the lot of the young mother [sic]' (1979, p. 290), the first woman to benefit from this gift from on high being, of course, Mrs Skinner! Skinner, unlike Watson, had the good sense to restrict a full-blown operant regime for children to the realm of story. This he did in his utopian novel of an experimental commune, *Walden Two* (1948). In that text, babies progress from auto-crib at around one to a communal nursery and on into a kibbutznik-like childhood. To be fair to Skinner, whatever his own domestic arrangements, in '*Walden Two*' child care was not only communal but also gender-fair. Further, Skinner used *Walden Two* to promote a number of then radical ideas about young people, from deschooling to a respect for young people's (hetero) sexual rights. The publication of *Walden Two* coincided in the United States with the anti-communist witch hunt of McCarthyism. Skinner may well have been lucky to survive it. Ironically, however, it was the Left which gave him the hardest ride. At the time it was widely condemned as a prescription for a Fascist totalitarian dys-topia. Yet, in the 1960s *Walden Two* was not only rehabilitated, it be-came the model of at least one apparently successful commune 'Twin Oaks' (Kinkade, 1973). Skinner's theorisation did not fair so well, it fell victim to a late-modern flirtation with structuralism, particularly over its treatment of language (Chomsky, 1967).

There are several aspects of Skinner's approach which can be easily recast into a social constructionist gaze – not least his critique of explan-ation by the postulating of intra-psychic essences. Indeed, one input into our own critical polytextualist stance was the work of Steven Brown (1980) on a empirical programme that treats 'experience' as *operant subjectivity*. Skinner also shared with social constructionists a flair for deconstructing sacred cows. In *Beyond Freedom and Dignity* (1971), he took on the liberal-humanistic discourse of persons as free agents and the democratic structures built upon it. For Skinner, the adult condition, just like that of the child, is to be controlled. The moral issue lies in the direction, effects and effectiveness of that control. If that is the test, then many later followers seem to have misread Skinner badly. In the hands of some practitioners 'behaviour modification' has taken on not a utopian cast, but a distinctly social control orientation in which 'clients' often turn out to be the already oppressed and disadvantaged inmates of total environments (which, of course, includes children, particularly those with learning difficulties, cf. Watson, 1989, and more recently those subjected to the notorious 'pindown' regime, Staffordshire County Council, 1991).

Mammonography

The second great marketable theme of early twentieth century US psychology was 'mental measurement'. One strand of the story begins in France, where Binet developed a low-bias means of identifying what we would now call children with learning disabilities. In the course of his work, he constructed (with Simon) an index of 'mental age', e.g. a child performing like a typical 8 year old had a mental age of 8, whatever their chronological age. It was a test of scholastic competence. In the hands of workers like Terman (1916 , the Stanford-Binet test), and drawing heavily on a eugenicist British tradition dating back to Galton in the nineteenth century, Binet's work became transformed into an index of a supposedly largely hereditarily determined faculty, 'intelligence'. To achieve this, Terman made use of a simple equation, harmless in itself, proposed by a German psychologist, Stern: Intelligence = Mental Age/Chronological Age. Expressed as as Intelligence Quotient (x 100), IQ enabled an index of personal and social worth, through which any individual's or group's deviation from the norm could be assessed with 'statistical' accuracy.

The political use of IQ testing and the interplay between right-wing politics and the Gods of the testing movement is psychology's best known and perhaps most salutary horror story (see, for example, Gould, 1981, Kamin, 1974, Rose *et al.*, 1984). IQ testing research 'findings' were, for example, used to justify the grossest kinds of racist social policies in areas as diverse as education and immigration control. For the child with learning disabilities, it was not enough simply to diagnose 'the severer clinical types – the mongol, the cretin, and the low-grade imbecile and idiot' (Burt, 1937, p. 88). IQ testing was to be used to pronounce upon their future prospects:

Where backwardness is the result of innate dullness, the teacher should be
warned that it is not only a waste of time but positively harmful to press
the child on in the hope of raising his [sic] attainments to the normal.
Capacity must limit content; and if a child is born with a low measure of
innate capacity, it will be as foolish for the teacher to try and instil in him a
full amount of knowledge and skill as it would be to try to pour twelve
ounces of medicine into an eight-ounce bottle. (*ibid.*, p. 136)

This quotation shows more than Burt's particularly naive and literal-
minded version of the alembic myth. It demonstrates something more
general, the view that psychometricians like Burt took for granted: their
gaze and their narrative. It is one of various dialects which make up the
dominant tongue not only of developmentalism, but our whole modernist world view. Like modernism itself, it is imbued with tensions well
identified by Rose *et al.* (1984):

> The contradiction is between the ideology of freedom and equality and the
> actual social dynamic that generates powerlessness and inequality. The
> mode of coping with it is a reductionist natural science that develops
> simple models of social or biological causation, providing fundamentally
> flawed explanations of social reality. (p. 80)

Through buying into a discourse of competence determined entirely out
of nature and a nurture (varying their roles according to one's politics),
the modernist so construes (and hence evidences) this as the condition
of the young, arguing they cannot escape the limitations of their genes.
Hence it locates them into a reality in which this constraining rhetoric is
the only language-game around. It is a cosmology not lost in the last
great 'God' of modernism.

The ghost in the machine

Developmentalism has ever been open to metaphorical use of the technology of its day. For Locke it was the *tabula rasa*, for Freud, it was
nineteenth century hydraulics (mind as a fixed-energy machine). Between the wars the mind as a telephone exchange had its vogue. Today,
the metaphor which haunts us is the information processing system. In
this, an ancient discourse has been recovered from the archives and
given new clothes. This is 'faculty psychology' which has its roots in
medieval theology. Faculty psychology filled the mind with separable
systems that intervened between sensation and action – inner functions
such as a general sorting and integrating system for incoming sensations
(the common sense), a temporary repository of these integrated sense
impressions (imagination), a faculty of memory and one of reason. Some
version of faculty psychology emerges whenever questions arise as how,

say, stimulus-response links actually 'work', how learning takes place and is retained. In the 1930s and 1940s, these kinds of concerns led to some complex but totally speculative 'mediational' theories. However, the advent of clever electronics and ultimately the computer led to the growth from the 1950s onwards of what is now known as the information processing approach (IPA) to the mind. In this, faculties are modelled upon and paralleled to units and systems in the construction and operation of computers. It is an inner world of channels, stacks, registers, loops, filters, working memories, retrieval processes and long-term memories. It is the home of 'cognition' and the locus of 'cognitive development'.

As a child psychology, the IPA is concerned with the development of the faculties. In this respect it is another variant on the development of capacities theme. Progress over age is plotted in terms of developing larger short-term memories, more selective attention, ever improving recall and retrieval, better informational organisation and so on. The indexing of a variety of faculties certainly gives it a degree of flexibility in the conceptualisation of developing faculties, seldom found in work on intelligence, and markedly different from the rigid Piagetian stage model. IPA workers also incorporate a limited notion of reflexivity in the form of studies of meta-cognition (i.e. the accounts children give of their faculties), a technique which can and is extended into areas beyond cognition, such as meta-knowledge about emotion (Harris, 1989). However, the approach retains a variant on the nature-nurture theme through the metaphor of hardware versus software. Its overall focus on the flow of information in and out of individual minds thus leaves it very weak in terms of accounting for the social nature of knowledge and recognising the cultural-historical locatedness of the faculties and *their* meta understanding.

The shaking of the temple pillars

There are several inter-textual positions from which the end of an era of 'Grand Narrative' theories of the child, grounded in bio-science, could be heralded. One is the claim that its cloaking *episteme* (modernism) is itself now collapsing, transmuting or fragmenting into postmodernity – a condition in which grand narratives themselves can no longer operate (Ibañez, 1991). Another is that evidenced by the approach we have taken in this chapter, namely that *as stories*, scientised accounts of the child are losing credibility. Not only is their fundamental warrant now in doubt (part of a general dis-ease with science manifested in such diverse movements as anti-vivisection and Green politics), but they have been over-told and over-sold to the point that they have lost their essential cachet. As a result, they now invite as a 'top of mind' gaze, not awe, but ire.

One further sign of the fragmentation of child theorisation under modernism, and of the weakening of bio-social developmentalism in particular, has been the taking up by disciplines such as sociology of agendas traditional developmental psychology eschewed. We have already quoted Denzin (1977) as a key text in the emergence of the social constructionist perspective. It was that symbolic interactionist text which drew attention to the effect of the hegemony psychology had exerted over childhood. As he began his book: 'There does not exist, nor has there ever existed, a sociology of childhood' (p. 1). Just how rapidly that situation has changed is attested to by the range of material that constituted 'contemporary issues in the sociology of childhood' as brought together by James and Prout (1990) – except, of course, it is not sociology as traditionally understood. The paradigm is explicitly social constructionist – more evidence, we would argue, for a postmodern shift towards transdisciplinary enquiry (BCFC, 1991).

However, one of the most convincing indices of the decay of grand scientific narratives of childhood development is what has happened to their telling. In human science itself, they are no longer presented as governing the cutting edge of research (even as a source of hypotheses to be critically evaluated). Indeed, developmentalists of the meta-story school are no longer the central players in what has recently called itself, once more, child psychology. The new child psychologists are, most often, scholars of infancy. Their concern is narrow and specific, the mental (now often called subjective) life of the neonate. As Bradley (1989) wryly notes: 'Two decades of demonstrating how Piaget underestimated the intelligence of infants mean that the baby is now deemed to be able to conceptualise in the womb, if not the gene' (p. 151). Bradley associates this infantiolatry with a mythic constitution by child psychologists of early life as a time of innocence. This discourse of pronatalism is well illustrated by Desmond Morris whose latest book *Babywatching* asserts: 'It is not an exaggeration to say that the human infant is the most remarkable life-form ever to draw breath on this planet . . . Small, vulnerable and wordless the baby may be, it is at the same time power-packed with astonishing potential' (promotional preview in the *Sunday Times Magazine*, 10 November 1991). However, if *'from the scientist's point of view* infancy is very much an empty book or memory theatre in which a great and conflicting variety of things may be said about the basis of human nature' (Bradley, 1989, p. 175, emphasis in the original); if '[t]he scientific value of observing babies is *rhetorical*. It allows scientists to draw conclusions that they would not otherwise be able to draw' (*ibid.*) – then the new pro-natalism is not science as it used to like to portray itself, but a moral and ideological arena. All that is needed is an injection of reflection, and it can be seen that: 'The science of babies reveals first and foremost the way in which scientists become conscious of babies' (*ibid.*, p. 176). Moved towards an interpretative discipline – a moral, hermeneutic, rhetorical arena – the new child psychology from its infancy can no longer aspire to be a grand narrative. To Morris must be added doubt: 'there is no answer to questions about infancy which can always and everywhere be taken as true' (*ibid.*, p. 180).

We have earlier criticised Bradley's particular moral analytic as a directive to conduct, but his analysis of his own discipline is a powerful account of the dissolution of developmental grand narrative within the human sciences. This reading is widely endorsed by other, more radical, critical observers of developmentalism (e.g. Broughton, 1987, Morss, 1990). However, as bio-social science has troubled its own claims to be the site of grand narrative, that authority has been arrogated by other social raconteurs. In particular, the mongering of grand narratives of childhood has fallen into the hands of feminists such as Firestone (1972) and therapists such as Miller. The claims for a feminist meta-narrative we have critically addressed elsewhere. However, whether one reads such agendas with respect or otherwise, their dislocation from any scientific, indeed scholarly, warrant is patent. Each offers its own, singularising, ideologised representation of the child, and however powerful their impact on the construction of issue-led debate (particularly that on child abuse), with no pantheon to which to be elevated, they can at best be seen as semi-divinities, local and domestic, *lares and penates*. This then, is where the 'end of modernity' has left the theorising of the child. If, as a society, we are still to act with concern, it has to be done without 'gods', and, if we wish to avoid singularising our discourse (and hence our conduct), without even the sense of local certainty a demigod can conjure up for us. How that can be lived, we return to in Chapter 11.

7

Being had: Biosociology and the production of new children

Ideas often do strange things if pushed to extremes. In the case of the bio-social sciences there has been a tendency, in particular at their outer fringes of genetic biology and cultural anthropology, to separate out and singular-ise just one assumed causal element. This – respectively either nature or nurture – is then treated as the *only* causal element of importance, with the counter pole suppressed into insignificance. Phenomena previously at-tributed to the suppressed element are then drawn under the explanatory power of the valorised one. In the first half of this century, this showed itself in the nativist eugenics movement and, predicated upon that, the resistance movement that came to be known as cultural determinism.

> In 1912 Burt published a paper in which he avowed the belief, which in later life he was to support with quite unprincipled eristic fervor, that 'mental inheritance . . . moulds the character of individuals' and 'rules the destiny of nations'. It was against this very doctrine that Boas had been struggling since 1894, and that Margaret Mead, beginning in 1928 with the publication of *Coming of Age in Samoa*, was, as a leading Boasian, to fight with the 'whole battery' at her command. By the second decade of the twentieth century, then, the nature-nurture controversy, in which two fervently held half-truths contended vainly for outright mastery [sic], was about to enter upon the most active phase of its existence. (Freeman, 1984, p. 35)

The 'eugenic' and the cultural engineering practices of Hitler and of Stalin (and each pursued both policies) rightly dampened academic en-thusiasm for such polarised positions for around twenty years beyond the end of World War Two. However, as memories faded and cultural-intellectual climates changed, the old extremes emerged again from the woodwork, led as before by the nativists. A key marker here is Jensen's (1969) resurrection of the inheritance of IQ debate (cf. Taylor, 1980, for a telling critique). However, old nonsense has less cachet in the narra-tive world than new nonsense and the 1970s were to see the emergence of a wonderful example of the genre. We are talking here of sociobiology, where nature is accorded such sovereign causal influence that the impact of nurture is relegated to a minor, ephemeral 'civilising' gloss over humankind's true, biochemical nature.

When exploring stories of childhood, this propensity for placing all one's eggs in a single explanatory basket matters because it is frequently associated with naive ideologisations of conditions of change. This, we would argue, is particularly the case with sociobiology. Sociobiologists such as Wilson (1975) have developed their thesis from the biological determinist tenet that the function of behaviour is to reproduce and thereby perpetuate an individual's genes (for an earlier formulation see *Genesis* 38:9 and the story of Onan). Truly successful fatuity requires such a simple and non-refutable thesis – and, if we accept conventional stories of the march of knowledge, sometimes generates quite unexpected pay-offs (e.g. alchemy leading to the discovery of new chemicals).

In order to expose some of the dangers of 'all or nothing' polarisation, and issues raised by sociobiology in particular, in this chapter we will have a little fun by turning this story on its head. We will exploit our weakness for a good story ('being had'), to a serious purpose – an exploration of the initiating stage of social construction as a child – how the child is 'had' in the first place, in other words, reproduction. In doing this we will offer some other 'teasers'. The first is a playful alternative to sociobiology – which we have called biosociology. We will explore what kind of story emerges when instead of suggesting that children are the reproducers of *nature* (i.e. their 'selfish genes'), we treat them as the reproducers of *culture*. The second is to treat not genetic reproduction but childhood itself as a competitive game. What can that tell us about childhood? We look at this in the context of reviewing the power of story-telling to make choice and conduct seem 'inevitable'. And finally we will use the idea of cultural (rather than biological) evolution to speculate about what kinds of childhood are coming to occupy the cultural ecology of a postmodern world. Of course our teasing has serious purposes: to offer a half-convincing, half-disturbing counter-narrative to the wealth of bio-scientised determinist stories around on the basis of 'why should they have all the best stories?' And, by lampooning in this way, to deconstruct these other stories further and to further open the space for trans-disciplinary alternatives.

Biosociology

In this story we cannot, of course, have any truck with notions of motivated genes or heritability, nor mechanisms for conduct like drives, libidos or wired-in programs. Culture is all that is necessary – culture can ensure its own reproduction and perpetuation via the child, and can evolve to accommodate changes in social environment by producing new kinds of children, adapted to those new conditions. Specifically, we will adopt as axiomatic that: *Children are the means by which cultures transmit themselves, mutate and evolve.*

Biosociology requires a number of mechanisms to operate. These include ensuring there are:

- reproductive systems which create or obtain children with which to perpetuate culture;
- evolutionary mechanisms to modify these systems (and the children they produce) to meet new cultural conditions; and
- regimes of knowledge that serve these vectors.

Reproductive systems

The religious community known as the Shakers (John Fowles' novel *A Maggot* (1986) gives an account of their early British origins), like Onan, eschewed insemenatory sex, putting their energies instead into dancing for the 'Glory of God' and inventing better household appliances. But sadly, the Shakers are no more, the last group closed up in the 1930s. Cultures that do not reproduce children inevitably die out, unless they can survive by others means such as recruitment. While it might be argued that celibate communities like Christian monks and nuns form a counter case, it rather looks as though that at the time they were saving 'civilisation' for us (Clark, 1969), they were also far from celibate, and did their bit to generate perpetuating children (Lilar, 1967). A similar process seems to be operating today with the more radical (and hence innovatory) monks and nuns getting back into the habit (as it were) of *cultural* perpetuation via a rejection of celibacy. Furthermore, unlike the Shakers, the monastic orders have, for at least a thousand years, developed systems like oblation (see Chapter 5) and offering schooling, to reproduce their cultural elements through recruiting children:

> It was not until the eleventh century that there was any education to speak of outside of monastic schools, and not until the thirteenth century that there occurred marked changes in the character of education given in any institutions, for until then practically all of the schools were taught by monks. (Monroe, 1906, p. 261)

However, it is the family which is the prime site for reproduction. Indeed, the power of families to reproduce their cultural elements is so self-evident that we could be in danger of overlooking the fine-grain detail of how families manage to produce not just children, but *future-family-making* children. However, for our western industrialised world this is precisely what developmental psychology has laid out for us – a functional account in which childhood is the seed bed for the reproduction of the family. In more traditional cultures in other contemporary locations, or in western culture in historical times, similar notions are and were deeply sedimented within traditional wisdom – 'the child is father to the man [sic]' and children are to be found 'playing mummies and daddies'.

Within the psychodynamic approach, this goal orientation for childhood is quite explicit – the function of childhood is seen as the production of an adult who can (in Freud's concept) 'love and work'. In Erik Erikson's life-span expansion of the Freudian sequence (e.g. Erikson, 1963), the childhood stages of development can be seen even more clearly as essential building-blocks for the first and second adult stages, specifically concerned with the achievement of a relationship within which to have children, and then with the establishment of a caring and educative 'nest' for rearing them. Erikson's last stage prescribes an idealised older person, who avoids becoming an interference to the next generation in their repeating of the cycle. Thus the family's purpose is to provide a location for growing up, and the purpose of growing up is to provide children who will go on to provide new families.

The family system thus has to be made to endure, and resist all contingencies which might disrupt it. This, culture achieves in a number of ways. In the past, and in some locations today, it can make dissolution of the family immensely difficult (e.g. legally, or by religious proscription). It can base the whole system of welfare provision (from state benefits to 'care in the community') upon the assumption that everybody is a member of a family. But perhaps the most critical mechanism of all is the cunning story culture has come to tell about how the family is constituted – out of an elective choice, based upon romantic love. Mount (1982) views the family as the ultimate subversive organisation: 'The family is the enduring permanent enemy of all hierarchies, churches and ideologies' (p. 1). We do not need to share his interpretation to see that the story culture tells is that whatever the vagaries or demands of social, political and economic contingencies, 'love conquers all' and will survive anything – revolution, parental and societal disapproval, whatever. Many a tear has been out-jerked by the likes of David Lean's movie of *Dr Zhivago* around just this motif. The apparent revolution whereby the loving marriage has been challenged by the loving relationship can be seen as very much a continuity glamouring as a change.

Under the complex socio-economic arrangements of modernism, bio-social science can be seen to have played a part in knowledging the continuance of the reproductive family. More specifically, empirical developmental psychology has taken just such a broadly functionalist stance, in assuming that families operate to transmit cultural values from one generation to the next – i.e. not just to produce a new cohort of any-old-how family-making children, but particularly to produce a new cohort of individuals adapted to that family's culture, and thus capable of reproducing it:

> Lower- and working-class parents stress obedience, respect, neatness, cleanliness, and staying out of trouble – precisely the characteristics that their children will need to adapt to a position within a blue-collar economy. In contrast, middle-class parents are less restrictive and authoritarian and more likely than low-SES parents to stress independence, creativity, ambition, and self-control – the attributes their children will need for success in business or the professions. (Shaffer, 1985, p. 637)

Not just class but gender (sex-role development, gender identity), ethics (moral development), and sexuality (dating, premarital heterosexual behaviour) have been carefully studied as largely taken-for-granted cultural elements in reproduction.

Selfish teens

If children are the agents of cultural reproduction, then culture needs to make sure they are set up for this role. As the latest in a long line of authorities, developmentalists have certainly done their bit to assert that they are: 'Boys or girls of sixteen are as old in both wisdom and physical development as their parents were at nineteen or twenty . . . Except financially, they are ready for marriage' (Cole and Hall, 1970, p. 372).

If we accept Mount's (1982) definition of 'popular marriage' as a seemingly elective rather than legal pairing (with the costly 'nest-building' the latter usually signals), Cole and Hall in fact do no more than describe the condition of the majority of contemporary western young people. By age sixteen, large numbers of them are sexually experienced (Ives, 1986) and begin a pattern of serial 'popular marriages', often with tacit or explicit family support. While sometimes presented as a 'sexual revolution', this early coupling is revolutionary only within a very narrow historical and cultural gaze. As regards age, Renaissance canon law seems to have generally set the age of contractual consent (i.e. to marriage) at twelve for a young woman and fourteen for a young man (cf. the ages of Shakespeare's Juliet and Romeo). This was also the locally operating notional age of the start of puberty (taken from the Romans who were not beneath a peak under the toga to make sure (Darmon, 1985) and, hence, of ability to consummate (Casey, 1989). Over the history of serial 'popular marriages', Houlbrooke (1984) notes:

> The length of the period between sexual maturity and the termination of
> service or apprenticeship meant that courtship was often a protracted
> process, and that an apprentice often had a succession of partners. . . .
> That the pattern of successive courtship partners was already old [by the
> seventeenth century] is suggested by the numerous medieval and sixteenth
> century marriage cases in the church courts in which more than one plain-
> tiff laid claim to the same man or woman. (p. 73)

Thus we can see plenty of evidence that in the past, as now, while there
may be (or have been) strong cultural invectives to delay reproduction
until later in life, there also exists (and existed) counter-narratives which
(albeit somewhat subversively) encouraged the required activity (sexual
intercourse) as soon as it is reproductively feasible. There are a number
of ways this tension serves culture's purposes very well indeed. First, by
making sexual activity a marker for adulthood, and by making adulthood a desirable state to be obtained (culture has been pretty active in
creating all sorts of stories to push these ideas, and all manner of conditions that make them 'real'), the young are made to view sexual activity
as something to be got into as fast as possible. On the other hand,
culture needs to make sure that the young are not encouraged to do so
until they are ready to rear the children produced as a consequence.
Prior to the availability of effective contraception, it achieved this by a
graded sequence of controls. These varied from making virginity a culturally prized commodity, by promoting compelling stories that 'good
girls save themselves for marriage', to the production of such ritual as
'bundling' in which all else but penetrative sex was warranted. With the
advent of contraception (at least prior to the HIV virus) these cultural
mythologies mutated to ones stressing 'responsibility':

> We realize that for some young people, sexual intercourse is part of a
> joyful, non-exploitative relationship. This does not deter us from our main
> and most generalizable conclusion: Primary prevention programs [sic]
> must enhance self-acceptance, discourage sexual intercourse among teen-
> agers and promote contraception and prophylactic use for those young
> people not impressed or affected by our conviction. (From the Preface to
> *The Sexual Adolescent* (second edition) Gordon, Scales and Everly, 1979)

Culture is being very clever here, for what it is doing is playing both
sides to the middle. It is priming young people for parenthood (i.e.
making them ready to produce the next generation) by getting them
hooked on sex (either as a present reality, or an aspired-to potentiality),
while deterring them from parenthood until they are in a position to rear
the next generation. As we know the narrative best, it is wrapped up in
its ubiquitous tales of romantic love, and courtship and dating rituals. It
moves the story along with a youth culture imbued with conservatism, in
which options like celibacy and homosexuality, even just not being 'sexy'

or caring more about schoolwork than sex, are sure routes to ridicule or worse. For obvious reasons, in terms of their relative reproductive roles, this enchantment is somewhat gender differentiated. Particularly for girls, it uses every device to hand, from music to movies, teen-mags to television, to make absolutely sure that young people, as soon as they begin to put childhood behind them, know that 'falling in love' and finding a sexual partner is their greatest preoccupation, and that all the other goals to which they may aspire must give way lest they compromise this quest (Walkerdine, 1987). The fundamental biosociological axiom does not require that all young people are entrapped within such mythic stories, only that the large majority that are, will produce families in which the children, in their turn, will reproduce it.

Consolidating culture

The next element of our thesis is to make sure that established culture gets to perpetuate under the best conditions for it to retain its dominance. The challenge that culture faces is to ensure that as many babies as possible are conceived where culture has its strongest hold, and as few where its dominion is most tenuous. Hence, culture in the past stigmatised the outcome of unsanctioned sex – the bastard child – and created the double standard, whereby the cuckolding wife was seen to be far more condemnable (indeed, open to far more stringent punishment, including death) than the errant husband. However, this cultural mechanism only worked when contraception was unavailable or highly fallible. The recent emergence of a combination of reliable contraception and, when that failed, relatively easy access to abortion, meant that culture had to adapt. It did this by a three-pronged attack – it sanctioned non-reproductive sex, made popular marriage (cohabitation) respectable (i.e. appropriated it into culture), but promoted a powerful belief that reproductive sex is the 'obvious' long-term goal of both of these. Consequently we now have a system in which 'living in sin' as a subversive, counter-cultural activity becomes 'living together' as a culturally normative activity, but one assumed either to be the first stage leading to a permanent relationship (Mullan, 1987) or as a 'testing ground' to discover whether it can become one.

It is at the stage of 'wanting to have children' that more formal contractual families generally emerge. Increasingly this is not a legal marriage, but is generally viewed as a long-term commitment. Codifying culture, the Children Act 1989 introduces specific mechanisms to regularise cohabitative parenthood. Culture also has some other neat tricks up its sleeve, however, if the relationship does break down. Pair-bonding is so powerfully prized that the normative response is to try again, and to mark the significance of the new relationship with a second crop of children. And the way a man demonstrates his dominant position in society is to capture a young, fertile 'trophy wife' – and 'get her' pregnant. By contrast, those with counter-cultural lifestyles (e.g. single people and lesbian and gay couples) are strongly enculturated to believe that parenthood is 'not for them', and if they try to challenge this wisdom, will be made to face considerable opposition if they seek help in obtaining children to enculturate (whether by AID or adoption). Culture teaches us that their wishes are 'selfish' and they cannot create the right environment (that is, they cannot provide a hefty enough dose of normative culture) in which to rear children, so they do not have the same entitlements to these services as 'proper' (i.e. culturally correct) couples.

Wanting may be elective (giving up contraception) or *post-hoc* (e.g. a decision not to abort a contraceptive failure). Complex age, career economic and social contingencies mediate what amounts to a major rite of passage – for having children constitutes a major change in lifestyle for women in particular (Gittins, 1985). Nevertheless, culture makes sure it is a change which couples expect, and are expected to make. Culture provides plenty of clearly articulated stories about when to have children and how many children to have – indeed, cunning stories of an (obviously nonsensical, but none the less useful) 'biological clock' that *impels* women to want to have children 'before it's too late'. At the same time, it writes few (and not at all attractive) scripts for not complying with what remains, for most, a 'taken for granted' state ('having a family') (Busfield and Paddon, 1977). Thus children come about through a rather paradoxical dynamic of choosing (and even striving) to do that which one is *expected* to do (a key ingredient of any good conspiracy of course.)

Family planning

In economic terms, after housing, the major investment made by families is in their children (Franklin, 1986). In the past getting married and 'starting a family' were usually synonymous. Today the availability of highly effective contraceptives means that getting pregnant usually needs positive action (i.e. *not* contracepting), particularly as this now usually follows a pattern of 'living together'. The present birth rate, in other words, reflects that in addition to a residual level of biological roulette, a considerable amount of explicit decision-making goes on. Given choice (in some meaning of the term), families continue to produce children (chapter 9 in Busfield and Paddon, 1977). The euphemism of 'family planning' is, for once, accurate. For most couples, contraception is used to plan and limit family size, not to set it to zero. Culture uses a pressing *more* which renders the production of children *the* major definition of what constitutes 'a family' – as in 'Do you have a family?' Indeed, infertility is generally seen as a problem, for which couples turn either to a market in children (i.e. adoption or surrogate parenthood) or to medical science for solution. Having children is no longer a matter of sheer inevitability, rather it is a cultural element transformed into a social need – couples almost invariably want to have (a few) children: 'I think marriage without children is a very empty life, and I think there's absolutely no point at all in marriage without children; if one gets married it should be for the purpose of creating children' (participant quoted in *ibid.*, p. 135).

A brief intromission

Culture, having primed its agents when young, apprenticed them until ready to 'settle down' and then convinced them they want to 'start a family', now needs to make sure they can competently produce the goods. It needs no recourse to innate ability, yet again culture is all that is needed. Indeed, sexology has given us plentiful accounts of individuals whose deficient enculturation has left them without the understanding to copulate. For example:

> But the delusion still survived that where love and affection reign, sex will take care of itself. Van de Velde's patients illustrated the disastrous consequences of this delusion. He learned from them that no matter how loving a couple may be, sexual response is *not* automatic. (Brecher, 1970, p. 84, emphasis in the original)

It is worth noting that in the past the Christian construction of 'female innocence' in fact demanded such a state of virtuous ignorance. Darmon (1985), discussing seventeenth century 'impotence trials' (for Catholic marriage dissolution) notes the following lawyer's interrogation tactic upon a purportedly still virginal wife:

> He did demand of her, in the presence of several witnesses, whether her husband had caressed or kissed or embraced her. She replied that he had. 'And who then did tell you that this does not suffice?' he asked her. 'Where did you learn the rest? If your virginity be intact, as you proclaim, you ought not to have any awareness that your husband is impotent.' (p. 91)

However, for most people, socialisation does seem to provide basic copulatory knowledge. It does not do so terribly effectively, but it seems however, good enough.

Getting it together

However, a knowledge of embodied possibilities does not guarantee action – or more accurately, does not guarantee female-male copulation (ideally in a settled-down pair-bonded relationship, though this is not always essential to culture's purposes). Fecundational sex is obviously critical to culture's needs, and it uses a variety of cultural thematics to achieve it. It problematises the alternatives – masturbation and homosexual copulation. These do not require absolute anathematising (although sometimes this is a cultural element), merely that they are made 'dodgy' or difficult. The particular cultural means vary. Homosexuality can be rendered a moral/legal offence, a sickness or 'merely' the target of social prejudice (homophobia). Masturbation (see also Chapter 10) can be made unrewarding (for females) by clitorectomy, it can be turned into a nameless vice of self-abuse (promoted as an established cause of madness, as noted in early modern European culture by Tissot) and a behavioural problem to be tackled by juvenile chastity belts (Stainton Rogers, 1989). Culture also needs to give the desired conduct itself a valorising gloss. This can be achieved by making it a critical social rite of passage (as we have already considered). It can also be fostered by a mythology stressing the mystical union of male and female (e.g. the Greek relinking of the severed Hermes and Aphrodite into Hermaphroditus). The more this can be linked into a powerful iconography, the better (whether in Hindu temples or the popular media) – even better if this iconography can incorporate a level of genital coyness (the odd fig leaf, thong or g-string). Coition also needs to be constructed as a goal in its own right. This often seems to be the agenda of the genre of 'marriage' guides and handbooks. Willy [sic] (in a 1933 translation of an undated original) devotes a chapter to 'the wedding night' and 'defloration' [sic] as culmination:

> We have already said it must not be a rape, and that the man must on the contrary apply all his tact and skill to persuade his bride to co-operate with him in the culminating act. In other words, he must by caresses and love-play stir her passion to the required pitch . . . Granted all this, there remains a last obstacle, the hymen. (p. 324)

Culture must create a favourable opportunistic environment for copulation. The privacy of the honeymoon suite and then the marital home is obviously the best location. Failing that, cultural inventions like the haystack, the automobile, the student dorm and the motel can offer alternatives. But as well, individual acts of coition need to be made to happen. Again, within the ideal situation regular sex is expected, and seen as a marker that the relationship is working out. Just to help things along though, culture has invented parties and festivals, residential courses and holidays, spiced them with a range of disinhibiting drugs like alcohol and hashish, and provided activities like dancing which encourage pre-coital conduct.

Being fruitful and multiplying

Finally (and obviously) sanctioned copulation has to be made effective (i.e. child-producing). This can be achieved by formal sanctions against alternatives (e.g. against non-penetrative sex, anal sex and withdrawal as well as contraception) or by reducing their consumer acceptance (e.g. by poor opportunities for personal hygiene). It can also be fostered by menstrual taboos which schedule copulation into more fertile times in the cycle and cultural beliefs and practices which restrict male ejaculatory opportunities and so raise sperm count. At the same time, the risks of child-bearing to women, and the costs of child-rearing to them need to be played down, and their benefits extolled. One suspects that a culture which made masturbation (as a private or shared activity) sound half as much fun as coition would be well on the road to extinction! In a culture like ours where there is effective fertility control, the copulatory desirability of the child-bearer needs to be focused on their most effective child-producing years, and the state of motherhood endorsed as attractive: 'The campaign to "glorify, dignify and purify motherhood" and to transform this image into reality [infant welfare] began in earnest soon after the Boer War . . . when it became part of the drive to improve the quality and quantity of the population' (Lewis, 1980, pp. 13, 15). This prizing of motherhood has had, in a world of more equal gender divisions, to mutate to a valuing of parenthood, and has demanded of culture the evolution of a new kind of person – 'new man' whose fatherly, nurturing qualities are now extolled in advertisments (which virtually treat the child as a designer accessory), magazine accounts as well as bar-room gossip. Culture rounds the whole scheme off by asserting parents' rights to bring their children up as they think best (i.e. as their culture dictates), and making intervention (read interference) which is culturally insensitive the height of political uncorrectness. Thus the new generation is all set up to play 'happy families' and raise the new crop of recruits to culture's clever conspiracy.

Telling a good story

Under the biosociological myth, culture thus ensures its reproduction (and the avoidance of its extinction) by a kind of Scheherazadian plot –

the continued telling of good stories. People think they are choosing what to do, and have some free will in the matter, but in fact they are merely acting as passive agents of culture. The control of the putatively elective can be theorised in various ways but may, perhaps, be most easily approached by the notion of plausibility (a concept proposed by the social constructionists Berger and Luckmann, 1967). Culture regulates an apparently free social market in conduct by eliciting actions within a set of plausibility structures. We can think of each of these as a social world and a network of social practices, which render those actions obvious and unquestioned. In turn, those actions in that 'reality' help to maintain a subjective reality – a powerful sense of who one is and a personal and interpersonal myth of high conviction. In other words, cultural perpetuation works through a 'language game'. The question now becomes one of unravelling what it is that maintains a dominant social reality in which 'having children' is taken for granted. We have now reached a point where more hidden agenda to our game is beginning to surface. It is becoming easier to see how strongly enculturated stories gain plausibility. It should be easier too to spot the slippage between social constructionism as an analytic, as a deconstructor of taken-for-granted, and the use of constructionist talk to convey a crude conspiracy theory into plausibility. It is indeed, time to begin to disentangle ourselves as writers from the game we have been playing.

Crying 'Wolf'

Many writers, who, no doubt, would baulk at our game of vulgar biosociology, nevertheless employ forms of cultural determinism (varying in conspiratoriality) in seeking to account for the evolution and/or maintenance of the 'having a family' reality in which children are (re)produced. In diametric contrast to Mount in these discourses, the family generally gets told as the site at which power, as the villain of the piece, is perpetuated. Williamson (1987), for example, stresses its 'crucial importance . . . as an institution in maintaining the State . . . agreed upon by radical feminists and government ministers alike' (p. 115). This kind of approach draws heavily upon notions of the power of cultural idealisations – family myths (e.g. dream babies, earth mothers, madonnas, holy families, the nuclear family, the bourgeois family) – that present ubiquitous ways-of-being abstracted from individual, mundane circumstances:

> The representations of the family as an autonomous emotional unit cuts across class and power relations to imply that we all share the same experience. It provides a common sexual and economic goal: images of family

life hold out pleasure and leisure as the fulfillment of desires which, if not thus contained, could cause social chaos. (*ibid.*, p. 116)

Such representations-to-identify-with are, of course, counter-balanced by equally pressing representations-to-identify-against (e.g. the wanker; the old maid, the problem family). Such panoplies of descriptive, prescriptive and proscriptive exemplars no doubt have a powerful, culturally archetypical power, but it is important now we have given up our biosociological ruse *not* to concretise them any longer as *deus ex machina* of popular and professional discourse. Rather, we need to see such representations as integral aspects of discourse. The debt owed to feminist theory for its challenging of (and thereby highlighting of) such elements of 'patriarchal ideology' (e.g. Gittins, 1985) should not beguile us into failing to recognise that patriarchy too can easily drift from being a critical, analytic category into a reified biosociological explanation. When we hear of child abuse, for example, being spoken about as ' a problem of this, patriarchal, society' (Hearn, 1989, p. 79) we are moving into the margins of this slippage point. As a constituent of reality-maintenance, myth enables a kind of rhetorical melodrama, a set of character and story templates upon which 'actual' persons and biographies (ours or others) can be mapped and morally located, as in terms like: 'bundle of joy', 'little princess', 'little more than children themselves', etc. This is clearly shown, for example, in descriptions of the characteristics of 'abusing parents' [sic], as in, for example: 'They are often very young when they marry and pregnancies follow rapidly' (Jones *et al.*, 1982, p. 89). Such condemnations tend to gloss over the observation that such characteristics seem strangely not to lead to becoming an abusing parent if you are the future Queen of England, only if you come from a 'severely deprived background'.

Clearly, there is here a kind of casting power, but one that only results in an assumption of agency if we allow our working tale (whether a culture seeking its own perpetuation, a patriarchy, or an economic system) to become dogma, and thus to construct a hidden director or producer (whether culture, or anything else). As a description (i.e. as a story), melodramatisation is a feature of what we may call life-games – those plots around which tales (including biographic fables) are told (Berne, 1967). What we are suggesting is that life-games (e.g. first love, leaving home, finding a vocation, having children) do not merely serve reality-maintenance functions, but enable each new generation to constitute a sense of being *authentic* – authentic through collective identification with archetypal experiences that are reconstrued as both profoundly shared *and* deeply individual. They are also authentic because they bring into play skill, chance/hazard and high-level costs and pay-offs – all sources of the 'highs' and the 'lows' for which game-players play games (cf. Schiebe, 1986) All these elements are highlighted in the melodramas of parenthood, from *Oedipus* to *Neighbours*. Deconstruction they may merit, but such a challenge needs more than iconoclasm, it needs to address and to foster the positive possibility of new texts of identity.

Playing the child game

These texts of identity, as they relate to child players, we have speculated a little upon elsewhere. Our aim in this section is more modest – it is to continue to make good our escape from biosociology, and to clear the board for the next chapter, by playing games with 'being had'. The child game draws in all sorts of players, and turns up in biographies of most of us (critical polytextualist or otherwise). To qualify as a player by the most normal route begins with a genetic and fertilisation lottery. Never even reaching the board can be a matter of 'natural' or induced abortion. Where not so terminated, there follow months of risk to both mother and child, many of which are newly reconstructed for us (e.g. listeria, rubella, teratogenic agents). These risks vary by social location, and they include elective choices (e.g. over smoking). Yet they contain so much that is unpredictable that few players need to feel that all the cards are stacked against them at this stage. Pregnancy enables new players to be brought into biography (e.g. doctors, ante-natal paramedics) and reconstitutes current significant others (e.g. parents, siblings). Birth itself not only forms a risk-focus (including very real costs to the mother in terms of pain and possible death). It also sees a new player joining the table – the baby – and a fundamental change in the game itself.

From now on, the initial player or players are necessary but no longer sufficient movers. Like opening batspeople in cricket, they are there to play for a time until the nascent star player is ready to take the pitch. Children as players are left in little doubt as to their position in the stochastics of the child game, as we used to chant over our plum stones in pre-feminist dialects of the game: 'Tinker, tailor, soldier, sailor, richman, poorman, beggarman, thief'. Childhood is both a time of learning life-games and their melodrama (play), and a time of deadly earnest lifegames-personship. Children's social life can be (to adult sensibilities) brutally frank about those who already look like losers (the physically and mentally challenged, the ethnically marginalised, and those with compromised identities): 'The kids used to call me "bastard" in the streets and say things like, "Don't go with her she ain't got no father" ' (Irene Roberts, quoted in Humphries, Mack and Perks, 1988, p. 128). And it can be overtly brutal for those who get into the side play of the bully and the bullied. As childhood moves into adolescence the position of parents becomes more and more like that of coaches or trainers with a hefty investment in their champ and, for the more cynical, laid off bets on the outcome! Just in case they experience the player's attributional bias *vis-à-vis* the coach, to be more blamed for failure than given credit for success. To be so positioned is easy – move the mother counter round the board! 'A mother's place is in the wrong' or as Thomas and Chess (1980) labelled the psychobabble version, the '*mal de mere*' syndrome. Old players, to a person, and bearing the scars and injuries to prove it (though broken hearts outnumber broken noses), they gather round the ring. And from that ringside they whisper words of warning, encouragement and strategy to those now on the moving canvas (who largely ignore them, being convinced against all evidence that the game is new) and worry about 'blows under the belt' as the referee is left behind and the lights go out. But by then the preliminary rounds of a new generation of the child game have already begun, and, of course, there is always the grandchildren game to look forward to – or rather there might be.

Lacking in determination

In this chapter, even in the above analysis where we have added chance into the metaphor, it is easy to see that cultural determinism (like biological determinism) can enable stories that are fun to tell. It can even make some telling observations. But these tales tend to leave their characters (and hence must cast their tellers) as mere puppets – at best cynical commentators (like a Greek chorus) upon dramas that are decided elsewhere. What, of course, got somewhat lost along the way was the notion of active, humanly negotiated change. And yet it was such a change which got us to this position, the shift from children-that-just-happen to children-that-are-chosen. In other words, the child game as outlined above is, in many respects, a new game – or at least one where the rules have recently undergone dramatic change. And, while it may be played with a level of nomic predictiveness, that order is still painfully nascent, which is why it invites a light satire upon its developing manners.

The production of new children

Culture, before we finally discard as milked-dry our original jokey axiom, 'uses' children, not just to perpetuate itself, but as vehicles

of change. Thus contraception is a cultural innovation in so far as, paradoxically, it does not just 'stop' pregnancy but also produces children
who are different. They are different because they are fewer, both generating an ageing population (cf. Muller, 1969) and generating smaller
and (hence richer) families. This shift from the inevitable mass production of the young to an elective techno-craft has set the parameters of a
child game that is a true product of the twentieth century, in the industrialised western world, at least. In it, 'new children' are being crafted.

A place of their own

Children, our grandparents were prone to say, should, 'know their
place'. As we are using the term here, the notion of *place* allows for
many other readings over and above the Victorian sense of a singular
location in a taken-for-granted social order. It impinges upon, for example, notions of 'place' as it features in other proverbial/gnomic
phrases – such as 'feeling out of place', or 'taking the place of', and so
on. A *place* can be electively occupied, but it may also be a location we
are stuck with, either through the actions of others – as when we are
caught in such situated identities as a Fool, or because we have 'dug a
hole for ourselves' or 'got stuck in a groove'. The notion of *place* is
crucial to the narrative approach to young people developed in this
book. Characters in the script of a play, we suggest, will be convin-
cingly perceived as children to the extent that they take part in ex-
changes in which their placements are *children's* placements. This is
not a dramaturgical analogy (Goffman, 1959) but a polytextual analytic. For constructionist purposes, a 'real' child too is a child because
s/he enters into the particular patterns of self-placement, placement-
by-others, placement-of-others and alter-placement which, with their
unique commonalities and discontinuities, constitute the discursive location of a child. Of course, each child's precise structuration of placements will be unique to that child and her/his autobiography, but it is a
uniqueness bounded by the repertoire of the placements available in
their culture.

Adopting a critical polytextualist position demands great caution
about offering a singular story about childhood (i.e. assuming their
placement reflects properties that are biologically or culturally fixed).
None the less, it in no way prevents (and can often facilitate) an analysis
of such meta-narratives – stories that imply a particular pattern of placements of biography-in-culture. Late modern childhood, we argue, is
constituted around meta-narratives that represent a major shift in placement from earlier childhoods – not least in the degree of self-placement

allowed the young. The wanted children of modern families in the afflu-
ent west, the 60–70 per cent who do not belong to the new poor or the
old poor underclasses, or to traditional sub-communities, are experien-
tially and, hence substantively, new children. Or, more accurately they
are new children in some of their locations – for a late modern childhood
is inevitably a mosiac of positionings: some well sedimented; others
fitting the descriptors of postmodernity. Their special condition reflects
the many parameters of the new child social tectonic. We can observe
the direction and focus of these shifts in the placement of the new
children of modernism within the following points.

*Greater resources being directed towards (and hence a sense of greater
investment in) each child.* This feeds a burgeoning market in child
nurturance (e.g. in toys, child-specific entertainments and foods, child-
and youth-focused fashions in clothes) and in child management (i.e.
developmentalism).

A transformed home environment. New children are likely to have
their own allocated space (including an unshared bedroom) and the
heightened sense of privacy and possession that goes with this. Home
has become vastly more commodity rich, in terms of entertainers and
mass cultural agents like television, video, and hi-fi.

Changed family dynamics. New children relate with their parents as
singletons, dyads or triads rather than as a larger group. Usually close
together in age, new children (at least when younger) are more likely to
experience events (e.g. vacations, trips) 'as a family'. However, while
family life can be richer and more intense than in the past, it is also more
fragmented. If not in their own families, then certainly via the families of
their friends, new children experience new reconstituted family relationships as the norm, although conversely children are less exposed to
parental death and orphanhood.

Values which are secularised and contingent. New children are constructed in families which generally run without absolute religious or
ethical authority, and that operate by pragmatism rather than by dogma.
Even child-rearing itself is recognised as subject to fashion and as an
activity that is informationally updated.

Decay of traditional children's oral culture. Rather like a traditional
people subject to the intrusion of development, new children are losing
their local and relatively stable oral culture of games, songs, etc., and
taking in their place the output of a global industry of entertainment and
commodity production. In some respects, this is a functional response to
increasing geographic mobility. New children may experience moving
home, area, country, even continent, and still find much that is constant
in juvenile culture. Even juvenile argot (at least in English) has a global
gang to speak it.

Segmentation into markets. Both as the targets of expenditure and, over time, increasingly as consumers in their own right, new children experience their lives as segmented. Thus what they do (e.g. experience as schooling, and as recreation) is time-staged in a way that reflects and constructs the stage-development plotted by child psychology. Such a segmentation (and the age closeness of siblings) promotes constant product redundancy and hence a buoyant market in new goods and new activities. However, their lives are not only segmented over time but also within time. They are required to, and expect to, move between a range of situated identities on a day-to-day basis.

Development planning. New children are exposed to a regime which is pragmatic and probabilistically orientated. Child-rearing reflects a risk analysis approach, in which strategies are constructed around perceived likelihood of events and perceived costs/benefits. For instance in terms of health, this process begins with a monitored, scheduled pregnancy, proceeds through Well Baby clinics to immunisation schedules and a medical gaze which runs from head-lice to veruccas (with intervening excursions into fluoridation and orthodontics) and ends in the latest 'wisdom' on contraception and sexually transmitted diseases. Risk analysis has also dramatically reduced certain traditional freedoms. New children are kept off the streets (away from both traffic and 'dangerous adults') to an extent unique to our times and place.

Increasing sexual egalitarianism. New children are exposed to a culture in which, at least notionally and often more, boys and girls are treated as equal but different. Shifts in adult-gendered identities too, distance new children from narratives resting on more traditional man-child and woman-child dynamics both within and outwith their families.

A changing condition of selfhood. The more fluid the lives of the young and their families, the more appearance itself is rendered plastic – the greater the demand for the self to be constructed around the metaphors of breadth rather than that of depth, performance rather than substance.

All these culturally produced changes which constitute the 'new childhood' have some impact upon those 'new children' coming into culture. But living in culture means making culture as well as being made by it. It is a creative as well as a constrained condition, open-ended as well as predictable. Conspiracy theorising robs us of one of those moments or reduces action outside of the order to mere resistance, and for all our biosociological language games in this chapter, it is important to remember that we have told our story as a rhetorical device, a game with plausibility in order to worry 'taken for granted' wisdom. As we have said all too often to our own children (as our parents said to us) do not take it too seriously – it *is* only a game.

8

A minority group: The condition of childhood

In this chapter our concern turns to what are generally termed the 'agents of socialisation' for the young – the family and the school. However we will explore these not as agents, but as locations constituent of the conditions of childhood. They are the places where the young serve out their time until they cease to be a minority group and acquire their majority. And, equally, they are the positions where the competences that make adulthood are instantiated. In keeping with our agenda, we do not offer a formal review of the social psychology of childhood conditions but instead have sought to perturbate their construal.

Starting conditions

In a typical post-industrial society most people 'go to' one of two locations – school or work. There are of course exceptions – the 'school refuser' and the child educated at home; the 'unemployed' and the houseperson. But for the majority, their time is almost equally shared between that work-world (of schooling/working) and two other great domains of reality, the home-world and the sleep-world (time is also taken up, of course, in the transitions between them). For the infant, however, only the latter two realities will be on offer. Furthermore, there are social bridges to be crossed even before that dichotomous condition can be realised – 'parenting begins before birth' (Rapaport, Rapaport and Strelitz, 1977, p. 130). Infants are brought into social life through a family (or some simulacrum of one) which, normally, is 'expecting' them and whose expectations and capacities will help to mediate their life track. Granting children this 'social being', in other words, is seldom delayed until the moment of birth, but is attributed from that point after conception where they are recognised as the 'baby to come'.

123

The constitution of a family to enter into is, of course, one of the parameters of 'fertility motivation' (see Hoffman and Hoffman, 1973) which help to bring about the condition of being 'my' or 'our baby-to-come' following the decision to 'start a family' or expand one. Pregnancies which are held not to be routes to the potential birth-mother's family are more likely to be terminated or result in adoption, e.g. of the 'school girl' pregnancy, of pregnancies of the mad or those with learning difficulties. The specimen case of the pregnancy 'for adoption', both in its early modern form as the lot of the unmarried mothers and in its late modern aspect as surrogacy allows us to see that only under certain conditions will the 'child to be' in our culture enter a parentally constructed track before its birth (Tanner, 1987).

None the less all 'foetuses-for-the-having' are potentially headed for some track. It is the predictability of these future stories that has constituted a great deal of what once passed as the 'sociology of the family'. Much of the available data makes unsurprising reading, because it maps our ordinary understandings of the social order. Children at the point of birth and even earlier are bound for actuarily different biographies according to their location at birth in terms of gender, social class, family constitution, nationality and so on – and these differences cover everything that constitutes the social order. Probabilistically speaking, the tracks anticipate things like: health; education; life opportunities; even criminality. Such evidence is, of course, historical, and only extrapolatively predictive. Any particular track might lose its predictability, were aspects of the social order (as they impinge on its location) to be disrupted dramatically. The baby-in-family, for example, can meet unexpected points which change its tracking, if for instance the family experiences upward or downward social mobility, which will, of course, often be a matter of extra-familial conditions and events: economic depression; civil war; and government policy.

For the critical polytextualist, this apparent lawfulness in the reproduction of the social order is, of course, itself constructed. If the advantaged beget the advantaged, that contingency can be told as a story about the powers that render the social predictable, just in much the same way as the lawfulness of traffic at traffic intersections. It is the acceptance of the order that makes the order possible. Every discourse permits a particular form of materiality – but not, of course, in the naive sense that any given contingency is open to unique and isolated change. All is intermeshed, rule into rule, so that to change, say, the side of the road which a nation drives upon may require virtually every element in a traffic system to be changed. So too with the young. Each child location brings with it not just a material reality, but also an identity-story, culturally enmeshed through multiple connections. That will offer, at a minimum, notions of both development individualised (a construction of the child) and of identity in the social (a construction of that family as culturally located). The powers of any particular family, or of any particular growing child, to negotiate both objective and subjective realities will always be limited and conditional. It may be as difficult to avoid the material and the representational realities that construct a prince[ss] as it is those that construct a pauper:

> Economic stress magnifies the perception of kids as monsters . . . The proximity caused by lack of space, lack of work, lack of minders, lack of time intensifies the deeply felt helplessness of adults facing baby power, child demands. The innocent becomes menacing, the hapless malignant. (Warner, 1989, p. 42)

Also important is the impact of the received order upon embodiment. Conditions predating any given conception may well have set probabilistic tracks which can impinge on the embodiment of both the child-to-be (e.g. the nutritional history of the mother) and her/his caregivers (e.g. the likelihood of orphanhood). At the same time co-termination of tracks can be challenged. That history which constitutes the bodily disadvantaged (e.g. unhardy) mother-to-be can be (and sometimes is) decoupled from its often assumed current contingency with either problematic mothercraft skills or the experience of inferior ante-natal care.

Children in families, then, are subject both to life-story tracking through the material reality in which their nurturance is located, and via its impingement as subjective representations. In turn, their own constructive activities will be both enabled and bounded by those realities. For the early years of life, home (and its extensions and complements such as forms of day care) will be the major focus of these social tectonics, in what has been traditionally called *primary socialisation*. Rejecting as we have dualistic biological/social accounts of primary socialisation, opens up the challenge to write an alternative story of early life construction. To do so, we first need to allow that babies are born into a socially constructed location. Typically, their caregivers bring to the 'expected' neonate both a general cultural (and often a more specifically instructed) knowledge of babyhood. Little is demanded of the young infant, save that its embodiment meets a general template for caretaker action. This is all that is required for enough neonates to survive their infancy for population replacement. Of course, where the individual infant is valued and the material aspects of culture permit it, all manner of contingent risks to survival may be countered. Perinatal mortality becomes a focus of cultural concern and a locus of interventional action (both medical and social). However, the presence of a baby does not merely engender immediate actions, it also opens up a futurity. The baby is expected to 'become' in predictable ways (the local story of childhood), and that extrapolation leads to an expectational responsiveness on the part of care-givers. How those expectations are explained in the impinging systems of child-knowledge does matter, of course, but not as much as the expectations themselves. To take an example, theories of how language emerges clearly can engross language theorists and create an agenda for, say, nature/nurture analyses. But such theory does not need to be contained within general cultural understandings as a necessary pre-condition for infants to begin to speak. They will, in all cultures, whatever the child-stories that culture tells, because all these stories create expectations of speech. Such universality is enough for a critical polytextualist treatment. We have no need to causally explain that universality because our elected task is not to causally explain but to analyse causal explanation.

> No mysterious underlying cognitive structures or 'language acquisition devices' need be called on to explain this process . . . [its] origins are lodged in the social order that he [sic] is born into and not in physiological structures, innate needs and drives, or in age-specific developmental phases . . . The child is, as Lewis argues, truly a speaker born into a universe of fellow speakers. (Denzin, 1977, p. 91)

What essentialists would call the beginnings of the acquisition of language by infants, are to Denzin's constructionist gaze, entry into discursive practices and hence to the social knowledge they engender. Again, in a critical polytextualist analysis, this does not require explanation – it *is* what language utilisation means. It may, if we so wish, be studied, and such studies can bring an appreciation of the social worlds which child actors are involved in bringing into being. But no amount of study can bring us into direct touch with 'child thought', 'child language' and 'child culture' as separable thinghoods – except in the form of particular, and always deconstructable, operational definitions (which bring them into being as objects for study). Of course, not only professional (e.g. developmentalist) stories use operational definitions – so too do popular knowledges of the child. It is these, ordinary, gazes which enable the social at large to confirm the social tracking of the young. When five or six year olds enter a school, their expressed location (e.g. in terms of race, gender or social class of origin and the differential indexing of powers concomitant to those markers) is patent to their teachers and is generally reflexively endorsed.

The knowledges at the disposal of pre-school children, then, reflect their locations: their home; their friends; their siblings; their nursery/day care; and, indeed, any positioning they occupy and have to handle. Life-tracks vary in the locations they bring to the young, and these in turn create varied opportunities for self-tracking. These life-worlds both link and diversify, fragment and re-integrate. Some contingent cultural competences are local in definition – to take an obvious example, an English child's competence in cricket may have little meaning if that child is moved to the United States. On the other hand, others may be very widely applicable, like competence in the exchange of money for a chocolate bar. Competences are always reflexively constituted. What a child is attributed to be doing impacts upon what is done to the child, and such dialectics are both drawn from the ongoing reality (e.g. the economic exchange system) and draw the child into that reality (e.g. create an identity as a consumer). Specific features of the child's embodiment (e.g. their attributed gender) are usually part of the impinging local realities, giving rise to, for example, gendered locations and concomitant gendered identities. In turn, features of embodied tracks, such as a gendered identity will tend to enable some self-tracking competences (e.g. being a person who can plait hair) and to problematise others (e.g. being a person who cannot use a hammer). Self-tracking by the child is both elective and contingent. It is also a value which will vary in salience and polarisation from one local order to another according to the operating stories of childhood (e.g. a liberal-humanistic location may well seek to enable self-tracking).

Cross-cultural confusions

The preceding section, indeed this book as a whole, has focused upon the child as understood in the post-industrial world (indeed, often within that, in the English speaking or textualised-into-English world). This is not because we set out in some ideologically blinkered way so to do. Rather, it is, paradoxically, an inherent feature of the critical poly-textualist approach. This results from two concerns. First, in rejecting developmentism, its foundational nature-nurture myth and its ethnocentric gaze, we can find little to gain from that large bulk of cross-cultural work which is so grounded (e.g. Wagner and Stevenson, 1982). A more recent example of the genre is that brought together by Jahoda and Lewis (1989) who, in criticising the early work of Hall make the following grounding observation:

> [A] generation earlier Galton had already displayed a more enlightened [sic!] attitude, devising a questionnaire requesting information about children of 'savages' who had been removed from their parents and brought up in 'civilised' conditions. His aim seems to have been to explore the relative contributions of heredity and environment. (p. 30)

Secondly, if socialisation is the reflexive construction of cultural competence, then to study that socialisation in any specific collectivity requires a competence in that culture on the part of the researcher (cf. Rabain,

1979). Our problem is that we have no such competence outside of the social worlds contingent upon our location as British parents and academics. Hence, when we address other locations, it is as those have been translated for us into our local cultural codes. To do more, requires a multi-culturality. Without that, the resultant research is prone to disaster, as we shall see in a later section of this chapter on cross-cultural studies of schooling.

One bi-cultural location for some western academics is that brought about by the creation of a Jewish state. Central to much mythologisation of Israel (and understandably there is a potent need for such mythologisation) are the kibbutzim. Unlike the fictional thought experimental world of Nema, kibbutz life appears (to essentialists) to provide a natural (i.e. factive) experiment in socialisation. It has also been, of course, a significant influence on the storying of childhood in the West. The young of the kibbutz, have enjoyed powerful and influential 'second childhoods' through such movies as *Exodus*. Equally, the kibbutz experiment has been a significant influence upon science fiction. Ursula Le Guin's anarchic planet of Annares is an obvious example, and Annaresti principles of non-ownership are vividly brought to mind by the following quotation from Bettelheim (1971) thanking the kibbutznik:

> Who let me have his own room, let me sleep in his bed, at considerable inconvenience to himself. (While it is a misnomer here to speak of his 'own' bed, since it is merely the bed assigned to him by the kibbutz and not his private possession, this does not alter his generosity a whit.) (p. 11)

The quotation is from *Children of the Dream*, Bettelheim's report on seven weeks of study of communal child-rearing on kibbutzim. Like so much cross-cultural research of its time, it is a book with many agendas. The first is a commitment to the bio-social myth, in terms of the kibbutzim providing (as his first section is entitled), 'an experiment with nature'. Another is a predicated critique of then current angst about the condition of children in the United States: 'Among the pressing problems still unsolved in American [sic] child rearing are those of the slum child, of the restless dissatisfaction of youth in general, and of particular disturbances amongst them, like drug addiction or juvenile delinquency' (p. 18). A third is the location of a US citizen (by naturalisation) who is also Jewish and a holocaust survivor: 'Certainly, the six-day war vindicated kibbutz child-rearing methods and made it once again a symbol of all that is best in Israel' (p. 28). Finally, like many writers, he shows a fascination with 'the dream' – the story of the kibbutzim. However, Bettelheim is far from just presenting recruitment material for the kibbutz – it is, he concludes: 'a fine system for some and not for others' (p. 266). Some clue as to whom those others might be, and a clear indication that the kibbutzim story is not an emancipatory text directed at the young, comes from the following passage:

> For example, although there is officially small concern with premarital sex, teachers are much concerned if a youngster is tired because he [sic] is having sex relations at age seventeen or eighteen . . . The true attitude to extra-marital sex, as opposed to the one given lip service, shows up in the reaction to extra-marital pregnancy. The severest sanctions are reserved for those whose pregnancies show that they took sex to be as 'natural' and 'good' as they were told . . . the kibbutz here displays a double standard, despite their avowed belief in equality of the sexes: the boy who got the girl pregnant is criticized but that is all. (p. 213)

Indeed, total communities like this, while they are extremely useful for the social analyst, because they add to our stock of alternative realities, seldom seem to turn out the 'dreams' their makers hope they will be. They are singularities (zealotic productions), and hence cannot offer blueprints for better childhoods (or, indeed adulthoods). This has not, of course, stopped them from being seen by external observers as such, a cultural dialect of the 'golden age' or 'noble savage' hypotheses, in which the wholesome, unworldliness of romanticised childhoods of other cultures are held to be superior to our own. A good example is given in a recent reader entitled *What do anthropologists have to say about drop-outs?* (Trueba, Spindler and Spindler, 1989). The latter two authors lead off with a singularly naive paper entitled 'There are no dropouts amongst the Arunta and the Hutterites.' This despite the statement made by a Hutterite young man interviewed by Spindler and Spindler (1989) who said 'you couldn't stand to be a Hutterite for three seconds' (pp. 9–10).

What we can glean from this first level approach to the conditions of childhood, is that nobody – child or adult – can ever be universally culturally competent. Hence socialisation is always partial, and relocation can reveal this at any life point. Collectivities only expect relative competences, and these themselves are location dependent. This is as true for us, as cultural analysts, as it is for our children. However, throughout the industrialised world at least (and indeed for kibbutzniks and Hutterites), age markers, usually set around five or six years old, are institutionally established as 'readinesses' for schooling, just as they once were for work in historical times.

In a class of their own

In this section we will examine an aspect of childhood which, in the West, is virtually universal – schooling. Often cited by sociologists as *the* major site of secondary socialisation, it marks the domain of childhood whereby the child is subjected to systematic and intended, state or institutional, social intervention. As such it provides a location both for the moulding of the young by a directed social force of 'education', and as one from within which to explore the nature of nurture somewhat paradoxically outside of the gaze of developmentalism, as will become evident when we turn our attention at the end of the chapter to studies of schooling in nations which have drawn upon an alternative ideology to western capitalism.

It is easy, but misleading, to see the education of the young as synonymous with their schooling (Illich, 1973). All the world's children are in some way educated (i.e. are impinged upon by the social such that they acquire cultural competences that will enable them to come to pass more or less effectively as adults). Only some are schooled to a greater or lesser extent (i.e. experience a specific institutional regime of enculturation which has an overt syllabus of testable knowledge). Nevertheless, for most western children and for their caregivers, education is equated with a State imposed 'right' to be schooled. Another way of looking at it, however, is around ten years of forced conscription into an army of the young. Such a deconstruction does not require that we see schooling as a 'wrong', but it does allow it to be envisioned within a critical gaze. Compulsory, universal state-provided and/or monitored schooling is a comparatively recent cultural innovation, in the West dating from the mid-nineteenth century. None the less it parallels so many other structural innovations that society, as we know it, would be unworkable without school. In telling stories of schooling, therefore we are recounting facets of a whole range of societal processes that concern much more than (and need not parallel) any analysis of the best interests of the young, even where that is read as their education.

On one reading, universal schooling was made possible and perhaps necessary by legislation which removed the young from paid work and paved the way for the alternative containment of (unpaid) school work. Although working conditions in nineteenth century schools were harsh by modern standards, at their best they were also vastly safer and less arduous than the conditions existing in industry of that time. Furthermore, schools came to reflect a concern for the health, the physical development and the diet of their child workers that few, if any, early capitalists even aspired towards for their employees. Universal schooling is one of the key factors in the constructing of a modern work-force. On the one hand, it acts directly and indirectly as a training ground for knowledge, skills, values and attitudes transferable to – if not directly salient or useful to – the demands of adult labour and the requirements of labour consumption. At the same time it ages as it educates the young, and thus emancipates and empowers the work-force. It thereby contributes to greater powers of the labour force in industrial and inter-familial relations. Overall, it provides a cheap or even free 'child mind-ing' service (and thus has been a crucial mechanism for enabling parents – read women – to join the work-force). And it has acted as a powerful mechanism and environment for social control of the young. Nothing perhaps illustrates this better than the changing personnel of industries like fabric milling, where between about 1820 and 1920, the work-force shifted from children to 'mill girls' (of all ages). In these and other ways (e.g. clearly a proportion of the work-force is directly or indirectly em-ployed by the schooling industry), the lineaments of work are predicated upon the lineaments of schooling.

Since its initial introduction, schooling has increasingly eaten into the world of work. Not only have school leaving ages been raised, but the proportion of the young population remaining in full-time schooling beyond the compulsory minimum leaving age has also grown. This has the effect of increasing the span of the young's ultimate economic de-pendence (but not their childhood which may well be moving in the opposite direction). Perhaps the best characterisation is that the bound-aries between schooling and work are dissolving. For the latter years of schooling, the western young may well gainfully work part-time. Equally, first jobs usually involve training, and frequently some type of day-release for more formal schooling. The growing importance of adult education, and growing recognition of continuing education across the life-span and within the world of work, have also served to muddy the boundaries between education in childhood and beyond.

Although its economic benefits may be compensatorally large (if hard to calculate) schooling is massively expensive as an item in a country's budget (or indeed in a family's if they are in a position to elect to buy education). The equation is easier to sustain if additional, non-financial benefits, can be argued. All nation states seek to direct schooling towards national political goals and within those states, is-sues of education are always politicised. The school and the process of schooling impart specific values through their institutional structures and their personnel, and are required so to do by their funders. These values may not always coincide (since the schooling industry is a politico-economic force in its own right), but by and large schooling is a recognisably *national* enterprise, if subject to a greater or lesser degree of federalism. The state school finds itself charged with a tacit, if not explicit, syllabus which follows (in form although not in content) the already established and continuing patterns of religious schooling – the construction of a total institution for indoctrination. The strong argument of the school as total institution, once raised, needs, of

132   *The condition of childhood*

course, to be challenged. Otherwise, we run the risk of confusing the analytic with a reifying causal model.

The story of schooling as conspiracy is only workable if one accepts as axiomatic a broader understanding of society as conspiracy (e.g. a Marxist or feminist analysis). Such a singular certainty of analysis does not sit comfortably with critical polytextualism's radical doubt. Rather, ideologies are regarded as tools so that while we can be, in any particular instantiation of method, say, Marxist-informed, overall a critical polytextualist account is a stylistically heterogeneous collection of stories. What this can open is a sensitivity to schooling *vis-à-vis* the young as a series of alternations between one reading and another:

- Homogenising *and* heterogenising (i.e. both constructing children that are alike and constructing children that are diverse).
- Reproductive *and* innovatory (i.e. both perpetuating the status quo and changing it)
- Exploitative *and* exploited (e.g. both controls the young and is used by them for their own purposes)
- Reactive *and* subversive (i.e. is a nexus of power which can be taken unchallenged or deconstructed).

These and similar tensions are quite general in a pluralistic culture. They will be differently read, of course, from one ideological gaze to another. A move from gaze to gaze will reveal not only that their meanings shift, but that the whole notion of 'tension' is also fluid. We are not obliged (except by ideological fiat) to see these tensions as 'leading' anywhere or following any particular 'laws' of resolution. The workings of societal apparatuses, like the workings of biological apparatuses (even if themselves construed as lawful) need not be held to carry a forecast of their future, nor need to implicate any ability to foretell from the past and the present, the course of evolution. Rather, in constructing stories around such tensions, we are likely to detect imbalances of power, when one pole acquires a greater or lesser strength according to cultural-historical location. Equally, the workings of these tensions are likely to strike us as varying child by child, covarying with such socially constructed markers as gender. 'Evolution' is a matter of what we understand we can do, and what we, through ideology, construe we should do with these analyses and understandings, the actions or inactions they engender in a system which is constrained but undetermined.

Homogeneity/heterogeneity

An apparent ability of the schooling apparatus to produce sameness or to produce diversity in its students accepts no simple political analysis.

Sameness in knowledge (e.g. a state controlled curriculum) may have 'left-appeal' or 'right-appeal' according to the knowledge concerned. The lure of peace studies syllabus is usually a good bait for the radical; while the reactionary responds to a quite different attractant: e.g. education for social responsibility. In general, ideologues approach the supposed homogenising powers of schooling not so much as ends *per se*, but as means to the realisation of a particular political utopia. Because a belief in these powers is necessary for their utopia, they are equally paranoid about the hazards of those powers falling into the wrong hands and being used for dystopian purposes. Hence, de-schoolers/anti-schoolers can also be found right across the ideological spectrum, wherever pessimism exceeds optimism!

A similar analysis also prevails over the purported heterogenising powers of schooling. For the right, this is subsumed under notions like 'choice' and 'selectivity'. For the left, heterogenising is more likely to be favoured where it enables children to 'develop their own unique potentials', or in terms of a respect for ethnic and cultural diversity in education. For others with more specific agendas, it is seen as the means by which traditions can be preserved (whether of language or religion). Again, the focus is not so much upon means as upon ends, and the means are seen as capable of 'being subverted' for the 'wrong ends'. In the 'real world', schooling can be also be read as displaying both functions. State intervention has yielded homogenising national curricula in both, say, welfarist Sweden and post-Thatcherite Britain. Equally, heterogenising selectivity has been a consistent part both of British and Soviet education. Hence, rather than accepting a traditional political analysis (in which, incidentally 'a voice for the child' has seldom been a salient input), a critical polytextualist account needs to challenge the conventional 'utopian' agendas underpinning the management of schooling.

Reproductive and innovatory

Within a critical polytextualist analysis, the past is not a singular thing – history – but is itself a matter of tensions, dilemmatics, and alternative and competing discourses. In that sense the history of radical education discourse is part of the status quo, just as much as is the discursive history of the British public schools. They may differ in their levels of current representation to us, but they both go towards making up the received. Over its socio-historical existence, the apparatus of schooling has reproduced the status quo in so far as it has been managed around the tensions of society itself, in particular the orthogonal tensions of homogenising/heterogenising and left/right utopianism. All that may happen within those given gazes is that changes which have been conceptualised one way (e.g. the liberal concept of selectivity as placing each child in a potential matching context) may go on to be subsequently reconstructed (e.g. as perpetuating class divides and advantage/disadvantage). So it is no great surprise that it has been in the privileged private educational sector, through its relative insulation from State monitoring, where some pioneering experiments (e.g. the free-schooling of Summerhill) have taken place.

Within those tensions, schooling has certainly 'moved with the times', but it is a movement which is renovational rather than radical. Schooling provides the new persons to replace the old within the national enterprise, and as that enterprise is differently conceptualised, so too are the apparatuses of renewal recast. But the telling of such a functional reproductive story does not preclude alternative accounts that see other things from different gazes. Schooling can also be a context of innovation. It is so whenever 'education' is led into a critical polytextualist gaze. This may be because the teaching craft itself is infiltrated by a few personnel who see it as a subversive activity (cf. Postman and Weingartner, 1971), a place to foster 'crap detection', and other constructionist skills. It may also result when originally 'safe' domains of the syllabus (like nature study) reach a critical mass of problematics in which it becomes clear that there is very little nature actually left to be studied! Meta-perspective enters analysis, and the safe becomes the site for subversive challenge to the received order. Change may also be imposed upon the system by apparently happenstantial outside events, like the emergence of HIV infection. This has recently been seen to generate new educational needs (i.e. for sex education) and reconstruct the student body (i.e. which must now be acknowledged as constituted of sexual, even potentially homosexual, persons). And finally, it can result from a change in the raw material of schooling itself – the young.

Exploitative and exploited

The apparatuses of schooling, like any structures of power, are easy to read as mechanisms of control. By and large, the success or failure of schooling is measured upon available control indices like high examination success and low truancy rate – not upon whether the students' needs (as they might define them) are met. Equally, it is those indices which are promoted (or obscured) by schools in their own publicity. Furthermore, it is the power-structures of the school that strike both researchers and more casual observers through their permanence and patentness –

areas are segregated by gender, by status within the undergroup (the students) and by undergroup/overgroup divides (e.g. the staff areas). Rules define the flow of power and its exercise. In this sense, school is easy to equate with other total institutions. Nor would it be a mistake to accept this analysis for what it can tell us. The school as an anti-human device is well-established in our cultural symbolism (e.g. in films like *If, Zero de Conduit* and *The Wall*) as well as in the biographic myths of many of us. Schooling not only enables specific adult powers over the young, but may also foster legitimated (e.g. prefectorial) and under-ground (e.g. bullying) forms of power by the young over the young (cf. Stainton Rogers, R., 1991; Stainton Rogers, W., 1991). That the weight of power favours the institution cannot easily be denied, but to stay with such a singular treatment alone is to deny the powers of the young to employ the apparatuses for their own devices.

Any experience of a school with an eye to its use by the young will reveal that it is a medium for the development and testing of student powers outside of those constituting the formal syllabus and curriculum. The socio-physical context that is a school cannot prevent this (even where it may see some attempt at control as within its terms of refer-ence). The ecology of schooling – which includes journeys to and from school and extra-mural activities like trips and social events – offers a fruitful environment to the young for the development of groups and friendships, and the negotiation of sexual relationships. For some, the authority of the school itself also provides a valuable education in real-politik, and an opportunity to learn the workings of power and how it may be challenged, avoided and subverted. Students at times do exercise their powers individually or cooperatively 'against' either the system or individual teachers – and win. Such experiences may be normative rather than radical, but they do argue against any naive view of school-ing as a unidirectional power structure or one in which the young can be regarded as passive to their fate (a point made eloquently by Walker-dine, 1990, even with regard to pre-schoolers).

Reactive and subversive

As apparatuses of societal power, schools do indeed act as agents of reaction. They are, for example, open to establishment propaganda (e.g. from the police and the armed forces) in a way they are usually pre-vented from being open to counter-establishment propaganda (e.g. from peace groups or the gay community). Their libraries and their text books may be open to censorship by central and local authorities and by their governing bodies. Audio-visual materials are likely to be taken both from monitored television authorities and from largely unmonitored (but hardly unbiased) multi-national companies as part of their public relations budgets. However, in practice, the meanings taken by both teachers and by students of the informational inputs into the school, and the meanings taken by students from teachers, should not be read in terms of any simple, passive indoctrination. It is, for example, a cliché that some aspects of the school curriculum (e.g. classical music education, and Shakespeare) often act as a life-time turn-off to high culture! In a similar way, many an atheist will attest to the benefits of early compulsory religious study and worship in school. At the extreme, both experience of school in the generic, and specific subjects like mathematics, are not infrequently re-cast into 'phobia'. Complex discourses concerning health and illness as warrants to avoid unwanted commitments are acquired as cultural competences, in part, through their power to abrogate responsibility to attend school or parts of schooling (e.g. sport).

In addition to such negations of manipulation, we also need to recognise that schools – as marketplaces of young people – also attract entrepreneurs whose products often lie in tension to the ostensive educational curriculum. In urban areas, schools are often served by shops which are outlets for 'junk food', popular youth literature and cigarettes. Where schools have a youth intake, the school itself will serve as a locus for recruitment to parties, 'raves', music clubs and other teenage functions, both adult-legitimated and otherwise. In a similar way, the school also operates as a distribution network for the ideas and the literature of the youth wings of political and religious organisations, pressure and issue groups. Nor should we forget that schools and their environs also constitute a ready-made (and frequently used) catchment for the marketing of recreational and, sometimes, harder drugs.

Finally, secondary and particularly tertiary school groups have often proved, at times of overt social dissensus (e.g. the 1966 student riots in the West and those in 1989 in China) to be readily mobilised into the radical cause. (Note however that riots among students are not new phenomena: 'in 1818, by strange coincidence, rebellion broke out in all but one of the public schools' (Chandos, 1985, p. 178); in 1793 the army were called out to quell the Winchester school rebellion, *op. cit.*, p. 179.) The apparent stasis and apoliticality of the young *en masse* over relatively long periods of social time reflects a differential migration into a reality which merely *seems* to be the only reality around. The ability of the dominant realities of the young to pitch into the subterranean and vice versa seems an inevitable property of belonging to a culture which itself is constituted of a diverse multiplicity of cosmologies. The conditions which enable such 'quantum leaps' from one reality orbit to another (and whose negation often signals a leap back again) are specific to each subversive/liberatory event in the social calendar. But they usually follow some kind of value-added accretion of issues, events and evidenced vulnerability of the power apparatus. It would be historically and sociologically naive to judge any given meta-stable present by its overt indicators alone. Few (if any) observers of the schools and colleges of China in the early eighties (for example), had any inkling of the subterranean seething of ideas which erupted into the social quakes which followed.

The grass is greener?

Thus far, we have discussed schooling and its discontents very much in terms of tensions reflected in and reflecting western culture. However, that reflecting can also be applied to schooling extraneous to our experience. When it is, the results can illuminate our own discursive preoccupations, or at least the discursive preoccupations our appointed observers take with them!

China checkers

The emergence of Communist China from isolation in the early 1970s enabled a number of self-conscious explorations of Mao's new empire as a natural experiment in socialisation. In 1973 a number of the leading lights of American developmentalism – including such figures as Urie Bronfenbrenner, Bettye Caldwell, Jerome Kagan, Eleanor Maccoby and George Miller – travelled through China over a three-week period as part of a thirteen-strong 'American delegation on early childhood development in the People's Republic of China'. Their findings, reported in 1975 under the title *Childhood in China* (Kessen, 1975), is both a fascinating piece of social history and an extraordinarily self-mutilating document. As their report develops, it becomes dramatically clear just how local and contingent are these 'experts" own understanding-systems of children and their social world, and how open to culture shock they were. For example they noted that 'young Chinese children are extraordinarily poised and well-behaved' (p. 39). They also seem remarkably insensitive to discursive devices which transform such observations into negative contrasts to prevailing western norms, as in this passage: 'The children were generally docile and conforming, displaying little of the restlessness, rough and tumble play, grabbing of property, or the pushing and striking of peers that are common in American homes and schools' (p. 56); and then invert them again: 'They were far less restless, less intense in their motor actions, and displayed less crying and whining than American children in similar situations. We were constantly struck by the quiet, gentle and controlled manner of Chinese children' (p. 69).

Faced with facticities about Chinese childhood which do not map onto their constructions of the young (e.g. 'The skill and expertise of the children in executing the songs and dances is phenomenal' (p. 92)) they seek for causal agency behind these 'major mysteries': 'How are such skills taught? By what pattern . . . are the abilities acquired?' Wherever the received dogmas of developmentalism seem confounded (e.g. when they see six year olds drawing with perspective) they again look for hidden hands: 'The children had obviously been taught certain skills that contributed to the maturity of their drawings' (p. 94). At times, even explanation seems to elude them and they regress to simple simile: 'The Chinese children we saw seemed to have an ability to attend with laser-like focus to what adults were saying to them' (p. 107). They were equally unsuccessful in seeking the 'signs of unhealthy adjustment' that their culturally engendered exchange theories seemed to demand as the 'psychological price' of Chinese enculturation practices: 'the obvious signs of tension, depression, or apathy were rare compared to those in groups of Western children' (p. 142); 'we saw the continuing development of children . . . without the disorders of behaviour we have come to expect at a steady low base rate in American schools – hyperactivity, impulsivity, isolated withdrawal, and neurotic symptoms' (p. 146). Further, their taken-for-granted, western, pathologising approach to children seems to have left their hosts bemused:

> We had little success in communicating the concept of hyperactivity. We would describe the symptoms and first grade teachers would agree that some children . . . might have some difficulty settling down to the routine of a classroom; such difficulty, they said, might last for as long as three weeks or a month . . . Chronic hyperactivity, however, was simply not a familiar problem to them nor to teachers of higher grades. (p. 144)

Only in their overview, do we begin to see the faintest precursors of a reflexive, constructionist reading:

> Put in its most simplifying form, Chinese children behave the way they do because that is the way children behave! The contrast with common American practice can be easily made. An American teacher (or parent) considers how he or she will effect a change in the child, what should be done with the child to make a difference . . . If the instruments of education, whether they are problem setting, positive reinforcement, or modelling, are ineffective, then change is difficult or distorted . . . Chinese teachers have uniform expectations of what children at one or another age

can do and . . . they behave with the virtually certain knowledge that the children will come to behave in the expected way. (p. 219)

How might this expectation (and its associated effects) come about? Kessen leaves us with a fascinating shot in his own foot:

We were struck by the generally nonanalytical (educational theorists might even say 'unscientific') posture of Chinese teachers toward their children. There seemed no commanding need either for theories of classroom 'management' or, let it be emphasized, ideas of child development. (p. 220)

Seldom has the historical and cultural specificity of the developmentalist gaze upon childhood and schooling been more succinctly (and one suspects less self-reflectively) stated (though to be fair, Kessen, 1990, tells a very different story).

From Russia with love

Shortly before Kessen *et al.* were to stun western developmentalists with their study of education in China, a not totally dissimilar reflection on Soviet socialisation (also with US practice as the contrast) was produced by a prominent member of the Kessen team, Urie Bronfenbrenner (1971). There is little doubt that Bronfenbrenner was one of the most respected social developmental psychologists of his time and *Two Worlds of Childhood: USA and USSR* was widely seen as capping that reputation with 'one of the important books of this generation' (review by John H. Fischer quoted on the dust cover). What we are actually treated to is a powerful critique of the failures of US socialisation: 'the unmaking of the American child' (to quote the title of Chapter 4). Indeed, according to Bronfenbrenner, only one country 'exceeds the United States in the willingness of its young to engage in antisocial behavior . . . [t]hat country is England [sic], the home of the Mods and the Rockers, the Beatles, the Rolling Stones' (p. 116). On index after index, the literal (and figurative) Young Pioneers of the great Soviet experiment, who stare out at us in full socialist realist colour, bright eyed and bushy-tailed, are found to be superior to their US counterparts. They were: more morally and socially responsible; less cruel, inconsiderate or dishonest; more polite, orderly and helpful; less selfish and with a greater sense of responsibility.

Social scientists throughout the twentieth century have proved particularly naive over the workings of authoritarian regimes and the ability of those regimes to fabricate a reality for their visitors. It would be unfair to single out Bronfenbrenner's paean to Brezhnev's USSR as in any way unusual. However, as a text designed to influence policy *Two Worlds of Childhood* is a political discourse, and it should not be allowed to escape the ironisation that more recent geo-social history has brought to it. Here is Bronfenbrenner engaging in a little futurology and a little nostalgia:

> All of this suggests that Soviet children of the future will continue to be more conforming than our own. But this also means that they will be less anti-adult, rebellious, aggressive and delinquent. During our family sojourns in the USSR, we have learned to our surprise and pleasure that the streets of Moscow and other Soviet cities were reasonably safe for women and children, by night as well as by day. They say that New York was that way once. (pp. 90–1)

So indeed, we might say now, was Moscow that way once! Our teasing is not aimed at Bronfenbrenner's failure to predict the details of the break-up of the Soviet empire, it is directed at his apparent inability to think it possible because it was not so socialised. Look at videos of Moscow August 1991 and you will find a good part of the crowds protesting the attempted counter-coup are made up of Brezhnev's/Bronfenbrenner's children! Where is all that conformity now? Look at the new street markets, the new generation of wheeler-dealers, the crime, the 'drug problem' – it could almost be New York. Hence, when he tells us that: 'We have sought to demonstrate that the behavioural sciences, though admittedly limited in knowledge and theoretical grasp, can, nevertheless, illuminate both the problems of a society and possible directions for their solution' (p. 165) we know that US society did not listen and survived; we also know that 'Marxist-Leninist' educators did their best to socialise a whole society into an enduring collective, and failed. Arguably, the USSR fell because it was an economic disaster. The United States, despite the horrors that a free market visited and continues to visit upon its under-class young, flourished. Bronfenbrenner's fundamental mistake was not that he was fooled by the political propaganda of the USSR, it was to put his faith in socialisation as constituted under western social developmental psychology. Paradoxically, had he taken a more Marxist position and wondered how human relations are constituted out of economic arrangements, he would never have seen the US/USSR contrast as a natural experiment with socialisation as the key differentiating variable. The error began when he equated the USSR with the US as facing 'similar problems as an industrialised nation with highly developed systems of technology, education and mass communication' (p. 2). It was not similar, hence both the collapse of the Soviet dream and the demise of Bronfenbrenner's fantasy of the power of behavioural science. Both were myths of modernism and few, outside of their respective party apparatuses, will mourn their passing.

9

Childhood's end – overlords and underlings

In this chapter we direct our attention to how and why the boundaries are drawn between childhood and adulthood. As we have already noted, this borderline is unique – unlike other forms of social demarcation (e.g. between social classes or castes) it is specifically time-limited. Once beyond the transit point at which the child becomes an adult – childhood's end – it dissolves.

> So endeth this chronical. It being strictly the history of a boy, it must stop here; the story could not go much further without becoming the history of a man. When one writes a novel about grown people, he [sic] knows exactly where to stop – that is with a marriage; but when he writes of juveniles, he must stop where best he can. (Mark Twain's 'Conclusion' to *Tom Sawyer*)

It is true that by *Huckleberry Finn*, Twain may seem to have changed his mind. But between the 'play' of *Tom Sawyer* and the deadly earnest 'games' of *Huckleberry Finn* (from its use of heavy dialect, to Huck's near murder by his drunken father) there is a major shift in focus. Twain's point not merely survives his writing of the second book, it is reinforced by it. The young people who inhabit *Huckleberry Finn* have been transported to the other side of 'childhood's end' before the novel begins. So too, has its audience. Today young readers are now asked to reflect upon *Huckleberry Finn* against the background of their implied locations as apprentices in social concern:

> Is Huckleberry Finn a valuable classic of American [sic] literature, or is it racist, sexist and immoral? According to some of the parents and students at George Mason High school, the book should be banned and the principal – not for the first time – agrees to remove the offending item from the library shelves. But that's just the beginning of the story. (Cover-jacket text to *The Day They Came to Arrest the Book*, Nat Hentoff, 1987)

It is not only the weavers of fictive stories like Twain who face dilemmas over the boundary location of the young. The construction of childhood's end constitutes a problematic for all who seek to account for childhood.

Absolute markers

Broadly the absolute point of transition from child to adult is marked in one of two ways: either by a biological event; or by a chronological one. In those traditional societies where childhood's end is indexed in terms of embodiment by biological clocks – the wisdom of the body – it is generally located amongst the changes that are constituted into the process of puberty. In its modal form, changes in embodiment (most notably the menarche) are construed as not just the signs of biological change, but also as the signals for rites of passage which lead to the acquiring of a new social status and identity. This new identity may not be perceived as bringing full adult rights and responsibilities, but it is clearly seen to betoken them. For example, for young women, it often amounts to a time of sexual segregation and protection prior to the rites of marriage (as in traditional Jewish, Islamic and Mediterranean societies). In other traditional cultures it may open up a period of social and sexual exploration, as described in Margaret Mead's controversial accounts of coming of age in Samoa (Mead, 1928 as criticised by Freeman, 1984 or Elwin's less challenged report of the Muria (1968) and Turnbull's of the Mubti (1976)). Both sides of this tension share a construction of the embodiment marker as indexing a state of 'readiness' whether to be controlled or released (see Crawford, 1984, for an analysis of these two perceptions of embodiment).

In bureaucraticised cultures, although the changes of puberty will be subjected to detailed examination (one is almost inclined to say loving examination – talk of the 'budding' of the breast suggests a caring gardener), by developmental researchers such as Tanner (1978), it is chronological age which is used to mark the transition into adulthood – attaining of the 'age of majority'. Generally set at about eighteen, this has varied historically (we, the authors, had to wait until twenty-one) and varies geographically. For instance, in Scotland, young people enter a state of *pupilage* (at age twelve for a girl and fourteen for a boy), when they acquire a limited set of adult legal entitlements before full majority at eighteen. The actual 'date stamping' of this passport into the adult world tends to be warranted not by the biological 'readiness' heralded by puberty but by the intellectual 'readiness' assumed to be necessary for participatory citizenship. The basis for setting the cut-off point is partly informed by historically sedimented concepts of the child as a politically *performative* incompetent, but has more recently been warranted by a developmentalism which portrays children as *cognitive* aliens, for whom enfranchisement would be beyond their capabilities.

Discount conditions

However, childhood's end is seldom treated as an 'all or nothing' event. Rather, within bureaucratic societies, it is staggered. In almost all post-industrial countries, a number of 'discount' conditions are introduced, which allow otherwise-children access to adult entitlements or powers. A good example is the age of consent to engage in sexual activity. This consent typically precedes majoritorial enfranchisement, and for females has even existed without it. Consentability has varied historically (for girls in England it was twelve over much of the nineteenth century, but is currently sixteen). At present it also varies trans-nationally (see Ennow, 1986), and frequently differs for female and male heterosexuality and between heterosexual and homosexual activity. Chronological constructions of these partial ends of childhood generally make no claim to logic. They have emerged out of the unique historical contingencies of their locale and vary even within national boundaries (State by State in the United States, between England and Scotland in the United Kingdom). Perhaps most illogically of all, where male homosexuality is concerned, there is even a discount-up, with the age at which individuals are accorded the status of 'consenting adult' being twenty-one in the UK, despite eighteen being the legal age of adulthood.

Seldom, however, do chronological discount markers emerge from the social historical record as child-liberatory devices, instituted in recognition of the growing autonomy of the children concerned. Few, in other words, were accounted for by an acknowledgement that those who are still officially 'children' are entitled, none the less, to some limited forms of authority and choice. At best, they were instituted as compromises between a hard-won acknowledgement of the vulnerability of children to an unbridled capitalism and the demands of that social economy. This is true of such measures as those which restricted access to tobacco products or alcohol. More often, however, the stronger the vested adult interests, the more the exceptions have been made. Hence, the typical pattern in which children (as defined by law) are allowed to join the army, drive heavy agricultural vehicles, or forgo aspects of their education in order to perform as entertainers. In such cases the driving

144 Childhood's end

force is blatantly other than promoting the welfare or freedom of the child concerned. We may have moved on from the full horrors of the chimney sweep, the child coal miner and mill-child of the nineteenth century, but it is salutary just how similar are the arguments, advanced today in Britain, against a minimum wage (as this, it is asserted, would make young working people 'too expensive' to employ) to those put forward in the 1840s against reducing the working hours or improving the working conditions of eight year olds.

While administratively convenient (e.g. in running an education system or child benefit scheme), over many areas chronological markers are effectively unenforceable (e.g. over child labour, access to alcohol, and majoritorial male homosexuality) and arguably they may serve as much as incentives to the young to breach as they do as controls (cf. Winn, 1984). Indeed, despite legislation to accord children a 'protected space' from exploitation, where record keeping is poor, where records get lost or left behind, or where there is little motive to check, it has never been hard for under-age children in age-criterion societies to 'pass' as adult. This is not just true of relatively trivial hurdles like getting a drink but applied, for example, over entry into the British Forces in World War One:

> Joined up when I was sixteen. I went up the Colston Hall, an' the man behind the desk said: 'How old are you?' I said, 'Sixteen.' 'Too young,' he said, an' I went to walk away, but the recruiting sergeant called over to me and said, 'Go over to the other desk and tell him you're eighteen.' And that's what I done. Ended up in the trenches in France. (Humphries, 1981, p. 187)

In less bureaucratised societies and in guerrilla and resistance movements, those whom the society regard as children often none the less become full participants in adult activity without question (Townsend, 1980; see Chapter 11 for further discussion). While their competence in such roles often seems well established, it is a competence born of adult-perceived necessity, just as it was in the social history of our own society. Any notion that young people's competence should be established electively is alien to the bureaucratic–legislative gaze. We have already worked the story of civil rights gained in this way in the tale of Nema as a means of generating a narrative in which competence is the primary criterion of childhood's end. We had to do so fictively, as no actual society operates in this way, except under highly limited conditions, and almost always to serve adult purposes.

However, it is instructive to explore where western society is most prone to employ a competency discourse. The areas which immediately spring to mind are ones where competence itself is regarded as critical, and where performative excellence is highly valued. These include: classical music (the child prodigy as performer and/or as composer, e.g. Mozart); chess; and sports like gymnastics. Here, childhood is allowed to end in direct involvement in adult institutions (the concert hall, the tournament, the Olympic Games). Many, although not all, examinations are tests of competence, often without an absolute (though often practical) age barrier. Thus we see (albeit very rarely) adolescents able to study mathematics at university. What enables this often appears to be the idea of an 'innate' talent transcending the normal constraints of maturation or sheer age, so long as this does not too strongly challenge hegemonic professional power (we do not find adolescents studying surgery or social work). This is another product of the alembic myth. The negation of this thesis also operates, where people regard some individuals as 'adults with children's minds' – a state also usually seen as 'innate'. Such persons are not accorded a full childhood's end, but are seen as the subjects of adult interventions 'in their best interests' e.g. to be sterilised (Kamin, 1974).

In this we see one of the problematics of a competence criterion. It is potentially élitist – it accords privileges for 'the best', penalties for 'the worst'. In our kind of society, competence passing is also very much domain specific – a fifteen year old with a degree in mathematics still cannot vote or buy a drink or consent to sex of any nature. Where there are gross disparities in opportunity, a competence criterion is likely to increase rather than reduce inequalities, for example, as in the UK eleven-plus examination.

However, three domains, in particular, are strenuously denied to children: sexuality, the utilisation of wealth, and political enfranchisement. Whatever partial entry into adulthood children may be accorded, these are the no-go areas from which children are excluded. In terms of sexuality, there is a highly specific adult reluctance to see performative or cognitive competence as a warrant to allow quasi-adult status. Whereas the highly skilled child gymnast or ballet dancer is proffered to us as a spectacle of desirable (if unattainable) accomplishment to be wondered at, an equally proficient child prostitute would not be admired for her or his dazzling ability. And, whereas with other domains of competence acquisition, popular wisdom has it that what children need is lots of opportunities to practise, over sex, it asserts they need the opposite! We take up this issue of children and sexuality in more detail in Chapter 10. As far as wealth is concerned, the adult world is similarly extremely careful to prevent children from any real control over 'serious' money or substantial material goods. Where children do acquire large incomes (as entertainers or by inheritance or by the awarding of damages in a lawsuit, for example), the law specifically prevents them from holding authority for its disposal. Instead, adults hold and administer their assets for them. The most crucial exclusion even wealthy or well-paid minors face is a lack of access to credit and hence to the very business of business itself.

The age of majority is also a specific marker for political agency, since it is the point at which an individual acquires voting rights, and the power to engage in any effective manner in participatory democracy. Thus the principle 'no taxation without representation' is breached for children, long after all other taxed groups have gained enfranchised status. More generally, the political disenfranchisement of the young is found in the severe lack of any power for young people to influence public policy (e.g. decisions about environmental issues) or even the running of the very institutions intended to serve their interests, notably schools. The recent 'Parent's Charter' for schools says much about the rights of parents, and very little about the rights of students.

Warranting exclusion

Under a conflict theory analytic, these exclusion areas represent the key defences of the adult world. So long as they hold, the young are (at least in law) prevented from acquiring any serious power over their own lives, or indeed, over adults. Put another way, these are the major rewards of joining the masonry of the mature. They are, in the classic language of conservative politics, the 'rights' that compensate for, and complement, the 'responsibilities' of adulthood. To challenge the foundations of that last great fable, the axioms that ground adulthood itself, is that which cannot be allowed – cannot even be thought. To protect them, any price, including the continued oppression of the young, can be justified. Under a consensus analytic, however, this is not the state of affairs at all. Concern for the young continues to advance forward and is evidenced all around us. It is certainly the case that recent legal moves have accorded children certain new entitlements. The Gillick appeal ruling established that a child under the age of sixteen could have the legal capacity (i.e. competence) to consent to contraception (Gillick v. West Norfolk and Wisbech Area Health Authority and the DHSS [1986] AC112). This ruling did not, however, alter her legal lack of capacity to consent to sexual intercourse! Harris (1989) notes that this judgement:

> seems to establish that while it is illegal for a girl under sixteen to consent to become pregnant in the usual way via sexual intercourse, she may legally consent to become pregnant via various forms of medical intervention. . . . Thus young girls [sic] may consent to being made pregnant by doctors but not by their lovers. (pp. 138–9)

Nevertheless, the aggregative impact of such judgements can be seen in the England and Wales Children Act (1989), in which considerable competence is allowed for. For example, specific provisions are included which accord a child 'if he is of sufficient understanding to make an informed decision' [s. 44(7)], the right to refuse a medical examination – even one ordered by a Court. We see then a strange set of competency judgements, in which children may be accorded the right to control their own sexuality or have others control it (by receiving contraceptive advice, or refusing to submit to a medical examination), but are not accorded rights to promote their own sexuality.

The tension between the readings of childhood's end offered by the conflict and consensus analytics may well not be a resolvable one. Rather, it represents the polytextuality of the discursive arena itself. That concourse is no respecter of the boundaries between the factive and the fictive, for the dilemmatics permeate all our cultural doings. An interesting, if disturbing, fictive exploration of competence which explores the combination of age markers and performativity is told in the science fiction book *Rite of Passage* (Panchin, 1970). In this story the first-person hero, Mia Havero, is introduced to us as a twelve year old child aboard one of seven massive star ships, that (along with several anarchic colony worlds) constitutes the post-holocaust human race. We follow Mia's life as she is trained up for her 'Trial', since in this story, at fourteen all young people (for it is a gender-egalitarian rite of passage) are cast onto a colony world for a month either to die or to survive and so gain adult status. Mia proves a survivor, as she confronts adults in their own, violent, *realpolitikal* terms, and so gains her maturity – a transition which is marked, as are so many of our own competency trials, by the establishing of a sexual relationship! The key, and as yet unresolved, issue of course lies in how competence is to be assessed and against who's criteria of maturity. However harsh the 'Trial' Mia and her peers faced, it was a test for which her culture prepared her. Reflected back onto our society, the question which emerges is: how far do we fairly prepare young people for the competency trials we may impose upon them? Also, Mia was allowed to cooperate with others undergoing the rite in order to work towards success. How many doctors or magistrates, one wonders, will allow young people in Britain the help of their peers in establishing competence?

Adolescence

The tensions of childhood's end are also made explicit by the social construction of a limbo-state between childhood and adulthood –

adolescence. If being textualised into being is the mark of social construction, then of all 'children' so constituted into being, *the adolescent* is the specimen case. While the term adolescence is of fifteenth century French origin, as Kett (1977) notes, it was only used very rarely as late as the middle of the nineteenth century, acquiring its specifically modern meaning, and its subsequent diffusion of usage, through the proselytising theorising of doctors and educators. However, interestingly, two completely different stories are told about its gender origins. Kett (*ibid.*) characterises it as initially a female phenomenon: '[T]he concept of adolescence was the creation of a distinctive mind set, an expression of a mélange of nostalgia and anxiety, and in its crudest mold an embodiment of Victorian prejudices about females and sexuality' (p. 143). The rationale for Kett's female gendered analysis of the production of adolescence is grounded upon the adolescent girl as a textualised concern:

> [F]or most of the nineteenth century, teenage girls were a more interesting literary and psychological topic than their brothers. Adolescent girls were stock figures in novels from *Charlotte Temple* in the 1790s to Fenimore Cooper's *Tales of Fifteen* in the 1820s to Oliver Wendell Holmes, Snr.'s *Elsie Venner* on the eve of the Civil War. In a sense, girls were the first adolescents; only much later in the nineteenth century were the normative implications of adolescence applied primarily to boys. (pp. 137–9)

The key psycho-social crisis (to borrow Erikson's term) facing the adolescent girl (or put another way, the problematic brought to her by the newly emerging human science practitioners) was that of 'naturalness' versus 'precocity'. It is a tension which was to endure for over a century. As Musgrove (1964, p. 102) reports of his own research, while precocity (being 'too forward', 'too sophisticated', etc.) was never ascribed by adults to male adolescents, it was attributed to female adolescents by over one third of his sample. Nevertheless, Musgrove, writing of Britain rather than the United States, tells a quite different, male gendered story of the constitution of the modern adolescent: 'School stories such as *Tom Brown* (1856) and *Eric, or Little by Little* (1858), *The Boy's Own Paper* (from 1879) and *Stalky and Co.* (1903) addressed themselves to, and helped to create, a specifically (middle class) adolescent world' (pp. 33–4); 'The nineteenth century public school redefined, and, indeed, re-made the adolescent' (pp. 54–5). The differential cultural referents of these two authors may well account for their distinctive dialects about adolescence. Where Kett, Musgrove and many other authors agree, however, is in locating the origin of modern adolescence in the work of Rousseau. As Musgrove puts it: 'The adolescent was invented at the same time as the steam-engine. The principal architect of the latter was Watt in 1765, of the former Rousseau in 1762' (p. 33). It is none the less a very Anglicised Rousseau who so invented the adolescent (cf. the very different story told by Donzelot, 1979). The adolescent who railroaded *her* way into North American consciousness was soon to be joined by her brothers in the foundational text on adolescence by G. Stanley Hall (1904). He was largely responsible for establishing developmentalism itself as a prime and primarily North American academic and practitioner discipline. Hall's belief in development recapitulating evolution viewed the adolescent as an uncivilised savage (at least one step on from the primitive animality of childhood) wherein 'adolescence is pre-eminently the criminal age' (p. 325). What emerged was a class-divided image of adolescence, with the youth movements of the middle class (whose child rearing style was seen as 'civilizing') such as the Boys Brigade and the Boy Scouts contrasted with juvenile delinquent working class youth (Gillis, 1975).

Not surprisingly then, Hall had a critical influence over four key areas of the policing of US youth: youth clubs; parental youth-handling manuals; youth teaching; and vocational guidance (Kett, 1977, p. 221). This regulatory activity towards adolescents was further facilitated by the chronological coincidence of North American adolescence with North American high schooling. As Kett again notes 'the high school became the age escalator of adolescence, as a stage of life was defined in terms of a stage of schooling' (p. 238). Under US cultural imperialism, the High School became a key adolescent location, not just for North Americans, but for all who partook in the products of the US communications industry – from the youth of Europe through the movies and later television, to the academics who consumed the journals and textbooks. From petting and proms to jives and juvies the adolescent pilgrim's progress is grounded upon the North American experience. When, for example, Margaret Mead's controversial work in Samoa is under discussion what is not so often explored is the taken-for-granted contrast – US adolescence. Again, much of the storm and strife of the gifted adolescent in so much fiction is predicated upon the studies of gifted youth in the United States by Terman (e.g. 1937). Finally, we have discussed in Chapter 8, the use of North American education as the critical foundation from which the Communist Chinese and Soviet systems of education have been explored.

The critical polytextualist device of shifting location enables us, as authors, to move our own positioning. Having argued how adolescence has come to be naturalised within developmentalism, it is also valuable to shift the story-telling perspective into an acknowledgement of the unique position of the adolescent *vis-à-vis* the alembic myth. The adolescent can be seen as just a later stage in that alchemy (i.e. a staging-post to childhood's end): 'Some of the storms of adolescence may be due to the ding-dong battle between these two sets of hormones, the one working towards completion of growth and the other inhibiting growth' (Pickard, 1965, p. 12). At the same time, most writers have made use for some considerable time of the 'self-evident' historico-cultural emergence of adolescence to distinguish it from puberty *per se*, however otherwise dubious some early analysis:

> It is characteristic of the *primitive* economy that the transition from child to adult is abrupt. In a savage tribe there is not time for ten years of adolescence, and in particular the adolescent girl seems to be a modern, even a recent, phenomenon. (Wall, 1948, p. 9)

The result is that adolescence can be seen as an under-resourced location in an economy of power. The corollary is that the adolescent condition can be brought into being in adults by changes in social contingencies:

> It is interesting to note that where adults (as in static units in the Army) are placed in an environment which deprives them of a measure of independence, puts restraint upon sexual activity, and offers frustrations and thwartings similar to those which modern conditions impose upon the developing boy or girl, the result is a marked increase in moodiness, in horseplay, in increased alcoholism and seeking for excitement, and in sex behaviour which is markedly 'adolescent' in its expression. (*ibid.*, p. 13)

Since which time, of course, the pejorative use of the descriptor 'adolescent' has joined that of 'childish' in popular idiom. That it is so used of teenagers (implying that they are often otherwise than adolescent) evidences something that more recent developmentalists have been at considerable pains to establish. Like other representations once mongered by biosocial scientists, the stereotype of the adolescent is now recognised as prejudicial:

> The prevailing stereotype of the pubescent is a negative one . . . Stanley Hall in 1904 described the period as one of storm and stress. While the strain may have been reduced since Hall's day by a more sympathetic attitude on the part of adults, a current writer [the reference is to Adams, 1969] described adolescence as a time of thrust and lust in a sociocultural animal. (Sommer, 1978, p. 3);

misinformed: 'The stereotype of adolescence as a time of identity crisis has been challenged, and the assumption that adolescents are usually in conflict with their parents would also seem to be incorrect' (Dunham and Jones, 1980, p. 27); and, misderived: 'Many of the crises of puberty are a direct result of change, not in hormones, but in status – change having to do with how one is perceived and responded to by others (Sommer, 1978, pp. 220–1).

What has transformed the reading of the adolescent is a typical symptom of the loosening of the alembic myth. The adolescent is now a concern in the social, indeed in the anthropological, for it is now to ideas of the adolescent as 'the alien in our midst', the *étranger* that theorists turn:

> This is a difficult time. The adolescent is 'betwixt and between'; he [sic] has outgrown his position as a child and not yet attained his position as an adult. He belongs to two systems of values. He therefore often presents characteristics of the 'marginal' man [sic]. (Muller, 1969, p. 228)

Not without reason did Kett (1977), always happy to tease his readers, entitle his historical study of adolescence *Rites of Passage*, for now it is not to the biological warrant of Darwin (see Morss, 1990) but to the anthropological warrant of Douglass (e.g. 1966) that the reconstituted adolescentologist now turns. As we have argued over the more general developmental model, this shift towards the social is not and should not be confused with radical deconstruction and reappraisal of the knowledging of the young. Indeed, it can result in quite the opposite. Anthropologising the adolescent (and their supposed non-existence in traditional societies) can easily result in this kind of conclusion: 'It may be one of the ironies of the human condition that any society must choose between social conservatism and rigidity, or the oppression of its young' (Musgrove, 1964, p. 149).

What seems often lost in discussions of the constitution of the adolescent under modernism, is that the persons who provided the driving force of the humanistic project itself often did not themselves experience a modern adolescence. This is true both for the middle class professionals and practitioners who knowledged the new order into being, and for the young proletarians whose labours fuelled its economy. The foundations of modernism were built in a culture which did not utilise age markers as we do today. It was not just in positions of gross exploitation that the young worker was found to exist, but also in professions such as the law and medicine (cf. Kett, 1977, Musgrove, 1964). Equally, whatever the horrors of early nineteenth century child labour, reform and changing market conditions produced by mid-century a situation in which earnings were sufficient to enable some young teenagers to leave home and achieve independence.

Between this situation and that of the age-tagged young person grading their way through twentieth century adolescence, a profound change seems to have occurred. That change reflects the emergence from around 1850 (most notably in the more stable liberal democracies – the United States and the United Kingdom) of a whole range of regulatory institutions, the bureaucratic machinery of a well-tempered social life. The events of 1848 had marked political upheaval and revolution in most of continental Europe. The United Kingdom had only just survived the risk of revolt during the 'hungry forties' and was entering the interregnum of Gladstone and Disraeli. For the young (and the liberal democracies were, demographically, societies skewed towards the young) these were the years that saw the introduction of Reform Schools (1854 in the United Kingdom, 1847 in Massachusetts), increasing legislation about the young and work, and a broadening and regularising of education (e.g. as marked in the United Kingdom by the publication of the Newcastle Report of 1861; the United States had rather more pressing social issues at that point). The emerging human scientists became the theoreticians and the practitioners of this legislative social hygienism, adding their warrants to the moral crisis-talk of more traditional mouthpieces for anxieties over social order. It was, for example, through the popularisation of the work of the German paedological theorist Froebel (1782–1852) that evolutionary ideas (later to be given a more scientific grounding by Darwin) were incorporated into educational thinking. The result, for those young people entering the twentieth century, was that they also entered into a powerfully age-marked system of regulation and containment – one that would have been both alien and anathematic to the youth of a century before. Adolescence had become: '[T]he most important and interesting period in the human life; for, after this, the moral habits are formed, and the organs shaped to a fashion in which they will remain ever after' (Walling, 1909, p. 205). Monroe (1906) neatly encapsulates the impact of bio-social science on the making of the new youthful identities demanded by being part of a liberal-democratic commonwealth:

> From the scientific tendency came the insistence upon a revision of the idea of a liberal education; a new definition of the culture demanded by present life; and the insistence stronger than ever when reenforced by the sociological view, that industrial, technical and professional training be introduced into every stage of education and that it all be made to contribute to the development of the *free* man [sic] – the fully developed citizen. From the sociological tendency came the commonly accepted belief that education is the process of the development of society; that its aim is to produce good citizens; that this is accomplished through the fullest development of personality in the individual; that this development of personal ability and character must fit the individual for citizenship, for life in institutions and for some form of productive participation in present social activities; in a word, that one must learn to serve himself by serving others. (pp. 748–9)

It was the contest of just that modernistic definition of freedom and youth which exploded for the young (and the not so young) in the mid 1960s. Coeval with and contingent upon that challenge, came the first hints of postmodernism, the beginning of the end for the grand liberal-humanistic adventure, whose vast social engine had, at last, begun to run down. If it is now harder to see adolescence today as a clear age-marked stage, it is because both the phenomenon and its apperception are products of modernity, subject now to fracturing and fragmenting before our gaze.

Devious ends

The idea of an ending of childhood is predicated upon a normative system wherein childhood itself is taken for granted. But childhood may also be 'ended' by narratives of personal or societal 'deviance' or by new stories reconstituting the modelling of childhood itself.

Juvenile delinquency

Few young people take their pupilage without some form of protest. Juvenile delinquency encompasses those forms of material, physical and sexual discontent most evident and most threatening to adults – because they are least childish – and its pursuit and prosecution brings into being the young offender. A century before s/he fell under the dubious eye of Cyril Burt, 'the young delinquent' was clearly an audience winner – as Dickens exploited so stunningly in *Oliver Twist* (1837–8). Indeed we can point to a well-established construction, quite resonant with that now contemporaneous, at the time Mary Carpenter wrote *Reformatory Schools for Children of the Perishing and Dangerous Classes and for Juvenile Offenders* in 1851 and *Juvenile Delinquents, their Condition and Treatment* in 1853 (see Manton, 1976). The (to us, familiar) biological/social tension in explanation of juvenile delinquency was also well established in liberal science by the second half of the nineteenth century, with Lombroso arguing the genetic case and Lacassagne – 'societies get the criminals they deserve' – environmentalism. Such discourses on the child as deviant reflect a much more general dialectic in the accounting of development of all our young and are reflected in specific legal practices which provide useful chronological markers in any social history of childhood and its end. Juvenile Courts were first established in the United States (around 1880), spreading rapidly around the 'developed' world (reaching the statute book in England and Wales in the Children Act 1908).

The really JDed and the merely jaded

The textual pre-eminence of North American bio-social science in the twentieth century (and hence the discursive generalisation of the social

Figure 9.1 *Adolescent dropouts from school* (From Psychology of Adolescence by L. Cole and I.N. Hall, 7th edn, Holt, Rhinehart and Winston, 1970)

location in which it operates) is powerfully reflected in what has come to pass for academic knowledge about juvenile delinquency. The wonderfully named F.M. Thrasher gave the US adolescent gangs of 1920s Chicago a hyperreal existence, as evocative of our early century's icon of modernity as the Artful Dodger's gang was of the parallel position of Britain's London in the early nineteenth century. From this point, the juvenile delinquent (singular or plural) has been reconstructed by every twist in fashion in bio-social science – from eugenics and psychoanalysis through to ethogenics and sociobiology. Our use of the term 'fashion' is far from flippant, for analyses of delinquency are highly sensitive to short-term social identities. In the supposedly respected seventh edition of Cole and Hall's voluminous *Psychology of Adolescence* (1970), there is a drawing of 'Adolescent dropouts from school' (Figure 9.1). The associated text reads: 'At an age when he [sic] should be up and doing, he is idle. The scene in Figure 23–3 shows the kind of aimless activity in which he is likely to engage . . . Many types of diversion are closed to him because he has no money, and those that are available often verge upon the illegal.'

There are, clearly, rich pickings here for cultural analysis. Just what are we to make of an area that has offered us: *Wayward Youth* or even better (?) *Wayward Girls* – perhaps friends to *Boys in Trouble; identification of potential delinquents at two to three years of age; Social Dynamite in Our Large Cities; use of surgical rehabilitation in young delinquents; Crooked Personalities in Childhood and After*? These (and there are thousands like them) were all taken from either book titles or journal article titles cited in supposedly serious academic treatments of juvenile delinquency! Rooted in ordinary social discourse, not only is the language of juvenile delinquency research moralised, it also manages to locate the delinquent with the same 'shock-horror', almost prurient fascination, which s/he enjoys in mass culture:

> Kick when he's down! Aim for the groin! Stomp or be stomped! These are the rules for survival in a kid gang . . . These are the rules that I lived by when I ran with a gang myself, trying to find out what makes a JD tick. (Harlan Ellison's New York-based *The Juvies*, 1961, back cover text)

> Gang girl is a proud name for certain types of chicks . . . they carry their stud's piece (or gun), they keep themselves available for bed duty . . . They've got a long-shoreman's grasp of the English language, and an idiot's grasp of the finer things in life. They swing, if you call that swinging. (*ibid.*, p. 166)

Indeed the considerable cross-textuality between the 'JD' of journalistic fictive documentary and the 'real thing' of academic participant observation research suggests that we are dealing with one of modernity's most powerfully sedimented scripts. Here is James Patrick's Glasgow a decade later:

> [S]oon accusations were flying that the Cumbie and Barnes Road were carrying blades, which allegedly had been smuggled in by their girlfriends. I sensed trouble and before long it had erupted . . . Tim led the charge, yelling 'Young team! Young team!' He was the first to reach the two struggling bodies; he kicked Sheldon's belly and face . . . I saw one large coloured boy 'stickin' the nut (i.e. his forehead) into the back of one of the attendants' head. The man fell forward into the path of a few boys from the Young Team who were making for the exit. Beano later described

what happened next: 'We did a Mexican dance oan' his face. Everyboady started playin' fitba' wi' his heid.' (James Patrick, *A Glasgow Gang Observed*, 1973, p. 54)

Discoursing delinquency

As a social issue and a matter of public concern, juvenile delinquency is by definition a time-delimited state – one cannot help but grow out of it. And in empirical terms, reported overall levels of delinquency (i.e. crime rate by age) show a general tendency to decline past around age 20. It is, in other words, a 'youth phenomenon'. However, it is not an inevitable one. Western culture expects and enables juvenile delinquents, much as it expects and enables licensed therapists and sociologists – and it does not expect and enable the young to be possessed of demons, or the analysis and cure to lie in shamanic practice. These expectations (although differently explained in the different accounts of social life available in our culture) are largely held in common, indeed taken for granted, across those accounts. Obviously, some young people are so placed as to be more or less likely to have built and to build such identity stories into their biography. Further, if we now have more young women delinquents and more young women car mechanics, this is part of what we come to collate together as 'social change' – in this case a change in the construction of gender identities. These changes permeate the various arenas in which identities are tried and tested, youth is a surface upon which cultural tectonics are both manifested and projected. We may not get the youth we deserve, but we do get the youth we have enabled and dis-enabled. It is a mirror which, in places, does not reflect well on the adult world, but we cannot alter that image by pathologising segments of the young. To so believe is one sediment from modernity that well merits the doubt we have sought to bring to it.

The final question we can ask is, what are the discursive functions of scientised delinquency discourse? Over its hundred year history, it manifestly has not brought to modern society the 'answers' to the 'problem'. Rather, it has become an industry in its own right, best read as reflecting back to society, not solutions, but a reflexive and evolving battery of accounting languages. It has yielded not control, but the discursive promise of understanding – and with that the promise of better things to come. Hoyles (1952) talks of a problem of anti-social behaviour needing address by 'modern science in light of Christian principles' (p. vii); West (1967) of a social disease requiring 'an unremitting attack upon a wide front' (p. 229); and Humphries (1981) of 'the resistance of working-class youth to powerful attempts to inculcate conformist modes of behaviour

... through various bourgeois agencies of control, manipulation and exploitation' (p. 1). And by the present day it has been recast yet again, to accommodate 'new kinds of delinquency' including the delinquent young of the middle classes. With a better class of delinquent, comes the demand for a better kind of treatment. The expert on delinquency is ever there to meet, in text and practice, the market's needs:

> There has been a differential response on the part of middle- and upper-class parents to their teenager's deviance. These parents, who are often psychologically sophisticated, rescue their children from the juvenile court's administration of justice and place them in mental health facilities. This process has significantly affected the status definitions of delinquency, statistics on delinquency, and led to an increase of mental health facilities and programs for delinquents.
>
> The emergence of a new delinquency has necessitated a complete re-writing of this book. However, this new edition, like its predecessors, benefits from my direct involvement with delinquents as a licenced therapist, as well as my research as a sociologist. (Yablonsky and Haskell, 1988, p. xii)

Meanwhile, a proportion of the young continue to rebel and to offend as they have done throughout the modern era. Where the identity-placements and the material context fit – whether in New York or Naples, São Paulo or St Petersburg – they will not just deviate, just meet childhood's end but murder and be murdered; be abused and abuse. And the delinquency industry will continue to story them, for that is *all* it can do.

Anarchy

The term anarchy is generally used (usually pejoratively) to describe the social conditions which would prevail under the breakdown of 'law and order'. But from a libertarian stance it refers to a utopian Cockaigne, without State or government. Applied to the problematic of childhood's end the anarchic resolution may be said to mean how childhood would end under conditions in which the young are in Bob Dylan's words 'beyond your control'; when overall social order collapses or is effectively de-regulated regarding the young; or in a political anarchy. The last is, of course, pure hypothesis and speculative utopias with an anarchic flavour like Ursula Le Guin's 'Anarres' from her book *The Dispossessed* (1975), often finish up dwelling not upon a childhood free of constraint but a childhood of political education:

> The knobby baby stood up. His face was a glare of sunlight and anger. His diapers were about to fall off. 'Mine!' he said in a high, ringing voice.

'Mine sun!' 'It is not yours,' the one-eyed woman said with the mildness of utter certainty. 'Nothing is yours. It is to use. It is to share. If you will not share it you cannot use it.' And she picked the knobby baby up with gentle inexorable hands and set him aside, out of the square of sunlight. (p. 30)

Faced with a planet poor in resources, Annaresti life is harsh. The young 'work' at their studies, experiencing a kibbutz-like life growing up in dormitories while their parents work away on various community projects. Although children are free to experiment sexually with either gender, such unfettered copulation seems not so much a liberation – a mark of childhood's end – as a lesson in non-ownership, the ultimate in avoiding being an 'egoising propertarian'. It comes over as a singularly joyless and highly partial emancipation, in which adult authority over children is largely unquestioned. It is salutary that Le Guin, in seeking to explore what an anarchic system might be like, seems to have created a childhood which is more – rather than less – controlled and constrained by adult power. Indeed, it is almost as though in order to create the conditions for a workable anarchy, childhood must be used to train its members into the right kind of anarchists! Similarly, in worlds closer to home a social system disrupted by factors like urbanisation may allow adult power to end childhood brutally and abruptly. From the fictional thief's kitchen of *Oliver Twist*, to the child slaves (sexual and otherwise) of, say, modern Bangkok (Ennew, 1986) such local anarchies destroy not only childhood, but even those freedoms (such as access to the peer-group) that even peasant or proletarian child-workers enjoy.

The form of anarchy where social order (and hence adult power) is removed, understandably leads to a different dynamic. Despite William Golding's highly pessimistic fictive (perhaps we should say allegorical) account in *Lord of the Flies* (1959), studies into actual communities of 'free children' (e.g. on the Children's Crusade; in the children's hut of the Muria; in continental Europe at the end of World War Two; and, with modern street children: cf. Allesbrook and Swift, 1989, Hoyles, 1988) suggest a marked level of sociality, order and community. We could call it a childhood's end, in that there is no providing adult culture to sustain a childhood. We might also so identify it because sexual bonds form among the older 'free children' whose units then offer some care of the younger. But because there is no salient domain of the adult, there is no sense in which such young people have passed from childhood into adulthood. Rather, we might say that they are a community of youth detached from the adult.

The most telling picture we know of an entré into such tribalism (and one constructed out of detachment from a dislocated adult order) is that experienced by Emily in Doris Lessing's *The Memoirs of a Survivor*

(1976). Yet, as we reread it, Emily's pubescent, drunken and near-coital 'hanging out' with the gangs and her subsequent 'taking up' with Gerald, sounds less a non-parental futuristic commentary, and more a parental meditation on postmodern childhood as many young people are now constructing it:

> Well, then, so there it was, she was infatuated. It was 'the first love' of tradition. Which is to say that half a dozen puppy loves, each one as agonising and every bit as intense and serious as later 'adult' loves, had passed; this love was 'first' and 'serious' because it was returned; or at least acknowledged. I remember I used to wonder if these young people, living as they had to from hand to mouth, who would never shut themselves off as couples behind walls unless it was for a few days or hours in a deserted house somewhere, or a shed in a field, would ever say to each other: *I love you. Do you love me? Will our love last?* – and so on. All of which phrases seemed more and more like the keys or documents of possession to states and conditions now obsolete. (p. 77, emphases in the original)

In many ways, this is the vision of the young that emerges from even the more intelligent books on parental angst, like Marie Winn's *Children Without Childhood* (1984). It is a story which might equally well be called 'Without Childhood's End' for its theme is that:

> something has happened to blur the formally distinct boundaries between childhood and adulthood, to weaken the protective membrane that once served to shelter children from precocious experience and sorrowful knowledge of the adult world. . . . Things are truly different for great numbers of children today as the traditional, hierarchical structure of the family in which children are children and parents are adults is eroded and new partnerships are forged. (p. 4)

Unlike age or bodily signs which are seen as emergent properties of the child, the anarchic approach to childhood's end tends to pick up upon the other pole of the individual-social tension, the 'outer' conditions which mediate that end. Running through all anarchic accounts, as the antithesis to the provided thesis, is the normative account of childhood (i.e. as a prolonged period of protection from and exclusion from the 'real world' of adulthood). At its simplest, that childhood is presented as maintained by 'traditional family life' and as overturned and negated by anarchy. While age and biological criteria are often seen to be differentially just or unjust (i.e. fairer to some individuals than to others), under the simple anarchic story, the implication is often that when 'anything goes', everything *does* go – with all children as losers. The thought experiment only results in a utopia for paedophiles, and those others who would use children for other ends like the catwalk, the sweat-shop and the battlefield.

Reconstruction

Taken more subtly, the anarchic story can be seen to dissolve the normative notion of childhood's end by dissolving the normative notion of childhood. A critical polytextualist concern with the condition of the young in general, and the specific conditions of some children in particular, cannot be based upon a premise of a 'true' childhood as used by angst analysts like Winn (1984). No more can it accept biological watersheds or chronological bench-marks as if they were indicators outside of 'the social' for the delineation of childhood's end. Nor can it find acceptable the use of reified notions of 'environment' or 'social conditions' as explanatory causal agents. Rather, the deconstruction of such notions is seen as a necessary, but not sufficient, condition for 'better childhoods' and hence better endings to childhood. One way to do so lies in a focus not merely upon the immediate condition of the young, but upon their future condition – children in Kellmer Pringle's phrase (1980, p. 151) as 'the seedcorn of the future'. While this is usually interpreted in unreconstructed Statist terms as Kellmer Pringle does, it can be taken in reconstructed readings as promulgating an 'open' view.

In other words, practices upon the child may have: a complex present impact (on what they do now); the power to construct futures (over what they do later – an obvious example is literal and metaphorical immunisation); and, the power to construct construction (e.g. lay down the literary powers to subsequently pen *The Rights of Man*[sic]' or *Mein Kampf*). Childhoods are continuously constructed and reconstructed as the present and hence history is reconstituted – so that there will always be doubt about whether children will reflect back upon their minority as a 'good' childhood or not. Our powers to 'control the future' are limited both by human and extra-human unknowables. Hence, our endeavours (e.g. attempts at socialisation) are always in doubt. For example, the emergence of the contraceptive pill and of an ethos of 'living together' may well have rendered much of the transmitted protectionist discourse of 'a Christian marriage of the previously sexually continent' with its associated horrors ('used goods', unwanted pregnancy), redundant. Equally, those in the 1960s who strove within that 'liberation' to also enable children's sexual rights had no prescience into the emergence in the late 1970s of HIV infection.

So we come to see that childhood's end can be reproblematised into 'childhood's end *for what end*?' Issues of what criterion or mixture of criteria should be employed to mediate the transition from juvenile to adult status are themselves reflections on the notion of what is desired and valued in the constitution of the adult. In late-modern liberal-humanistic sexual discourse, for example, the emphasis is not so much upon becoming 'grown up' because one has become, biologically, sexually mature, but upon the power of the resultant sexual relationships to help us 'become' as persons. Nature acts only to enable the necessary (but not sufficient) conditions for the serious, man- or woman-making potentials of 'real' sex. Indeed, nature as fecundity is seen as something to be thwarted – a shot-gun wedding is hardly compatible with an extended period of relational becoming, even though it might certainly signify childhood's end.

Arbitrary, normally well post-pubertal, 'ages of consent' can permit an escape from mere exteriorised biological construction of full personhood, into a more socially negotiable, and potentially fluid, boundary of competence. Where they are located in a culture of doubt and challenge (which also critically glosses the secular religion of human relationships itself), they can work for the emancipation of the young. For they come to be seen, by the young themselves, as a competence challenge. As things actually operate, by and large, if a young person is skilled enough to 'pass' they are often left to pass – not a perfect system, and one that certainly needs monitoring in a world where powerful adults may abuse and misuse if left unfettered – but good enough perhaps? Good enough at least, until we reach our final chapter in which the possibilities and the problematics of a critical polytextualist concern are explored in more depth and subjected to more thorough consideration.

10

Rearing its ugly head: Children and sexuality

Throughout modernism the conjunction of children and sexuality has been a focus of adult interest: sometimes a concern, sometimes a fascination (sometimes, one suspects, both). Accounts of – and in particular, visual representations of – 'sexualised' children (or perhaps it should be 'sexualised' images of children) can produce a highly emotionally charged reaction which is sufficiently distinctive to have acquired its own name, 'visceral clutch'. This term originated with the sexologists Masters and Johnson (see Faust, 1981) and refers to a profound, 'irrational' distressed reaction to sexual material. As authors we do not like that definition, but we do think the term is powerfully descriptive. There is then, a cultural equation which takes the terms: children + sexuality = visceral clutch. As a culture we voice concern that children should not become the objects of sexual abuse by adults and yet evince a fascination with the sexuality of the young. It is a problematic which permeates much of the current agendas of child concern as it has moved to encompass (often to seem to rotate around) issues of the child and sexuality (cf. Foucault, 1979). Where complex, highly emotionalised tensions permeate an area of concern and debate, that domain itself becomes a highly charged arena of discourses of feelings – and in our culture, the management of such affects is also their therapy. It is not surprising then that 'child sexual abuse' should have become an area where 'feelings' (of all sorts) have acquired a pressing centrality. This is held to be particularly true for those working in the field:

> Managing sexual abuse [cases] is a challenge that is testing the skills, knowledge and resources of all agencies to their limits. It is also testing the personal resources of everyone involved. Being a 'professional' does not provide any emotional immunity from the potent and intensely personal issues that underlie many of the professional dilemmas in this area of work. Unless we acknowledge and confront these acute pressures and our own feelings and reactions there is a risk of being overwhelmed by them. (Craig *et al.*, 1989, p. 59)

This accepted wisdom of its distress-potential for workers is paralleled by an equally strong (and almost universal) conviction among them that child sexual abuse has a peculiarly intense long-term emotional impact, as well as doing all manner of other harms. A typical illustration is Turner's (1989) description of the abuse survivor:

> The abuse which first took place in childhood dictates that in later life they will feel inferior, used and abused, with an overwhelming loss of self-worth . . . Like Peter Pan children who have never grown up, they have not been given the chance of the kind of love which enables them to grow and to move on into the future. Inside each and every survivor of abuse there is still the child which needs to be liked, which is still reaching out for someone who will not betray their trust. (pp. 82–3)

Indeed, for some writers, so powerful are the horrors seen to result from almost any sexual experience in childhood, that long-term trauma and psychological damage are unequivocally attributed to what might otherwise be seen as quite minor events:

> When Rita took a short-cut along an alleyway her parents had told her never to take . . . she was confronted by a man exposing himself . . . [S]he felt so guilty at having disobeyed that she was frightened to tell her mother . . . These intense feelings of guilt and fear are still triggered for her as an adult, whenever the memory surfaces. This triggering of the feelings associated with an incident of abuse is a common phenomenon for sexual abuse victims. (Hevey and Kenwood, 1989, p. 210)

At several levels of meaning, child sexual abuse has us in its 'visceral clutch'. At the level of debate and argument, to be in a hold, however understandable, may not be the best of locations. In this chapter, we intend to explore some leverage which may loosen the grip a little.

Hidden vices

The intercept of childhood and sexuality was as much a concern during the apparently sexually repressive Victorian era as it is under the purportedly enlightened present day. Neither this claim, nor the apparent paradox it leads to, should surprise us, because they both rest on one of the very features of modernism – welfarism. This argument owes much to Foucault's analysis (1979) of the institutionalisation of discourses on sexuality. In the name of individual and social welfare, sexuality can be repressed or it can be liberated, and each sustains its antithesis. The press for control, warranted through pre-modern authorities (such as religious doctrine and legal statutes), can be tracked from early historical times. It was the risk of incest (as both risk and incest were then understood) which provided the strongest moral imperative. Boswell (1991) traces this concern from Roman times into early Christianity, persisting throughout medieval times, its potential repeatedly cited as a problem which may ensue from the abandonment of children. The argument went that if a man resorted to prostitutes (male or female) he might, unwittingly, commit incest. The same motif recurs in a large number of myths, from Oedipus to Norse legends. The sexual use of children was itself no more censored than resulted from periodic attempts at regulation of adult sexuality in general. In slavocratic and patriarchal cultures, it was simply not an issue. The rights of the slave owner were seen as omnipotent, and generally the rights of a father over his children (even to pander them) were outside of challenge. Boswell however notes the difficulty of discerning historical views on morality *vis-à-vis* children when the terms used for 'child', 'servant' and 'slave' were largely interchangeable. He suggests, for example, that the arguments made about the acceptability of 'boy love' in Greek and Roman times, proffered in paedophile literature, may be misconstituted, since it is impossible to tell the likely age of the 'boys' concerned. More generally, sexuality with regard to children was made sense of within a much broader set of religious invectives against all forms of sexuality which were non-procreative. Thus, for example, childhood masturbation was seen as a vice, but no more (or less) offensive than in adulthood. Where injunctions existed against the sexual use of children, these related more to incest viewed as a sin. Adult-child sexual activity, *per se*, seems to have been largely an issue of little or no specific concern.

Foucault points out that the regulation of child sexuality was one of the very first targets of modern welfarism. In the nineteenth century this discourse of control was to be found in fields as apparently diverse as medicine (e.g. Tissot's campaign against 'masturbatory insanity') and the architecture of (boarding) schools. Similarly, in the United Kingdom, early nineteenth century campaigns against children working in coal mines were motivated as heavily by concern about the moral dangers of young persons of both sexes working together in minimal clothing as it did on the harmful nature of their working conditions. The pressure for housing reform was similarly moved by the perceived dangers of incest when bedrooms were shared across gender and parent/ child divides.

Modernism received from previous epistemes a set of moral injunctions concerned more with childhood masturbation than with the sexual use of children by adults (or indeed the resort of boys to women, within or outwith prostitution, cf. Chandos, 1985). It was within modernism itself that the press for control over children and sexuality was made manifest, as part of a larger project of bio-social hygiene. Concern over masturbation is emblematic of this venture. Masturbation was not only construed as a serious disease or precursor to disease (see Stainton Rogers, 1989) the source of its most vigorous persecution, it also acted as an unacceptable reminder of our newly accepted evolution from the apes. The blatant sexuality of young monkeys (at least in the overcrowded zoos of the time), too easily extrapolated to the young 'naked ape' as well. Advice given to parents over masturbation, from the evolutionary perspective, therefore stressed not its immorality, but its childishness, or developmental immaturity a discourse which persisted alongside much more draconian ones (as we shall come to) well into the twentieth century: 'Let him [sic] see you disapprove, that you think he is too old for such silly tricks, that grownups never do stupid things like that, but don't make too much of it – it will pass' (Gibbens, 1954, p. 151). However, it was Freudian theory (cf. Chapter 6) which gave childhood sexuality its particular place in modernist thinking, and propelled the notion of repression to its present polysemic power. Vulgar post-Freudian discourse refuted prior 'misconceptions' about the harmfulness of masturbation.

By the Woodstock era we can see another shift, this time towards the more 'liberatory' pole of the tension, part of a much broader emancipatory-humanistic worldview: 'Infants get the most out of their sex life. They play with themselves unashamedly, anarchistically, freely, and solely for the purpose of gratification . . . Sounds like the sex habits of the Underground, which is still, like children, narcissistic and guiltless' (Neville, 1971, pp. 223–4). In contrast to its previous location as a childhood vice, or as a childishly stupid habit to be cold-showered away, masturbation became 'wholesome curiosity' (Spock, 1963, p. 368).

Over the post-war period the gaze on childhood sexuality became one of growing liberal-humanism, with concern located in release as well as control. Attention thus became focused on sex education. The control element was directed towards helping the young protect themselves from pregnancy and from sexually transmitted diseases, and to avoid the emotional scars of irresponsibility – while the release element was dedicated to helping their naturally emergent sexuality to blossom (Rogers, 1974a). Crawford (1984) notes that the cultural shift in the West from the 1960s to the 1980s was a swing away from the dominance of the release discourse, back into the dominance of a discourse of control. Consistent with this trend, the spotlight of concern over children and sex shifted from a gaze of informed liberation to a gaze focused upon the danger of adult sexual misuse and abuse of children.

The currently fashionable story (see Mrazek and Kempe, 1981) is that sexual abuse by adults has always been 'there', but only recently has society had the courage to stop denying that it existed. This self-satisfied tale is a particularly irritating form of self-justifying rhetoric, whose logic is now itself under attack, with recent 'findings' that up to a third of the perpetrators of child sexual abuse are themselves children (Hollows and Armstrong, 1991). If we look at the location of the child *vis-à-vis* sexuality under both repressive and liberatory regimes, what we find are not the triumphs of a gradual journey towards enlightenment, but a continuity of adult power in monitoring, anxiety induction and confession. They form, as is typical under modernism, a false tension, a mere appearance of dialectic advance (Buss, 1979). Where once children were medically examined and psychologically inquisited in a search to uncover the vice of 'self-abuse' (i.e. masturbation), they now experience the same procedures in the scrutiny for evidence of sexual abuse. Likewise the induction of anxiety to protect the child from self-abuse has been replaced by the induction of anxiety to protect them from the sexual dangers posed by others. The adult gaze on the sexuality of the child still renders them 'subjects of study' and/or 'objects of concern', and the sexuality of the child is still reconstituted from adult confession. Adult tales of the resultant damage of childhood masturbation have been replaced by adult tales of the resultant damage of childhood sexual abuse.

Children and sex: Intertextual voices

We can explore these resemblances and differences by approaching the texts of the past in the context of our present knowledges and practices (much as we did for *Child of the Deep* in Chapter 2). For this, we have chosen the turn of the century writings of Professor Walling. His book *Sexology* (1909) offers a fascinating access into a turn of the century medical discourse on childhood masturbation and sex play, which has many instructive resonances with contemporary child sexual abuse 'talk'. It serves to remind us both of the socially constructed character of emergent moral concerns, and of the degree to which our present-day preoccupations recycle, unaware, parallel arguments, policies and prescriptions. What we have done to make this explicit is to introduce each section with a quotation from a recent text on child sexual abuse (widely varying in their focus and intended audience). These clearly establish the extent of discursive isomorphism.

Warrants to authority

First, contemporary authors usually begin with warrants of their authority:

This book is a decade review of the scientific knowledge about the problem of child sexual abuse. (Finkelhor *et al.*, 1986, p. 10)

To validate his argument, Professor Walling also claimed his book was based on: 'gems of knowledge gleaned from the entire field of standard literature and from the documentary evidence of eminent European and American men and women Physicians, Professors, Lawyers, Preachers and other brilliant minds' (p. 7). This served to set the stage for the multidisciplinary approach he saw as required.

We are not dealing with a purely medical issue

Sexual abuse does not fall clearly within the domain of one particular discipline. (Finkelhor *et al.*, 1986, p. 11)

Walling's assertion was: 'Remember, then, that this work is not based upon medical evidence alone . . . as experience has shown that knowledge not medicine, is needed' (1909, p. 7). It is needed, indeed for an often understated, unrecognised problem.

Fighting denial with proper scientific judgement

Child molestation . . . was none the less thought to be relatively rare . . . [however] . . . even the lowest rates indicate that child sexual abuse is far from an uncommon experience, the higher reported rates would point to a problem of epidemic proportions. (Finkelhor *et al.*, 1986, pp. 15 and 19)

For Walling too, childhood masturbation and sex play were not the rare events Jo Reader may have taken them to be: 'Those who accuse us of exaggeration will accuse us of extreme moderation if they will but consult the recognised authorities' (1909, p. 8). To make this case, Professor Walling saw a need to publicise the 'truth' in a clear, easily digested fashion.

Demystifying the 'facts'

Specially written in basic, non-jargon terms for a general audience. (Stainton Rogers, Hevey and Ash, 1989, back cover text)

Walling's *Sexology* also set out to instruct the reader with: 'the revelations of science in language deprived of ambiguity and cleared of the mists of technology' (p. 9). Among these facticities were the clear signs of the masturbator to the skilled observer.

Spotting the tell-tale symptoms

Other common behavioural characteristics of sexually abused children . . .
include . . . withdrawal from group activity; depression; . . . a sudden
change in academic achievement. (Vizard and Tranter, 1988, p. 68)

Walling (1909) assured his readers that: 'The writer could engage to
select the onanists of a school by a walk through the pupils' (p. 11).
However, detecting the self-abused child was also something anyone
could do by following a simple check-list:

Perhaps the most constant and invariable, as well as earliest signs of the
masturbator are the downcast, averted glance, and the disposition to
solitude. Prominent characteristics are, loss of memory and intelligence,
morose and unequal disposition, aversion or indifference to legitimate
pleasures and sports, mental abstractions, stupid stolidity, etc. (*ibid.*, p.
38)

Where these signs suddenly appeared, the almost certain inference was
that masturbation had done its evil work. 'Ninety-nine per cent of these
examples are cases in point' (p. 41).

Tip of the iceberg

The nature of the problem . . . inhibits discovery and discourages voluntary reporting. (Finkelhor *et al.*, 1986, p. 18).

However, as Professor Walling was quick to point out 'it is only the most
exaggerated cases that are brought to notice'. The result is that the 'vast
majority of cases escape detection' (p. 35). These laid, Walling argued,
the seeds for a host of adult symptomologies.

Long-term damage

Long term effects include depression, self destructive behaviour, anxiety,
feelings of isolation and stigma, poor self esteem, a tendency towards
revictimisation, substance abuse, difficulty in trusting others and sexual
maladjustment. (Wyatt and Higgs, 1991)

Similarly for Walling, the basis for concern about self-abuse was not just
its acute effects but its latter chronic consequences, it laid: 'the foundation of physical, mental and moral maladies, the causes of which are as
unsuspected as they are consequently persistent in their operation' (p.
34). Clearly, indeed, this was an area where early medical diagnosis of
the self-abuse is of critical importance.

The medical examination

> However, in a non-abused child masturbation [leaves] . . . very minor (if any) physical signs . . . vulvovaginitis . . . is suggestive of child sexual abuse. (Vizard and Tranter, 1988, p. 66)

It is here that Professor Walling's gynaecological expertise was drawn into the discourse. Quoting with approval one of his medical authorities, he noted:

> Deslandes says: 'I have every reason, from a great number of facts presented to me in practice, that of every twenty cases of leuchorrhea ('whites'), or of inflammation of the vulva or vagina in children [sic] and young girls, there are at least fifteen or eighteen which result from masturbation!'. (1909, p. 46)

Reluctance to disclose

Yet collateral evidence from the child herself may be hard to establish:

> Fear of disclosure . . . may completely prevent that child from putting a sexually abusive experience into words. (Vizard and Tranter, 1988, p. 89)

Similarly children, within Walling's discourse, could also be powerfully motivated to hide their masturbation: 'There is among children a sort of instinct, which leads them to hide and dissimulate their maneuvers before even they have found them to be illicit and shameful. The art with which they elude watchfulness and evade questions is often inconceivable' (1909, p. 47). Clearly then, Walling argued, we may need to seek direct evidence.

In Flagranti Delicto

> Sexually abused children from multiproblem families . . . may well demonstrate over-sexualisation in their play with the dolls . . . Very disturbed chaotic [sic] sexually abused children may become sexually aroused by the interview process. (Vizard and Tranter, 1988, pp. 96–7)

Here Walling was all for building up the strongest evidential case, using good observation and scientific reasoning:

> Let vigilance attach itself principally to the moments which follow the retirement to bed, and those which precede the rising . . . Often when suddenly approached, she may blush, and to be covered in perspiration unaccounted for by the temperature of their room, the warmth of the covering, or any other observable cause. The breathing is at the same time more precipitate, the pulse more developed, the blood-vessels fuller, and

the heart greater than in the natural condition. There is, in short, that sort of fever which ordinarily accompanies the venereal act. . . . However: it is not sufficient to use merely ordinary precautions of a judicial watchfulness; direct and skilled interrogation must be from time to time employed, in every suspected case. (1909, p. 48)

The pursuit of disclosure

> The passive presence of parents and relatives, who have been part of such an abusive household, will certainly inhibit the child from disclosure. (Vizard and Tranter, 1988, p. 105)

Walling took the view that childhood masturbation was often the result of 'instruction' by older children and adults, and promoted this analysis by a series of case studies. Quoting 'one of the most celebrated surgeons in the world', he recounted the sad case of a 'young girl of ten or eleven' suspected of masturbation because of her symptoms of 'increasing debility'. Sure of his diagnosis, despite the denials of the child, her mother and her governess:

> The physician, however, caused the child to be separated from both mother and governess. She was sent to her aunt in the country. . . . This aunt, taking advantage of the ascendancy which she had obtained over the girl's mind, subjected her to a secret interrogation. She was moved, embarrassed, discountenanced, but confessed nothing. Her embarrassment had already betrayed her, and from that moment, in the estimation of the aunt, her fault was assured. Soon the doctor arrived, who, directed against the child a last and vigorous attack. 'Mademoiselle,' said he, with a tone of authority, certainty, and conviction, 'the solemn moment has arrived to tell us here the truth, and nothing but the truth. It only remains to inform us who taught you this detestable habit, which has totally ruined your health, and how long since this fatal secret was revealed to you, which certainly did not originate with yourself.' At this severe and unexpected language the young child was much affected. Being urged, she hesitated, looked at her aunt and avowed all. It was her old governess who had taught her masturbation. (1909, pp. 44–5)

It is interesting to study the implicit theory guiding the search for the root offender in this and other cases Walling describes. The contrast with today is stark. In Walling's time it was the child – 'her fault' – who was the perpetrator of vice, having been taught it by her governess. The same child today would be seen as a victim, the governess the perpetrator, and the masturbation a 'symptom' of abuse, not abuse itself. However, this is not the only twist to the tale, as the shift is made from Walling's time to today.

The ideology of perpetrator spotting

Besides parental absence, conflict and lack of support, another parental factor – the presence of a non-biologically related father – has been discussed as a risk factor for sexual abuse. (Finkelhor *et al.*, 1986, p. 77)

Although Walling (1909) allowed that masturbation was often 'caught' by young children from older boys and girls, virtually the only adult instructors he identified are female. This was entirely congruent with his strongly anti-feminist and, indeed, mysogynist ideology. His comment on the case just discussed is instructive in its irony: 'After this, trust women, trust nurses, trust governesses, believe mothers!' (p. 45) Hence, it should not surprise us that the message which often comes over in Walling's text is 'beware – no woman is safe'.

Legitimate rage speaking out

Some women have been able to recognise that their struggle to deny their knowledge of the degrading things that happened to them in childhood is the cause of their often severe symptoms. They have given up this struggle and have started talking and writing of their experiences. (Miller, 1985, p. 324)

In one of his vignettes, Walling wove together the proposition of the long-term induced angry silence of the abused child, with the notion of victimisation by the matriarchy:

Another case, of a writer who states: At the age of eight he was lodged, at a watering place, in the same room with three girls, respectively, ten, twelve and fourteen years of age. The elder [sic] of these little misses succeeded effectually, during the few weeks association, in inducting her companions into the science of reproduction, while the male member [sic] of the quartet was aptly used in illustration of the subject. The matronly dignity with which this lady now chaperones her young daughters in the most fashionable circles of one of our most fashionable cities, does not, he says, in the least diminish the feelings of hostility with which he, as one of her pupils regards her, and which the publication of this anecdote is the first opportunity afforded him to gratify. His secrecy during his involuntary pupilage, was not the result of an innate sense of wrong or shame, but was induced solely by the subtle representations of his seductress. (Walling, 1909, pp. 13–14)

Protectionist work

Children are taught from the time that they are very young that there are ways to stay safe from dangers in the world . . . In the same matter-of-fact manner children can be taught strategies for staying safe . . . in case of abuse. (Elliot, 1989, p. 257)

As far as 'self-abuse' is concerned, Walling was critical of the head in the sand reaction of many parents: 'From false notions of delicacy, with a prudery as astonishing as it is criminal, the parents and guardians of boys refrain from all allusion to the subject, while in their hearts they must realise the imminence of the danger' (1909, p. 12).

Children, in Walling's view, were well capable of understanding such protectionist work without 'the gratification of a libidinous curiosity'. They faced 'dangers, whose advent they can easily and surely discern'. Although parents had a part to play in this, so too did the professional: 'In many instances the requisite instruction and counsel may best be imparted by the family physician' (*ibid.*). The alternative is a near certainty of the continued perpetuation of the vice.

Cycles of abuse

A number of male perpetrators of sexual abuse reveal a history of having been abused themselves . . . boys as young as nine years old . . . develop sexual activities with younger children. (Vizard and Tranter, 1988, p. 128)

The untreated self-abuser, for Walling, was not only a danger to themselves but to others: 'If a boy is an onanist he is sure to corrupt the smaller boys of his acquaintance whenever a safe opportunity presents itself' (p. 13). And, Walling argued, we should look to power rather than to consent as to the mechanism of such abuse: 'the power of mischief possessed by the older boy is increased in proportion to his size, and, alas! his experience' (*ibid.*).

The enabling culture of abuse

There is clear evidence of an overall decrease in parental vigilance about every aspect of children's lives, from the trivial to the life-threatening. (Winn, 1984, p. 22)

Walling was quite clear in identifying the role of the broader societal *Zeitgeist* in enhancing children's vulnerability. In his book he was explicit, for example, about the role of the mass media, expressing horror over those parents who: 'do not deem to scruple to place in the hands of their daughters the journals of the day, albeit teeming with advertisements and "news items" of the most revolting and indecent character' (1909, p. 24). Too often, he noted, boys and girls of school-age formed

liaisons unknown to their parents who were 'too indulgent or too care-
less to discharge their duties of supervision . . . not one word do they
hear of the good old-time veneration of voluntary virginity'. For girls,
one of the biggest dangers was the party and the pressures to grow up
too soon:

> It is now a common occurrence to hold these entertainments for little
> children . . . Each fond matron seeks to excel her acquaintances in the
> mimic pomp and fashion displayed, and a modern child's party differs
> from others only in the size of the dramatis personae. The newspapers
> pander to the unnatural performance, and the superb toilets of the misses
> and exquisite make-up of the masters are elaborately blazoned in the
> column of 'Fashionable Gossip'. Children from eight to thirteen are thus
> initiated into the mysteries of dissipation, including flirtation and liaisons.
> (p. 22)

Reflecting and refracting the Walling discourse

Read through the contemporary gaze upon children and sexuality, it is
easy to dismiss Walling as a pompous, opinionated bigot – someone very
few people, today, would let near their children. However, to so dismiss
him in this fashion misses the reading that he was doing little more than
acting as a spokesperson for a discourse well-established in nineteenth
century paediatrics and child welfare work. Placing him in that location
allows us to see his 'science' and 'good practice' as caught no more (and
no less) in the world-view and ideology of his times than the David
Finkelhors and Eileen Vizards of today. Within that cosmological
entrapment is the all-powerful assumption that one's own approach is
uniquely liberated by the march of knowledge from the errors of the
past, so that now (at last!) it is possible to get to the *truth*. Perhaps there
is such a progress – in which case the parallels and antitheses between
Walling's rhetoric and those used in contemporary child sexual abuse
discourse are only coincidental to growing knowledge. However, there
are rather a lot of coincidences – they include:

- whole gender blaming, now aimed at men rather than women;
- reliance on 'evidence' derived from adult attributions of current problems to childhood experience;
- an inevitable reluctance of the child to disclose (the 'child sexual
  abuse accommodation syndrome', cf. Summit 1983);
- interrogatory practices on a child who has been moved to an alien
  total environment to obtain a 'disclosure';
- genital examination to find symptoms which 'prove' the offence; and
- the assumption of an enabling culture and continuing cycle of abuse.

It is important to be clear about what is being said here. We are not claiming that because our culture now dismisses the turn of the century obsession with child masturbation as a mere 'moral panic' without sustainable substance, that this merits a similar dismissing of current concern over child sexual abuse. To do so would be to side-step the suffering of children it undoubtedly encompasses. Rather, we are directing critical attention to the resonances between the warrants that have been used – to the modes of production of first masturbation concern and subsequently child sexual abuse concern. Within both, there undoubtedly were and are children in acute and chronic distress. But also within both there were and are adults constructing a regime of concern to meet the distress adult activities have and had, themselves, produced (then, sexual guilt; now, the sexual use of children by adults). Within those regimes of concern, knowledges were constructed, unreflexive as to the impact of professional and sex/political ideologies. And in the application of those knowledges, children were further depowered and 'abused'. *That* is the agenda of the critique. Any of those shared warrants can be approached (and merit analysis) in terms of that agenda. However, of all the resonances, the most instructive in many ways is the continued reliance on the accounts of 'troubled' adults of troubled childhoods, often recovered in an ideologised/ therapeutic milieu or from the mitigating explanations of adult offenders.

Recovering the child within

While the notion that early experience can shape us for life forms part of both popular wisdom and the nature/nurture model it was only after around 1895 and Freud's evolution of a psychodynamic talking therapy that the recovery of such experiences and their use as evidential material became a professional craft. The accounts of troubled adults (as we have seen in Walling) became seen as factives supporting the psychodynamic model, and the recovering of those accounts became a critical feature of the talking cures, despite the way the credibility of psychodynamic theory and the plausibility of psychodynamic evidence underwent a series of seemingly devastating assaults. This scepticism was reinforced by investigations of the impact of 'brain-washing' by the Chinese during the Korean War and by later investigations of individuals caught up in cults. The general view existed in academic psychology that autobiographical data was so prone to self-serving biases (and case-study data so prone to 'suggestion' and selective reporting) as to be invalid as evidence unless cross-validated against other sources.

Talking childhood trauma blues

The question that now arises, is why is it then that so much of the current literature on child sexual abuse is reliant upon some form of therapised, explanatory discourse? To answer that question, we need to note that from the 1960s onward, there was a massive growth of interest in discourses of self-improvement (cf. Rosen 1978) and group identity (here feminism has been the key influence). Both were highly critical of established academic psychology and its scientistic dogma. Hence, both were able to find in the general narrative form of stories of 'the child within' the opportunity to generate extra-scientistic programmes for self- and group-reconstruction. The 'discovery' of child sexual abuse, opened up (for both these reconstructed narrators and for unreconstructed 'old school' psychodynamicists) a whole new arena of operations. For the feminists it tied in well with work with other 'survivors' of male oppression (raped and violently victimised women). Fascinatingly, even psychoanalysis, once an obvious target of women's anger for its patriarchal and patronising treatment of female experience, became reconstructed as respectable. Alice Miller (although she is currently distancing herself from psychoanalysis) became a widely quoted authority. Her reconstructive cure broadened the definition of abuse to the point that she argues that every one of us in adulthood has a hurt and hidden 'child within' which is the root of virtually all our personal and social troubles, and is the root cause of abuse itself. Evidence that those who sexually assault children can recount similar experiences in their own childhoods has then been used to validate an hypothetical 'cycle of abuse'.

Such claims worry us. We believe it is perfectly possible to have a concern to foster better childhoods or non-patriarchal social arrangements without accepting that such stories, *per se*, establish 'abuse' as an autobiographic actuality, or that the working through of such stories is necessarily the approach of choice for the children or women (or indeed, men) concerned. Indeed, both in therapeutic work with child sex abusers (cf. Wyre, 1989), and in the accounting of many practitioners in this field (cf. Worrell and Stainton Rogers, in prep.), the ability of individual's abusing to be explained in terms of childhood experience is recognised as a target for challenge, not as a justifying explanation!

What is so special about (children and) sex?

When one of us was working, a long time ago, in the area of sex education, a favourite publication was a booklet by Hill and Lloyd-Jones

entitled *Sex Education: The Erroneous Zone* (1970). What this lampooned was the 'groping prose' of sex educators and in particular the
need to 'specialise' sex – as in 'mummy's special hole', 'daddy's special
bit', etc. Yet in a wider sense, this precious language does capture in
highly literal form the unique location of sex in our gaze on the child.
The very need to sex educate speaks of the perceived absence of reliable
sexual information in the discursive world of the child, and its lack of
inclusion, as a matter of course, in the school curriculum. Both its generic absence and its deliberate insertion attest to its special-ness. Furthermore, as McKenna and Kessler (1985) point out, we do not talk
(although both reflect upon enculturation into adult concerns) of children's 'cheating play' as we do of their 'sex play'. Further, while children
are allowed to be playful about sex 'they are not allowed to share this
with adults in *any* way' (p. 266, their emphasis). It is a cheap point, but a
valid one that children (indeed adults too in the United Kingdom) can
watch on television how to load a machine gun but not how to arouse a
penis; how to tie a woman up but not how to stimulate her genitals.
Indeed, in some of the broadened definitions of abuse, to expose a child
to such sexual images would itself be regarded as a form of sexual abuse.
The same goes for involving a child as actor in those images (although
once again a child actor can be shown with gun or rope). Indeed, these
days about the only situation in which it is legitimate to even talk to
children about sex is within sex education or an investigation for alleged
abuse (*ibid.*). Anything else risks the accusation of being sexually abusive or the stigma of being erotically involved.

Children's sexual socialisation employs uniquely local definitions of
cultural competence, in which children are expected to gain some kinds
of knowledge (but not others) and *not* engage in some forms of behaviour. A child, nowadays, who acts out coitus in the nursery school
would be seen as 'precociously over-sexualised', and assumed to have
been sexually abused. Yet the same behaviour was treated previously by
anthropologists (e.g. Ford and Beach, 1951) as perfectly natural and
unproblematic in other societies. Even a child's linguistic cultural competence is a strangely constituted affair. Outside of obscenity, it can be
cast only in either a latinate formal language game of penises and va-
ginas or an infantilised language-game of willies and what? (in Hildebrand's guide (in Stainton Rogers *et al.*, 1989) to groupwork with
sexually abused children we are offered outside of the latinate and the
Anglo-Saxon these: 'Mary; little man in the boat [sic]; tuppence; fanny;
pencil sharpener; garage; crack; mash). Such language-games constitute
their objects such that while willies and penises share a 'signified', they
relate to separate domains of signification. In the latter the child is a
pupil, in the former an infant and, critically, an innocent.

Age of consent

The equation – children + sexuality = visceral clutch – can be put in another form – children + sexuality = taboo. The term taboo both implies straight prohibition and the tension between sacredness and prohibition. Historically, the story goes, children were (in so far as they were) protected from sexualisation by a social process which mixed religious prohibition with the valorisation of innocence/virginity. In early modernism, the taboo found a substitute scientific grounding in notions of the genetic costs of incest, the bodily dangers of early sex and in the supposed cross-generational 'taboos' in infra-humans. In the secularised liberal-humanism of contemporary welfarism, these analyses have been partly replaced by a formal moral argument based on the notion of consent. This is evidenced in the most commonly used definition of child sexual abuse as: 'the involvement of dependent, developmentally immature children and adolescents in sexual activities they do not truly comprehend, and to which they are unable to give informed consent, or that violate the social taboos of family roles' (Schechter and Roberge, 1976). Here we may observe that one of the value axioms built into much child sexual abuse work is that children are either lacking in the capacity to give such consent and/or so positioned by the power of others that true consent is impossible. This has the rhetorical (if not actual) capability to present all children as thereby innocent (i.e. sacred) and to shift all moral responsibility to the adult. As a located rule of thumb, this clearly has its uses. Were it followed exclusively, it would clearly abolish child sexual abuse instantly. However, singular understandings cannot be made to work in a plural social world. Sexual consent is also socially sedimented as something to be wooed, and something that flows from love, as apologists for 'child love' argue:

> Distinctions between two very different types of adult offenders is essential if rational action is to follow. Broadly, these groups are, on the one hand, adults who form happy and often affectionate relationships with children and are welcomed to sexual involvement; and, on the other hand, there are adults who manipulate events undesirably by applying physical or emotional pressure. (Brongersma, 1978, p. 78)

Here, the notion of 'consent' becomes problematic, for where it can be argued that a child does consent, then sexual activity between adult and child can be justified. So the axiom needs not just a failure to give consent, but *incapacity* to give consent. But this too is problematic, since it flies in the face of a growing willingness to accord children the right to make decisions for themselves (e.g. under the Children Act, 1989). And at least as compelling a difficulty is that the consent axiom makes little sense when applied to sexual activity between two children, i.e. the assumed non-consent-able with the assumed non-consentable. Either we must assume that this kind of activity is thereby innocent, or that the blame lies with some unspecified outside power. What we cannot do, within the consent axiom, is accord the child any moral power or authority, a position patently ridiculous once we compare sexual activity to almost any other form of social interaction like playground fights or playing sport. Those who would define the child as incapable of moral choice none the less would punish the bully, and praise the devotion of the child athlete. What is slowly being uncovered is the hidden agenda to the consent axiom – it is not a general moral analytic at all, but has been designed to fit a special case, the special case of adult/child sex.

Until quite recently the focus of the welfarist concern for the child (see Chapter 4) was on cruelty and neglect. Here issues as to whether the child consented to a beating or to starvation would be rightly seen as nonsensical as asking whether the victim of mugging consented to be mugged. The concern instead was with a failure to conform to basic minimum standards of fair and decent treatment (criteria which would also be applied to a dog under animal welfare law, and indeed was applied to animals before it was applied to children, cf. Stainton Rogers, W., 1989). These are developments which have gone hand in paw, so to speak. Under such populist morals, an adult who picked a fight with a child would stand condemned not because of issues of consent but because it infracted notions of a fair fight. Children could be seen to fight fairly together as could adults, so long as the protagonists were 'well matched'. Incidentally, it tends also to show the implicit parallel that is being drawn, between rape and child sexual assault, for it is only over an alleged crime of rape where the issue of 'consent' is also critical.

This argument is not an attempt to describe a 'golden age' of unproblematic moral choices, but an attempt to describe a reality largely lost to contemporary child protection work, with its heavy emphasis upon sexual abuse. It was in terms of such a straightforward, popular morality of 'fair treatment' that much of the history of child protectionist work against cruelty and neglect was conducted. That approach has been largely abandoned with the evolution of anti-abusive work, precisely because it cannot seem to work with sex. One reason is easy to pinpoint. Unlike being exposed to continual beatings or chronic malnutrition, children can, in ordinary understanding, be said to enjoy being exposed to sex (as well as initiating auto-erotic sex themselves). It is important here to define carefully what is being said (and accepted in popular knowledge). Children cannot be said to enjoy rape, to savour sado-masochism (broadly to experience a sexual assault). But sex *qua* sex they may enjoy: 'Because of the "hidden" nature of sexual abuse, it can become an activity which a child may want, and indeed from which he or she may derive pleasure. Only at a later stage may the experience feel abusive' (Bentovim and Boston, 1988, p. 18). Part of the problem faced by the anti-masturbators was that children can show every sign of enjoying self and mutual masturbation. However, the current tendency (and it is hard to see it as other than ideologically driven) is to see any and all sexual relations (genital or otherwise) involving a child as 'sexual abuse'. It is then asserted that extraordinarily large proportions of children experience sexual abuse, and soon we are led down a discursive path into believing that there is a 'problem' of massive proportions, requiring the most draconian actions to be taken. We take up these issues in Chapter 11. For now the key issue emerges – is there a better way to protect children, one which ensures that cruelty and neglect are still properly pursued, *and* addresses the equivalent 'hard core' of sexual assaults against children such as rape? Can we have care and concern without *The Crucible* (Miller, 1961)? Must a sensitivity to children's sexual rights also warrant the paedophile? Can we take the 'moral panic' out of the flashbulb glare of one sex abuse 'scandal' after another (or worse, rescue us from the concern-fatigue that is beginning to set in), and still do something about the undoubted numbers of children being sexually assaulted?

Dissolving the specialness of sex

It is time to make explicit a social tectonic that has been moving around just under the surface of this chapter from its start. We do not believe that there is something intrinsic to 'sex' which gives it special powers, neither in general nor *vis-à-vis* children. We have no problems seeing violent sexual assaults on children or sex under threat or coercion, however 'affectionate', as genuinely serious offences. We are appalled by the permanent injuries a small but significant number of children suffer from what we think are more effectively conveyed by terms like rape and buggery than 'sexual abuse'. It needs to become possible to see 'flashing' as wrong, without accepting that it will inevitably lead to serious harm. Why, it needs to be made possible to ask, was it assumed that it was the 'flashing' rather than the child-parental dynamics of disobedience-guilt which so 'fixed' this memory for Rita (p. 163)?

We need narrative mechanisms which allow us to talk about sex, sexuality and children outside of currently dominant discourses (including those promoted by child-sex offenders). We can do this via a thought experiment. Imagine a group of extra-terrestrials who have grown up in a culture without an understanding of the term sex. They understand everything else of our culture's knowledge about the world but nothing to do with sex. We get them to give us their views on 'child abuse' and to suggest a policy about how we should deal with it. What sort of recommendations might they propose? This, then becomes our analytic. Would the special status of child sexual abuse (as currently constituted) stand up to an enquiry looking to the 'best interests of the child' in the absense of a meaning to sex? In this summary ruling we have added, in italics, our interpretation of how the exercise would relate to children and sex.

The Judgement

1. In any practical operation, offences against the child need to be scaled between the profound and the trivial. *It cannot be assumed that the label 'sexual' indicates where on such a scale an offence should be positioned.*
2. Where offences occur within the home, criteria of risk *rather than the label 'sexual' or 'non-sexual'* must be the guide as to whether some form of separation of the child from the family is required.
3. Where separation is considered, the removal of the offender is to be preferred to that of removal of the child. *Such removals should be pursued without concern as to the sex of the child or of the offender.*
4. Serious attention should be paid to the views of the children concerned in the scaling of offences and in the seriousness attached to a specific offence. Seriousness should not be based upon the 'hearsay' of adult recollections of offences *labelled as sexual or otherwise.*
5. The pursuit of all serious *sexual and non sexual* offences must follow parallel procedures with equal emphasis on respect for the victim.
6. While as far as police work is concerned, there may be grounds for specialisation of function *(e.g. sexual offences against a child and an adult may call upon similar facilities),* attempts to divide child protection work between *'sexual'* and *'non-sexual'* specialisations is unjustified.
7. Children should be given a consistent status in law. It should be assumed that those who are capable of an offence and capable of knowing it to be wrong, are capable as full witnesses and are capable of consenting to *sexual or other* relations (and withholding consent) and of making *sexual or other* decisions.
8. In decisions over capability, demonstrated performativity may take precedence over age.
9. The greatest concern for the rights of the young people involved should be adopted in any consideration of *sexual or other* acts between young people.

10. Children and young people have equal rights with adults to know of the risks they face, to evaluate them and to take appropriate action, *whether those risks are 'sexual' or otherwise.*

The 'Catch 22' over such an enquiry, of course, is that to be able to hold it is tantemount to the condition of having deconstructed the speciality of sex. Given existing power relations, that may well be an 'idealistic' project (Parker, I., personal communication). However, unless we try, we will continue to have a concern over 'sex' obscuring a concern for the child.

Images and looking glasses

One of the vignettes we have used in discussing the social construction of child abuse (Stainton Rogers, W. *et al.*, 1989) has concerned a charac-ter Lou with a penchant for the company of pre-pubescent girls and an ability to capture them in photographic images of 'repressed desire' (Gernsheim, 1980) – the dénouement of the story being, of course, that we are discussing Lewis Carroll. Presented in 'case conference' terms, Lou sounds, at the least, one to watch, and it is hard to see present-day Oxford University accepting such actions from one of its dons. Never-theless, nineteenth century Oxford did, and one of the results was the *Alice* books. By an interesting coincidence of timing, Carroll's first meet-ing with Alice Liddell (daughter of his Dean), his emergence as a serious photographer and the birth of Freud (whose theories would be so influ-ential on latter analyses of both Carroll's books and his lifestyle) all occurred in 1856. The following year Carroll wrote *Hiawatha's Photo-graphing*, a parody after Longfellow, in which his understanding of photographs as icons is patent. For example, the Father, 'Volunteered his own suggestions':

> *He would contemplate the distance*
> *With a look of pensive meaning,*
> *As of ducks that die in tempests.*

It is a look well captured in A.B. Frost's illustration of the poem (Figure 10.1). Nevertheless, it cannot safely be inferred that the meanings we may read into Carroll's icons (from a gaze informed by over a century of further iconic sedimentation and interpretation) – particularly those of girls in which he specialised – are those that were read within their social and historical context by Carroll, by his models or by other viewers. What does seem to be the case is that the iconographic language Carroll employed was not an idiosyncratic one but common to his time and

"First the Governor, the Father"

Figure 10.1 *From Lewis Carroll's parody* Hiawatha's Photographing

shared by artists of both genders. Thus Carroll's photograph of Alice Liddell as *The Beggar Maid* (Figure 10.2) uses a costume very similar to that given to Sylvie by one of the Victorian age's classic children's illustrators Harry Furniss in Carroll's late book *Sylvie and Bruno* (Figure 10.3). Further, Carroll's much interpreted interest in drawings of child nudes seems to have resulted from that being a speciality of his friend E. Gertrude Thomson. Her work, for example, for Carroll's *Three Sunsets and other poems* would, one suspects, not find its way into a modern book in the same genre (Figure 10.4).

What a study of such images may provide, is not so much an insight into Carroll as into ourselves. The power of Carroll's images,

particularly of *Alice*, to our eye reflects what a century of iconography
has constructed: in photography as art, in advertising and in the cinema
(for a consideration of the continuing impact of Lewis Carroll on the
avant-garde treatment of the child in film, see Keller, 1986.) Over that
time, sexuality has been a prevailing cultural obsession – evidence, perhaps, that we have not so much enjoyed a liberation as an unfolding
preoccupation (Foucault, 1979). In this, language has enjoyed more freedom than image – typically we can describe more than we can show. One
consequence has been the development of a melodramatised non-verbal
encoding of 'adult' female sexuality through stance, a look that was
fostered by the demands of the silent movies as a specific medium and
was carried through into the talkies through a strict censorship which
denied more overt representations. Interestingly in this regard, much
'hard pornography' which is badly photographed, lacks this quality
(Faust, 1981). A second thread to the story centres on the market for
and marketability of 'youth'. The cosmetic and toiletry industry has long

Figure 10.2 *A drawing of Carroll's photograph of Alice Liddell as* The Beggar
Maid *(R.M Stainton Rogers)*

Figure 10.3 *Sylvie from Carroll's late book* Sylvie and Bruno

used images of the young (e.g. Pears Soap) as symbols of product purity and product benefits. The rag trade helped to construct 'the model', who over the years has got younger and thinner until the hebetic look dominates not only the cat walks but also the drawings on clothes patterns. In turn, the new young first subverted their own 'children's clothes' (one source of the naughty schoolgirl icon), then adopted the clothes of adults and finally required their own fashions. The result has been a heavy cultural overlay of visual images of pubescents and adolescents reflecting 'adult' cues of sensuality/sexuality/'availability'. Nevertheless, it would be a mistake to see this as a one-way flow from adult manipulators to an osmotic young. Here, for example, is the feminist researcher Valerie Walkerdine, describing six year old Janie:

> The pop song 'Oh Mickie' . . . was sung relentlessly by the girls in Janie's class in the Summer of . . . 1982 . . . Toni Basil, on the promotional video of the record is the epitome of the sexualised schoolgirl . . . She sings to Mickie to 'give it to me, give it to me any way you can' . . . But Janie does not only join in the singing. She is transformed in minutes from 'good' girl to 'bad' girl. She leaves the classroom and goes to pose in front of the

mirror in the privacy of the toilets to sing her own private version of 'Oh Mickie'. And her 'positioning' is transformed – from child to woman, from virgin to whore. (Walkerdine, 1986a, p. 74)

In contemporary iconography, the girl child oscillates between just these tensions and perhaps Alice as 'the beggar girl' fascinates us because there they co-exist within a single image, a conceptual illusion in which first one and then the other meaning emerges as understandings in complementary – like light as wave and light as particle, except that waves and particles are not moralised, whereas virgins and whores are. We can never know whether Carroll (who in so many ways anticipated twentieth-century cultural forms, cf. Phillips, 1974) experienced this tension, and it was that which caused him to cease photography. In any event, it is a tension we (i.e. those of us who are not overt paedophiles) not so much escape as compartmentalise, and our children aid us in this by a reflective compartmentalising. Walkerdine's Janie, at least notionally, 'whores' in private. This is sometimes achieved by a gender-specialised and function-specialised gaze, so that many (in another

Figure 10.4 *Naked children illustrating Carroll's* Three Sunsets and other poems

location) sexually iconographised images of 'children' exist in fashion magazines, fashion catalogues and other 'women's' publications. They may also feature in medical material and, ironically perhaps, as part of education in child abuse (Barnford and Roberts, 1989).

However, the tension is often most subtly resolved by dramatised explorations of childhood's sexual end (cf. Chapter 9). Here, the iconography of innocent/knowing is played out as a theme of symbolic transformation. Psychologised, and often overlaid with markers of signification, movies like *Summer of '42, The Innocents, The Company of Wolves* and *The Ice Palace* invite both empathy into and at the same time perspectives of distance from 'loss of innocence'. With actors a similar resolution of that tension may be played out through the publicised contrasts between (and the implicated commonality between) the 'part' and the 'person'. Jodie Foster illustrates this well with her transition from the 'sweet innocent' part she played in *Bugsy Malone*, through precocious sexuality in *Taxi Driver*, to playing an adult woman in *The Accused*. However, such resolutions are singular and biographic. One child may pass over, but 'the child' remains to pass.

Like any myth, it is 'magic' (albeit not more than the weak magic of collective entrapment in a created reality) but it is enough, no doubt, to result in some children being sexually assaulted by those self-located as under its 'spell'. But children were sexually assaulted before it under different 'spells' (e.g. via a monopolar 'innocence') and are so today. There is no reason to believe that by seeking to banish any particular myth we can thereby stamp out sexual offence. The sad but true condition of the young is that they are drawn into the social, no matter what that is, and all the social that we know uses the young for the old. Whether such a situation is unchangeable, we consider in our last section.

Beyond protectionism

At its most basic, the protectionist prescription works upon a utopia in which the relations between adults and children are foundationally asexual. This differs from the both the present and the past condition in which they are seen as, at best, asexual by external control and internal (to the adult) will; and, at worst, sexualised by failures of control and/or will. Like all utopias, the protectionist's ideal-world cannot be achieved, it can only be simulated and that simulation requires a regime of total policing – hints of which we have already seen in the texts and praxes of child sexual abuse protectionism. It is a profoundly conservative doctrine leading to a monitorial dystopia, in which the balance sheet, even for its purported beneficiaries (children themselves) is in considerable doubt.

Nevertheless, it is the currently dominant voice and finds support across a wide-spectrum of political opinion. It holds that position because it at least claims to put children first. It has also succeeded in wrong-footing more liberal voices into sounding, on the most favourable reading, more concerned with adult liberties than children's lives; and, on the least favourable, positively complicitous with the sexual abuse of children. As a result, the challenge it presents, for those who reject its doctrine, cannot be met by received anti-conservative agendas. Nor, in our view, can it met by a traditional feminist manifesto. Kitzinger (1990), for example, in her call for a radical reconstruction of childhood elegantly deconstructs both the ideologies of protectionism and liberal empowerment, but she still clings to a rhetorical rather than an analytic use of feminism – patriarchy remains the axiomatic enemy. Feminist cultural theory in contrast (e.g. Doane, 1982) in challenging through critical reflection, and adopting a culture-of-subjectivity approach (very much intertextual with critical polytextualist analysis), has much more to offer. Like the protectionist account, the culture-of-subjectivity approach, takes the present sexual mistreatment of children as given and inevitable. However, the inevitability is laid squarely at the door of cultural form itself and carries with it the possibility of and an agenda for cultural transformation. The pursuit of the individual perpetrator (and the rest of the protectionist arsenal) can now be seen as part of the culture that perpetuates perpetration, not the route to its change. This is not to argue against punishing sexual crime, but to see resisting reinforcing a worldview as a means to change its subjectivated praxes. However, this approach is quite distinctive in denying that the reification of *sexual* abuse is anything other than a cultural production, which needs analysis because it needs deconstruction. Exactly what can emerge from such a concern for the mistreatment of the young is as open-ended as what can emerge from any creative discipline. It involves, in other words, modelling child concern more on art than on science.

The idea that child mistreatment by adults can be best addressed by the deconstruction of old stories of their relations and the reconstruction of new ones is certainly radical! However, to recognise an obvious objection, is it practical? To argue its practicality requires an initial willingness to consider the possibility of two contentions. First, that the stabilities, the enduring features of adult-child relations, persist through enduring features of textuality. Secondly, that change is likewise textualised. Hence, the culture of subjectivity approach may well not only be practical, but be the only practical alternative to proceeding 'as if' we knew what to do, 'as if' the path to progress were not a *trompe l'oeil* painted upon the flat surface of theory but a three-dimensional *Camino Real* passing seemlessly from the past to the future.

11

On our own doorsteps and beyond our own backyards: Concern about concern

Traditional notions of ethics fare very badly under postmodernism, becoming either targets for deconstruction or transformed into an aesthetics of the ethical (cf. Shusterman, 1988). Probably the best-known attempt to construct a postmodern moral philosophy is that of Rorty (e.g. 1986, 1989), who does so via a narrative device, the construction of a character he calls the 'liberal ironist'. For Rorty, the minimum condition for making life better is an appreciation of human solidarity and that is something to be gained 'not by inquiry but by imagination' (1989, p. xvi). In developing his theme of abrogating the power of moralising from theory to narrative, he soon comes up against the treatment of the young. In taking as a specimen case Nabokov's *Lolita*, he comes to the following conclusion:

> The moral is not to keep one's hands off little girls but to notice what one is doing, and in particular to notice what people are saying. For it might turn out, it very often does turn out, that people are trying to tell you they are suffering. (*ibid.*, p. 174)

What Rorty is offering, and he is explicit about it, is a modernistic liberal-humanistic ethic stripped (and therein lies it postmodernism) of any foundation, of any possible metaphysical grounding. We doubt whether this ironising is enough to satisfy constructionist critics of liberal-humanism (e.g. Kitzinger, 1987) but more importantly, we doubt the future vitality of the liberal axiom that cruelty is the worst thing we can do to children. We would accept that it has done effective work – a similar liberal-humanistic ethic underpins The National Society for the Prevention of Cruelty to Children (NSPCC) in more than title. Nor would we deny that cruelty is bad (it is, under almost any current moral discourse – hence the humanistic bedrock).

But, specifically, critical polytextualism suggests it is meaningless to dub it the *worst*. Equally, it has a limited range of applicability: cruelty is simply not a very helpful term in many cases of child mistreatment. For example, it is inappropriate whenever an individual's actions are towards children in a general sense. We might call the manager of a chain store unmindful of, or even, knowingly oppressive towards, the children who work in sweat-shops producing clothes s/he sells. But we would not dub her/him cruel. Similarly a dentist who 'felt-up' an unconscious child under nitrous oxide gas is hard to label cruel, precisely because cruelty tends to be implicated upon communicated harm (as in the Rorty quote). And yet we would not want to forgo a moral analysis of such conduct. Again, the term cruelty also raises problems of the 'cruel to be kind' variety, e.g., male circumcision may be cruel (in some meaning of the term) but it could also be said to be kind because it renders the child 'one of us' (cf. Rorty, 1989, p. 191) with the solidarity-benefits that it is claimed to bring. Finally, a focus on the 'worstness' of cruelty is unlikely to be effective in a plural community in which liberal-humanists may be neither the majority nor necessarily the group most likely to perpetrate the cruelty (if such groups exist).

The alternative concept which we have used in this book has been 'concern', since its polysemy works well within a critical polytextualist analysis. Of course, concern for a child clearly can never be, within this context, a singular pursuit, secure in its analysis of the situation and neatly parcelled up, separate from other concerns and disconnected from the culture in which it operates. On the contrary, it will always imply a messy, deeply dilemmatic landscape, where exploration must be expected to trip us into unseen potholes and to leave us splattered with all the philosophical and ideological mud that surrounds issues of human conduct:

> [C]hild abuse [is] something that is produced by the decisions of people who are in contact with children . . . when we place the behaviour of adults towards children in a social context, it becomes available for labelling in a way which imposes a moral evaluation. . . . The point is that for some treatment of a child to be described as abusive or neglectful, an observer must recognise it, formulate it and label it. (Dingwall, 1989, pp. 158–9)

Such processes in social thinking – the generation of discourses of child concern – need themselves to become subject to polytextual reflection, for: 'Our concepts and our ideas reflect our own times, and they also reflect the history which has produced these current moments' (Billig *et al.*, 1988, p. 3). They also need to be subjected to a critical gaze. For example, the position of both children and women as objects of male power has resulted in the claim that only feminist theory can address certain areas of concern (e.g. child sexual abuse, see Saraga and Macleod, 1991). However, such a notion of commonality through power experience may perpetuate patriarchal equatings of 'women and children' while glossing over obvious conflicts of interest between women and children (cf. Ennew, 1986) such as a 'woman's right to choose' to abort or otherwise dispose of her child. Womanhood does not confer immunity against being ageist nor does it prevent oppression and mistreatment of the young. Traditional feminism, certainly, has no universal solution to conflicts of powers, for it is grounded in resistance to a specific power – patriarchy.

Equally, however, we are concerned about modernist moral analyses of child concern. These have tended to be preoccupied with issues of motivation and reasoning – assuming that the outcomes of particular conduct, policies and praxes are inevitably intended or at least accountable. They also adopt a naive pathology model, they assume there is a problem to be solved – that there are self-evident, concrete and particular issues to be tackled. This, incidentally, is as true of the institutionalised troublers of modernism (e.g. feminist analytics) as it is of its orthodoxies (e.g. welfarist analytics). The result is that whenever a concern about children is brought into public gaze, campaigns have been launched to seek out, expose and get rid of the 'villains' who were responsible. The consequence is either the pathologising of particular individuals or groups, or the blaming of particular institutions, professional communities, or other collectivities (e.g. ruling men, the state, capitalism). This kind of endeavour implies (when it does not explicitly claim) a credulous and singularised utopianism – that all that needs to be done 'to stamp out the problem' is to overthrow the patriarchy, or remove violence from television, or disband the social work profession, or liberate children from the shackles of adult power – and all our problems will be solved! Child concern thus becomes reconstituted as a moral crusade, not just by populist politicians and the press, but by the vast majority of practitioners, scholars and those who see themselves as advocates for the child.

To embark on a crusading quest for villains is to operate within a chimerical fairy-tale world in which, once the brave knight has slain the dragon, children can all live 'happily ever after'. Narratives of the 'real world' (whatever that might be) are not, we would argue, modelled at all helpfully by the teleological thema of melodrama. What we believe a critical polytextualist analysis can (and must) do is to get us away from this fixation and relocate our attention to consideration of the doubt that must surround both the problem-focused approach and the analytic of intention and consequences. Once the modernistic grand narrative claim that the social world is objective and lawfully predictable is discarded, it becomes self-evident that (almost) whatever we think and say and do about children could have some potential benefits for some, and do some potential harms to some others (depending also of course on shifting definitions of harm and benefit).

What this boils down to is a recognition that heroic 'child saving' or 'child protection' and villainous 'child mistreatment' are not two different kinds of action, with opposing mandates (to work for the good or for the bad of children). They are two alternative facets, or readings, of virtually *any* kind of conduct towards children. Similarly, children themselves are not either innocent victims of adult mistreatment, or culpable delinquents whose anti-social behaviour must be controlled. Rather these (and many more in between) are alternative placements that the adult world creates for children, into which individual children are located at different times, in different circumstances, according to the adult gaze adopted. All childhoods are oppressive, if by that we mean power unequal. As Berger and Luckmann (1967) put it: '[A]lthough the child is not simply passive in his [sic] socialization, it is the adults who set the rules of the game. The child can play the game with enthusiasm or with sullen resistance. But, alas, there is no other game around' (p. 154). At the same time, all children, virtually without exception, wield powers to manipulate, exploit and subvert adult control. An extreme example of such a positioning are the 'trust bandits' as described by Magid and McKelvey (1988): '[C]haracter-disturbed children can work a good con. They are manipulators who appear cute, loving, helpless, smart or beguiling, as suits their needs at the time' (p. 95). The behavioural control industry and indeed the warrant to adult authority in everyday child rearing requires us to be able to place our children within this discourse. In contrast, the operating wisdom and the practices (e.g. interrogation about sexual abuse) of child protection need children to be truly helpless and incapable of lying or fabricating evidence.

> We believe in the power of healing even after the most severe abuse. However, healing cannot begin until the reality of the abuse is openly acknowledged and victims are provided with an advocate who will believe them, be willing to hear their pain, and take action to stop the abuse. (Richardson and Bacon, 1991, p. 18)

Once we address a critical polytextualist analysis to concern, we have to transcend the limits of a singularising discourse, in which the 'goodies' and 'baddies' in the plot are so universally and uniquely identified, both in terms of the adults and the children concerned. What must be explored (and all that can ever be at issue) are prospective (and hence speculative) or *post hoc* moral cost-benefit analyses of the alternative readings of actions and conduct towards children, and of locating children themselves in different discourses of responsibility and blame. It is this perturbating doubt within an arena of plural textuality which must be the basis of child concern. In this chapter, we will round off the book by addressing this concern in two directions; first, towards those proximal children 'on our own doorsteps'; second, to those distal children 'beyond our own backyards'.

Proximal concern

Within a critical polytextualist analysis, the emergence into our local social awareness of new accounts of the childhood condition (e.g. the recent construction of the phenomenon of 'child abuse' and the growing importance of the concept of 'children's rights') creates new conditions of debate, new mechanisms and new practices. Such social tectonic activity results in shifts in the cultural landscape, movements along tensions and the social tectonic 'fault-lines' in discourse. However, unlike the geo-physical processes which mould the Earth's crust, such tectonics are humanly conditioned. True, social mountains (like major institutional masses of power) may be harder to dislocate than social molehills – but shift they do. As players in and contributors to the social mélange, the voices of individuals and collectives have an impact on a cultural landscape in flux.

In seeking to deny the determinism of 'conspiracy theories' of social process, critical polytextualism is nevertheless not naive as to the gross imbalances in the cultural distribution of the power to construct knowledge and the knowledge to construct power. Hence, its commitment to giving a more effective hearing to 'muted voices'. In this it comes into alignment with those 'children's rights' practices which are directed to, say, making children 'in care' active participants in the review meetings held to decide about their own care and future, or to seek the informed consent of children to medical examinations. However, its analysis must avoid any singular elevation of the children's rights discourse (as any other singular discourse) to the position of a meta-gaze. It needs to be remembered that abstract rights are a political construction and that how those rights are interpreted and turned into conduct will not be immune from the social tectonics that move politics in general.

The deliberate slipperiness of the term concern allows it to move across discourses of the child which are predicated upon differing constructions of childhood, and hence of 'child care' and 'child well-being'. It accepts as given that these discourses result in conflicting understandings of concern, and in the actions that reflect it. For example, a protectionist-focused concern which highlights the minimisation of risks and hazards (e.g. not permitting a child to play on a rubbish dump) may to an autonomy-focused concern amount to 'neglect by constraint'. Because its interest is upon stories of childhood, their weaving and their vicissitudes, conflict and tension (while not reified into dialectic) are nevertheless seen by critical polytextualist analysis as essential to the production of new understandings. The very complexity of such debates over construal and action constitute conditions in which concern is encouraged to child-openness – that is, to the incorporation of the notion that the child and childhood are inherently problematic.

Our own social history, and certainly the history we construct concerning the moral use (and its reverse abuse) of children, must thus be related in terms of the particular cultural practice of haggling the moral in an arena of competing moral discourses – of a tradition of public moral rhetorical debate. Over time, the 'losing' stories acquire a special implausibility – it becomes 'impossible' to think in them, and we consign the ideas they employed to the discursive archive (cf. Gleeson, 1991). The beliefs and the devices that made possible the judicial hanging, branding and transportation of child offenders have gone this way. As critical polytextualists, we have to accept that, had we been born in the seventeenth century that 'other we' would have found those moralities and practices alive (and probably have taken them for granted). Yet this relativity in no way alters their special implausibility to us as we are now, and, under the moral rhetorical rules in which we share, we can construct good arguments as to why the birching of youthful offenders or the use of straps and canes in schools are rightly being drawn back into the same unthinkability which now contains the juvenile gallows.

To such an extent, we can think in terms of progress. However, within critical polytextualism, our understanding of progress in moral practice and discourse cannot be based on the assumption that any particular construction of the child is of absolute value in that evolution. The understanding of the child as different from the adult (in say moral culpability) may well have made possible the ending of the hanging of children in Britain – a plausible action at a time when the ending of the hanging of adults was not plausible. However, it was just such an understanding of the child as different to the adult (in moral development) which made possible the corporal punishment of children in our post-war schools, but not the corporal punishment of adults in our post-war offices and factories!

Critical polytextualism thus permits us (locally and contingently) to consider how to achieve moral progress towards better childhoods. So far our examination has been very much focused on social policies rather than upon individuated actions (e.g. life in ordinary families and in the ordinary world). Clearly, in those domains of our culture, children do still get beaten, branded and killed – both by adults and by other children. In ordinary life, it would seem, the 'unthinkable' (and so it gets labelled by judges and other professional moralisers) still happens. Of course, it can happen in the public domain as well, but where it does, we can usually see 'rogue' world views at work as in regimes like 'pindown'. By contrast, most offenders against children seem marked by their relative ordinariness (or, at the very least, there are many who share their supposed characteristics without sharing their offence). Notions of 'inner pathologies' are not just anathema to critical polytextualists, they are singularly unhelpful in the control of child mistreatment. Which is why we need, in terms of the personal as well as the collective, to operate within an analysis of concern.

Critical to our analysis is the impact of a prevailing gaze, drawn from the alembic myth (and bolstered by its resonance with commonsense wisdom) in which the child is viewed as inevitably and inherently dependent, and hence needful of uniquely disenfranchised treatment. This gaze underpins much that may appear paradoxical in the locating of the young. The special treatment we mete out to children (like physical punishment) no less than those special protections we grant them, are grounded on notions of the child's needs. 'Spare the rod and spoil the child' can thus be read as warranting punishment, because it is supposed to meet the child's needs in terms of moral character-building. Hence, one way of challenging the mistreatment of children is to challenge the axiom of need, which is so central to the discourse of childhood dependency. Woodhead (1990), for example, goes so far as to claim that: 'our understandings and respect for childhood might be better served if "children's needs" were outlawed from future professional discourse, policy recommendations, and popular psychology' (p. 60). The critical focus here is not upon dependency *per se* but upon the way that discourse has traditionally placed children squarely within a patronising discourse which stresses their special 'needs', rather than one which acknowledges their human 'entitlements'. As Ehrenreich (1978) has noted in another context, there is nothing wrong with dependency, *qua* dependency. What matters within any society is 'the kind of dependency it generates, and its social impact'. What matters is that society 'can deal with [dependency] in a dignified and nurturing way' (p. 28).

The gaze which constitutes the child as dependent is intimately intertextual with and predicated upon a discourse of parental responsibility. For all the welfarism of today, popular understanding (and hence social policy) still operates from an historically sedimented view of a parental duty to meet the needs of their children, which is used to warrant denying their right to economic autonomy. New Right economics and old-style conservatism have found a common, self-serving, voice in the argument that young people should be dislocated from dependence upon the 'nanny state' and re-inserted into the economic unit of their family. The result is growing numbers of homeless young people on the streets. Social policies supposedly intended to support 'the family' can be plausibly retold as consequentially harming large numbers of young people. In other areas too, we see the most vulnerable young people being harmed the most. It is no 'law of social nature' that residential care for children removed from their families for their own protection has to be an abusive experience Yet the dependency mandate makes possible the disenfranchisement of the young (particularly if they are 'troublesome'), denying them the same rights to challenge authority as we give to adults (even those in other total institutions, like prisons).

Thus what we have today as institutional means for addressing child concern are not so much a set of policies, but the outcome of cultural tectonic activity in the social realities we inhabit. Although locally formalised, they have largely arisen by historical accretion, as a collage constructed out of adult discourse, which reflects that which the adult world has – and has not – been willing to countenance. We have not so much got the means to tackle child concern as an emotional market *in* child concern. Some locations become melodramatic 'hot spots' (e.g. the setting up of Childline and rows over 'ritual abuse'). Others, lacking such marketing or marketability, remain largely invisible (as with what went on in our children's homes until the Beck case and 'pindown' brought abuse in that context to our attention). Children still remain vulnerable to the vagaries of an adult world which is entrapped in living out fairy-story narratives. The lure of the 'quick-fix' acts to mute and to obscure the ongoing structural production of child mistreatment.

Hence, it is also naive to hope that we can find solutions in any simple shift in social policy, even if that included a radical reassessment of the fiscal and care policies adopted towards young people (though this would undoubtedly help some young people in some ways). The root problem lies much more fundamentally with the way we construct the young as inherently dependent, and the way we label them as 'victims' in one gaze, and 'delinquents' in another. This may at times and in some circumstances offer them special protection; it may, for the very young, accord them greater compassion and consequently offer them a larger slice of the 'generosity' cake with which we assuage our consciences. But for every coin in the collecting tin, and every cry of 'women and children first', there are many more children and young people for whom their culturally and socially constructed dependency is the root of their suffering and discontent. Similarly for every child believed in and cared for within a protectionist arena, there are many more less beguiling and winsome children and young people whose entitlements simply do not enter into our social conscience or consciousness.

Distal children – only pawns in their games?

The game of chess provides the cultures that play it with a potent range of metaphors for the use and abuse of power. The idea of children as 'the smallest pawns in the game' is used to entitle and to set the agenda for a book by Peter Townsend (1980) which documents a twentieth century social history of children in war and social chaos. It is a history which began with the deaths from disease of perhaps 10,000 Boer children in Lord Kitchener's 'concentration camps'; and ends with the continuing tragedy of Beirut. Not that the story ends there, of course. A further decade has added additional horrors in various parts of Africa and Asia, not to mention the Gulf War, the Intafada, the desaparecidos of Argentina and Chile and the death squads operating upon the 'street children' of Brazil. Further aspects of the tale are to be found in Cutting's more recent account of children in Beirut (*Children of the Siege*, 1988). Others (e.g. Cairns, 1989; various authors in Moorehead, 1989) have described how in all manner of subtle and unsubtle ways (e.g. as hostages tortured to persuade their parents to come out of hiding) children cannot avoid being caught up in the wars and terrorist campaigns being fought by adults. It is, then, a story not just of child suffering 'incidental' to adult conflict, but likewise of children in those conflicts as combatants. It is also a catalogue of torture, sexual assaults and exploitation that, though alien to the West in location, can be 'owned' once we are prepared to consider the critical narrative that implicates us through the national and economic involvement of our nation states in these conflicts and disasters. What rhetorical texts like Townsend's make possible is a gaze upon 'all the world's children'. Once engaged in this way, our specific moral panic over child abuse is shown to be just that – specific. Child abuse conferences have even been held in countries like Brazil, with a seeming blinkeredness to the paradoxes raised by enjoying services based on a regime of child labour and child murder.

It is not all that helpful to think of this catalogue of horrors as a specifically targeted, intended, perpetration of child abuse. Such horrors are an inevitable consequence of conditions that diminish concern for the human condition as a whole. This is not offered as a humanistic plea but a statement of how, when a global gaze is adopted, children cannot be isolated from the conditions around them. They can no more be cushioned from bombs and death squads than they can be from poverty, homelessness and deprivation. If we use recession, unemployment and cuts in public spending as politico-economic regulators in our own nations, or if we impose them upon Third World debtor nations, then we perpetrate mistreatment and neglect as surely as if we were the direct agents. If we allow 'the market' to determine the supply of goods, then we are bound to surround the world with the products of the armaments industries (i.e. war) and with the products of child labour somewhere in the world.

Our aim here is not to promote a 'guilt trip' approach to child concern but rather to argue for a moritorium on 'knee-jerk child concern'. This is the purpose of arguing that the mistreatment-sensitised western family, horrified by their country's child abuse statistics, are also the (albeit largely unwitting) agents of massive child cruelty and neglect. Their purchases, the investments in the arms, food and manufacturing industries of their pension funds and often their votes are doing just that. Even issues like child-slave prostitution in Thailand or the Phillipines are not simply attributable to their direct clients in the United States, Europe and the Pacific Rim (although they would not survive without them). Instead their origins can be traced to specific western policy decisions, albeit locally executed. If rain-coated wankers are more visible child abusers to us than pin-stripe suited bankers, it may be that we need to look to our cultural perceptual apparatuses, i.e. the communications media upon which we rely to see 'reality'.

These are political analyses – any macro concern for the young (indeed for anyone) cannot be anything else. They apply close to home as well as in locations distal to us. The same analytic would argue that it does not just happen that our cities harbour the young homeless, the runaways, the young prostitutes. They, and the other effects we have discussed, are not blemishes upon an otherwise healthy social body, they are reflections of the life we make our social body live (or allow it to live by default). And they require holistic treatment not symptomatic medication. The difficulty is, of course, that there is no 'new age medicine' to address the condition. It remains (and here the ironic doubt must out) that, despite it all, we do live in a Panglossian 'best of possible worlds' because we live in the only world possible. Certainly (and yet it could not have been said ten years ago), we now live in times when there seems to be no other viable socio-economic system around other than liberal capitalism. It is not a conspiracy but an immensely dynamic and successful constitutor of social and economic conditions that none the less happens to have the effect of not placing the human condition central to its purview. In that, it is like every other system of rule ever known. Unlike most other systems, however, it is pluralistic and dynamic, relying on information flow in that ongoing flux – which is both why this book is possible (at many levels of meaning) and, why the futurity of the young of whom we write is unknowable. It could be one in which texts like Townsend's become unneeded. Or it could get a great deal worse. Our message (if message we have) is that this system is no more – and no less – than a human product. It has neither reality nor force nor momentum of its own, outside of our discursive engagement in it. We have made and make it; only we can unmake and change it.

Bibliography

Adams, P., Berg, L., Berger, N., Duanne, M., Neill, A.S. and Ollendorff, R. (1972), *Children's Rights* (Granada: London).
Adorno, T. (1982), *Against Epistemology* (Blackwell: Oxford).
Alderson, P. (in press; 1993), *Children's Consent to Surgery* (Open University: Milton Keynes).
Allesbrook, A. and Swift, A. (1989), *Broken Promise: The world of endangered children* (Headway: London).
Ariés, P. (trans. Robert Baldick) (1973), *Centuries of Childhood* (Penguin: Harmondsworth).
Armistead, N. (ed.) (1974), *Reconstructing Social Psychology* (Penguin: Harmondsworth).
Attwood M. (1990), *Cat's Eye* (Virago: London).
Bamford, F. and Roberts, R. (1989), 'Child sexual abuse: 2', *British Medical Journal*, **299**, 5 August, pp. 377–82.
Banks, M., Bates, I., Breakwell, G., Bynner, J., Emler, N., Jamieson, L. and Roberts, K. (1992), *Careers and Identities* (Open University Press: Milton Keynes).
Bannister, D. (1966), 'Psychology as an exercise in paradox', *Bulletin of the British Psychological Society*, **19**, 21–6.
Barrie, J.M. (1928), 'Peter Pan', in Barrie J.M., *The Plays of J.M. Barrie* (Hodder & Stoughton: London) (original stage production 1904).
Barrow, R. (1978), *Radical Education* (Martin Robertson: Oxford).
Barthes, R. (1977), *Image-Music-Text* (Fontana/Collins: London).
Baudrillard, J. (1983), *In the Shadow of Silent Majorities* (Semiotexte: New York).
The Beryl Curt Fan Club (BCFC) (1991), *Textuality and Tectonics*, unpublished working paper.
Bean, P. and Melville, J. (1989), *Lost Children of the Empire: The untold story of Britain's child migrants* (Unwin Hyman: London).
Bell, S. (1988), *When Salem Came to the Boro* (Pan: London).
Bellah, R., Madsen, R., Sullivan, W.M., Swidler, A. and Tipton, S.M. (1988), *Habits of the Heart* (Hutchinson: London).
Bentovim, A. and Boston, P. (1988), 'Sexual abuse – basic issues – characteristics of children and families' in Bentovim *et al.*
Bentovim, A., Elton, A., Hildebrand, J., Tranter, M. and Vizard, E. (eds) (1988), *Child Sexual Abuse within the Family* (Wright: London).

Berger, B. and Berger, P.L. (1984), *The War Over the Family* (Pelican: Harmondsworth).
Berger, P.L. (1977), *Facing Up to Modernity* (Basic Books: New York).
Berger, P.L., and Luckmann, T. (1967) *The Social Construction of Reality* (Penguin: Harmondsworth).
Berne, E. (1967) *Games People Play* (Grove Press: New York).
Besag, V.E. (1989), *Bullies and Victims in Schools* (Open University Press: Milton Keynes).
Bettelheim, B. (1971), *The Children of the Dream* (Paladin: St Albans).
Billig, M., Condor, S., Edwards, D., Gane, M., Middleton, D. and Radley, A. (1988), *Ideological Dilemmas* (Sage: London).
Bloch, I. (1967), *Odoratus Sexualis* (Brandon House: North Hollywood).
Blos, P. (1970), *The Young Adolescent* (Free Press: New York).
Boas, G. (1966), *The Cult of Childhood* (Warburg Institute: London).
Boswell, J. (1991), *The Kindness of Strangers* (Penguin: London). (1st edn 1988).
Bowie, T. and Christenson, C. (eds) (1970), *Studies in Erotic Art* (Basic Books: New York).
Boyden, J. (1990) 'Childhood and the policy makers: A comparative perspective on the globalization of childhood' in James, A. and Prout, A. (eds) *Constructing and Reconstructing Childhood: Contemporary issues in the sociological study of childhood* (Falmer: London).
Boyne R. and Rattansi A. (eds), (1990), *Postmodernism and Society* (Macmillan: Basingstoke).
Bradley, B.S. (1989), *Visions of Infancy* (Polity: Cambridge).
Brake, M. (1985), *Comparative Youth Culture* (Routledge & Kegan Paul: London).
Brandstädter, J. (1990), 'Development as a personal and cultural construction' in Semin, G.R. and Gergen, K.J., *Everyday Understanding: Social and scientific implications* (Sage: London).
Brannigan, A. (1981), *The Social Basis of Scientific Discoveries* (Cambridge University Press: Cambridge).
Brecher, E.M. (1970), *The Sex Researchers* (Deutsch: London).
Brody, H. (1987), *Stories of Sickness* (Yale University Press: New Haven).
Bronfenbrenner, U. (1971), *Two Worlds of Childhood: USA and USSR* (George Allen and Unwin: London).
Brongersma, E. (1978), 'From a morality of oppression to creative freedom', *Civis Mundi*, **17**, pp. 108–15.
Brooke, B., Burgess, T., Dally, A., Hughes, G.F., Lawrence, M., Miall, S., Walker, K. and Wallbank, P., (undated c. 1965), *How Parents Can Help* (Caxton).
Brooks, P. (ed.) (1972),*The Child's Part* (Beacon Press: Boston).
Broughton, J.M. (ed.) (1987), *Critical Theories of Psychological Development* (Plenum: New York).
Brown, S.R. (1980), *Political Subjectivity* (Yale University Press: New Haven, Conn.).
Bryant, P. (1977), 'Logical inferences and development' in Geber, B.A. (ed.) *Piaget and Knowing: Studies in genetic epistemology* (Routledge & Kegan Paul: London).
Buck-Morss, S. (1907), 'Piaget, Adorno and dialectical operations' in Broughton, J.M. (ed.) *Critical Theories in Psychological Development* (Plenum: New York).
Burroughs, E.R. (1970 [1917]), *Tarzan of the Apes* (Hutchinson: London).
Burt, C. (1925), *The Young Delinquent* (University of London Press: London).

Burt, C. (1937), *The Subnormal Mind* (2nd edn.) (Oxford University Press: London).

Busfield, J. and Paddon, P. (1977), *Thinking About Children: Sociology & fertility in post-war England* (Cambridge University Press: Cambridge).

Buss, A.R. (1979), *A Dialectical Psychology* (Wiley: New York).

Butler-Sloss, E. (1988), *The Report of the Inquiry into Child Abuse in Cleveland 1987* (HMSO: London).

Butt, J. and Clarke, I.F. (eds) (1973), *The Victorians and Social Protest* (David & Charles: Newton Abbot).

Cairns, E. (1989), 'Society as child abuse: Northern Ireland' in Stainton Rogers, W., Hevey, D. and Ash, E.(eds) *Child Abuse and Neglect: Facing the challenge* (Batsford: London).

Campbell, B. (1988), *Unofficial Secrets* (Virago: London).

Carroll, L. (1982), *The Complete Illustrated Works of Lewis Carroll* (Chancellor Press: London) (original compilation publ. 1865–98).

Carter, P., Jeffs, T. and Smith, M.K. (eds) (1991), *Social Work and Social Welfare Yearbook, 3* (Open University Press: Buckingham).

Casey, J. (1989), *The History of the Family* (Blackwell: Oxford).

CCETSW (Central Council for Education and Training in Social Work) (1978), *Good Enough Parenting* (CCETSW: London).

Chandos, J. (1985), *Boys Together* (Oxford University Press: Oxford).

Chomsky, N. (1967), 'Review of Skinner's verbal behavior' in Jakobovits, L.A. and Morn, M.S. (eds) *Readings in the Philosophy of Language* (Prentice-Hall: Englewood Cliffs, NJ).

Christie, R. and Geis, F. (1970), *Studies in Machiavellianism* (Academic Press: New York).

Clark, K. (1969), *Civilisation* (BBC/John Murray: London).

Cohen, H. (1980), *Equal Rights for Children* (Littlefield Adams: Totowa, NJ).

Cole, L. and Hall, I.N. (1970), *Psychology of Adolescence* (7th edn) (Holt, Rinehart and Winston: London).

Coles, R. (1979), 'Foreword' in Schorsch, A. *Images of Childhood: An illustrated social history* (Mayflower: New York).

Cooter, R. (ed.) (1992), *In the Name of the Child: Health and welfare, 1880–1940* (Routledge: London).

Cormier, R. (1978), *The Chocolate War* (Fontana: London).

Coulter, J. (1989), *Mind in Action* (Polity: Cambridge).

Coveney, P. (1967), *The Image of Childhood* (Peregrine: Harmondsworth).

Craig, E., Erooga, M., Morrison, T. and Shearer, E.(1989), 'Making sense of sexual abuse – charting the shifting sands' in Blagg, H., Hughes, J.A., and Wattam, C. (eds) *Child Sexual Abuse: Listening, hearing and validating the experiences of children* (Longman: Harlow).

Crawford, R. (1984), 'A cultural account of "health": Control, release and the social body' in McKinlay, J.B. (ed.) *Issues in the Political Economy of Health Care* (Tavistock: London).

Cutting, M. (1988), *Children of the Siege* (St Martin's Press: New York).

Dahl, R. (1986), *Boy: Tales of Childhood* (Puffin: Harmondsworth).

Darley, J.M. and Latané, B. (1973), 'Bystander intervention in emergencies: Diffusion of responsibility,' *Journal of Personality and Social Psychology*, **27**, 100–8.

Darmon, P. (tr. P. Keegan) (1985), *Trial by Impotence: Virility and marriage in pre-revolutionary France* (Chatto & Windus: London).

Delarue, P. (1951), *Bulletin folklorique d'Ile de France,* Oct–Dec, p. 290 (q.v. Soriano, M.)

de Mause, L. (ed.) (1976), *The History of Childhood* (Souvenir: London).
de Mause, L. (1975), 'Our forebears made childhood a nightmare', *Psychology Today*, **8** (11,) pp. 85–8.
Denzin, N.K. (1977), *Childhood Socialisation* (Jossey-Bass: San Francisco).
Derrida, J. (1982), *Margins of Philosophy* (Harvester: Brighton).
Dickens, C. (1837–8), 'Oliver Twist' in Dickens, C. (ed.) *Bentley's Miscellany* (Bentley: London).
Dickens, C. (1862), *Great Expectations* (Chapman & Hall: London). (Part publ. 1860–1).
Dingwall, R. (1989), 'Labelling children as abused or neglected' in Stainton Rogers, W., Hevey, D. and Ash, E. (eds) *Child Abuse and Neglect: Facing the challenge* (Batsford: London).
Doane, M.A. (1982),'Film and the masquerade: theorising the female spectator', *Screen*, **23** (3–4), 87.
Donaldson, M. (1979), *Children's Minds* (Fontana: Glasgow).
Donzelot, J. (trans. Robert Hurley) (1979), *The Policing of Families* (Hutchinson: London).
Douglass, M. (1966), *Purity and Danger: An analysis of the concepts of pollution and taboo* (Pantheon Books: New York).
Doyle, P. (1989), *The God Squad* (Corgi: Ealing).
Drontner, K. (1991), 'Intensities of feeling: Modernity, melodrama and adolescence', *Theory, Culture and Society* **8**, 57–87.
Duffy, M. (1973), *Love Child* (Panther: St Albans).
Duffy, M. (1983), *Gor Saga* (Methuen: London).
Duffy, M. (1984), *Capital* (Methuen: London).
Dunham, J. and Jones, R. (1980), 'Understanding Adolescence' in Jones, R. and Pritchard, C. (eds) *Social Work with Adolescents* (Routledge and Kegan Paul: London).
Eco, U. (tr. Weaver, W.) (1984), *The Name of the Rose* (Picador: London).
Eekelaar, J. and Dingwall, R. (1990), *The Reform of Child Care Law: A practical guide to the Children Act 1989* (Routledge: London).
Ehrenreich, J. (ed.) (1978), *The Cultural Crisis of Modern Medicine* (Monthly Review Press: New York).
Elkind, D. (1979), *The Child and Society* (Oxford University Press: New York).
Elliot, M. (1989), 'Prevention and protection' in Stainton Rogers, W., Hevey, D. and Ash, E. (eds) *Child Abuse and Neglect: Facing the challenge* (Batsford: London).
Ellis, A. (1963), *A History of Children's Reading and Literature* (Pergamon: Oxford).
Ellison, H. (1961), *The Juvies: Life and Death of the Gutter Kids* (Ace: New York).
Elwin, V. (1947), *The Muria and their Ghotal* (Oxford University Press: Oxford).
Elwin, V. (1968), *The Kingdom of the Young* (Oxford University Press: Oxford).
Ennew, J. (1986), *The Sexual Exploitation of Children* (St Martin's: New York).
Erikson, E.H. (1963), *Childhood and Society* (2nd edn) (Norton: New York).
Eysenck, H.J. (1976),'The biology of morality' in Lickona, T. (ed.) *Moral Development and Behaviour* (Holt, Rinehart & Winston: New York).
Farrar, F.W. (1858) *Eric, or Little by Little* (Longman: London).
Faust, B. (1981), *Women, Sex and Pornography* (Penguin: Harmondsworth).
Featherstone, M. (ed.) (1988), *Theory, Culture & Society* (Sage: London). (Volume 5(2,3) of *Theory, Culture, & Society*, 'Special Issue on Postmodernism')
Ferguson, H. (1992), 'Cleveland and History: The abused child and child protection, 1880–1914, in Cooter, R. (ed.), *In the Name of the Child: Health and welfare, 1880-1950* (Routledge: London).

Feyerabend, P. (1975), *Against Method* (New Left Books: London).
Field, D. (1981),'Can preschool children really learn to conserve?' *Child Development* **52** pp. 326–34.
Finkelhor, D., Araji, S., Baron, A., Doyle Peters, S. and G.E. (1986), *A Sourcebook on Child Sexual Abuse* (Sage: Beverly Hills).
Finkelhor, D., Meyer Williams, L. and Burns, N. (1988), *Nursery Crimes: The sexual abuse of children in daycare* (Sage: Newbury Park).
Firestone, S. (1972), *The Dialectic of Sex* (Bantam: London).
Fisher, S. and Holder S. (1981), *Too Much Too Young?* (Pan: London).
Flekkøy, M.F. (1991), *A Voice for Children* (Jessica Kingsley: London).
Ford, C.S. and Beach, F.A. (1951), *Patterns of Sexual Behaviour* (Harper: New York).
Foucault, M. (1970), *The Order of Things* (Tavistock: London).
Foucault, M. (1979), *The History of Sexuality, Vol 1: An introduction* (Allen Lane: London).
Fowles, J.(1977), *The Magus* (rev. edn) (Triad/Panther: St Albans).
Fowles, J. (1982), *Mantissa* (Jonathan Cape: London).
Fowles, J. (1986), *A Maggot* (Pan: London).
Frank, A. (trans. B.M. Mooyaart-Doubleday) (1954), *The Diary of Anne Frank* (Pan: London).
Franklin, B. (ed.) (1986) *The Rights of Children* (Blackwell: Oxford).
Freeman, D. (1984), *Margaret Mead and Samoa* (Penguin: Harmondsworth).
Freeman, M.D.A. (1989),'Principles and processes of the law in child protection' in Stainton Rogers, W., Hevey, D. and Ash, E. (eds) *Child Abuse and Neglect: Facing the challenge* (Batsford: London).
Freeman, M.D.A. (1983), *The Rights and Wrongs of Children* (Frances Pinter: London).
Fromm, E. (1951), *The Forgotten Language* (Rinehart: New York).
Fuller, E. (1951), *The Right of the Child* (Gollancz: London).
Furstenberg, F.F., Brooks-Gunn, J. and Morgan, S.P. (1987), *Adolescent Mothers in Later Life* (Cambridge University Press: Cambridge).
Furth, H.G. (1969) *Piaget and Knowledge: Theoretical foundations* (Prentice-Hall: Englewood Cliffs, NJ).
Galton, F. (1869), *Hereditary Genius* (Macmillan: London).
Galton, F. (1883), *Inquiries into Human Faculty and its Development* (Macmillan: London).
Game, A. (1991), *Undoing the Social: Towards a deconstructive sociology* (Open University Press: Milton Keynes).
Gelman, R. (1978), 'Cognitive development', *Annual Review of Psychology*, **29**, pp. 297–332.
Gergen, K.J. (1973), 'Social psychology as history', *Journal of Personality and Social Psychology*, **26** (1), pp. 309-20.
Gergen, K.J. (1982), *Towards Transformation in Social Knowledge* (Springer-Verlag: New York).
Gergen, K.J. (1989), 'Warranting voice and the elaboration of the self' in Shotter, J. and Gergen, K.J. (eds) *Texts of Identity* (Sage: London).
Gergen, K.J. and Gergen, M.M. (1986), 'Narrative form and the construction of psychological science' in Sarbin, T.R., *Narrative Psychology: The storied nature of human conduct* (Praegar: New York).
Gergen, K.J., Gloger-Tippelt, G. and Berkowitz, P. (1990), 'The cultural construction of the developing child' in Semin, G.R. and Gergen, K.J. (eds) *Everyday Understanding: Social and scientific implications* (Sage: London).

Gernsheim, H. (1980), 'Introduction' in Ricci, F.M., *Lewis Carroll, Victorian Photographer* (Thames and Hudson: London).
Gibbens, J. (1954), *The Care of Children from One to Five* (5th edn) (Churchill: London).
Giddens, A. (1987), *Social Theory and Modern Sociology* (Polity: Cambridge).
Gillis, J.R. (1975), 'The evolution of juvenile delinquency in England 1890–1914', *Past and Present*, **67**.
Gillis, J.R. (1981), (revised edition) *Youth and History: Tradition and Change in European Age Relations 1770-present* (Academic Press: New York).
Gittins, D. (1985), *The Family in Question: Changing households and family ideologies* (Macmillan: Basingstoke).
Gladstone, D. (1991), 'Children in history' paper presented to the Libertarian Alliance Conference on "Children's Rights": London.
Gleeson, K. (1991), 'Out of our minds: The deconstruction and reconstruction of madness,' unpublished doctoral dissertation, University of Reading.
Godfrey, E. (1907), *English Children in the Olden Time* (Methuen: London).
Goffman, E. (1959), *The Presentation of Self in Everyday Life* (Doubleday: New York).
Golding, W. (1959), *Lord of the Flies* (Capricorn: New York).
Gordon, S., Scales, P. and Everly, K. (1979), *The Sexual Adolescent* (2nd edn) (Duxbury: Belmont, CA).
Gorman, T. (1991), 'Empowering children' paper presented to the Libertarian Alliance Conference on 'Children's Rights': London.
Gould, S.J. (1981), *The Mismeasure of Man* (Norton: New York).
Gramsci, A. (1971), *Prison Notebooks* (Lawrence & Wishart: London).
Griffiths, P. (1989), 'The investigation of suspected child abuse' in Stainton Rogers, W., Hevey, D. and Ash, E. (eds) *Child Abuse and Neglect: Facing the challenge* (Batsford: London).
Guthrie, R.V. (1976), *Even the Rat Was White* (Harper and Row: New York).
Habermas, J. (1971), *Toward a Rational Society* (Heinemann: London).
Haining, P. (ed.) (1975), *The Magicians* (Pan: London).
Hall, G.S. (1904), *Adolescence* (2 vols) (Appleton: New York).
Hall, G.S. (1923), *Life and Confessions of a Psychologist* (Appleton: New York).
Hardyment, C. (1983), *Dream Babies: Childcare from Locke to Spock* (Cape: London).
Harraway, D. (1991), *Simians, Cyborgs and Women* (New York: Free Association Books).
Harré, R. (1979), *Social Being* (Blackwell: Oxford).
Harré, R. (1983), *Personal Being* (Blackwell: Oxford).
Harré, R. (ed.) (1986), *The Social Construction of Emotion* (Blackwell: Oxford).
Harris, B. (1979), 'Whatever happened to Little Albert?', *American Psychologist* **43** (6) pp. 151-60.
Harris, P.L. (1989), *Children and Emotion: The development of psychological understanding* (Blackwell: Oxford).
Harris, R. and Webb, D. (1987), *Welfare, Power and Juvenile Justice* (Tavistock: London).
Harvey, D. (1989), *The Condition of Postmodernity* (Blackwell: Oxford).
Heinlein, R.A. (1967), *Farnham's Freehold* (Corgi: London).
Heinlein, R.A. (1968), *Stranger in a Strange Land* (Berkeley: New York).
Heinlein, R.A. (1969), *Podkayne of Mars* (New English Library: London).
Hendrick, H. (1990), 'Constructions and reconstructions of British childhood: An interpretative study, 1800 to the present' in James, A. and Prout, A. (eds)

Constructing and Reconstructing Childhood: Contemporary issues in the sociological study of childhood (Falmer: London).

Henriques, J., Hollway, W., Urwin, C., Venn, C. and Walkerdine, V. (1984), *Changing the Subject: Psychology, social regulation and subjectivity* (Methuen: London).

Herlihy, D. (1978), 'Medieval children' in *The Walter Prescott Webb Memorial lectures: Essays on Medieval Civilization* (Austin) see Boswell (1991).

Hersey, J. (1978), *The Child Buyer* (Panther: London).

Hevey, D. and Kenwood, D. (1989), 'The effects of child sexual abuse' in Stainton Rogers, W., Hevey, D. and Ash, E. (eds) *Child Abuse and Neglect: Facing the challenge* (Batsford: London).

Hildebrand, J. (1989) 'Group work with the mothers of sexually abused children' in Stainton Rogers, W., Hevey, D. and Ash, E.

Hill, M. and Lloyd-Jones, M. (1970), *Sex Education: The erroneous zone* (National Secular Society: London).

Hoffman, L.W. and Hoffman M. (1973), 'The value of children to parents' in Fawcett, J.T. (ed.) *Psychological Perspectives on Population* (Basic Books: New York).

Hollows, A. and Armstrong, H. (eds) (1991), *Children and Young People as Abusers: An agenda for action* (National Children's Bureau: London).

Hollway, W. (1989), *Subjectivity and Method: Gender, meaning and science* (Sage: London).

Holt, J. (1975), *(Escape from Childhood: The needs and rights of children* (Penguin: Harmondsworth).

Houlbrooke, R.A. (1984), *The English Family 1450–1700* (Longman: London).

Howitt, D. (1991), *Concerning Psychology* (Open University Press: Milton Keynes).

Hoyles, J.A. (1952), *The Treatment of the Young Delinquent* (Epworth: London).

Hoyles, M. (ed.) (1979), *Changing Childhood* (Writers and Readers: London).

Hoyles, M. (1988), *The Politics of Childhood* (Journeyman: London).

Hughes, M.V. (1977), *A London Child of the 1870s* (Oxford University Press: Oxford). (orig. pub. 1934).

Hughes, T. (1856), *Tom Brown's School Days* (Macmillan: London).

Hulme, K. (1985), *The Bone People* (Hodder & Stoughton: New Zealand).

Humphries, S. (1981), *Hooligans or Rebels?* (Blackwell: Oxford).

Humphries, S., Mack, J. and Perks, R. (1988), *A Century of Childhood* (Sidgwick and Jackson: London).

Hunecke, V. (1985), 'Les enfants trouvés: contexte européen en cas Milanais (XVIIIe-XIXe siècles) *Revue d'Histoire moderne et contemporaine* 32, 3-29.

Huxley, A. (1932), *Brave New World* (Harper & Row: New York).

Ibañez, T. (1991), 'Social psychology and the rhetoric of truth', *Theory and Psychology* 1(2), pp.187-201.

Illich, I.D. (1973), *Deschooling Society* (Penguin: Harmondsworth).

Ingleby, D. (1984), 'Mental health and social order' in Scull, A. and Cohen, S. (eds) *Social Control and the Modern State* (Martin Robertson: London).

Ingleby, D. (1985),'Professionals as socialisers: the "psy complex" ', in A. Scull and S. Spitzer (eds) *Research in Law, Deviance and Social Control* 7 (Jai Press: New York).

Ingleby, D. (1987), 'Psychoanalysis and ideology' in Broughton, J.M. (ed.), *Critical Theories of Psychological Development* (Plenum: New York).

Ives, R. (1986), 'Children's Sexual Rights' in Franklin, B. (ed.) *The Rights of Children* (Blackwell: Oxford).

Jackson, S. (1982), *Childhood and Sexuality* (Blackwell: Oxford).
Jahoda, G. and Lewis, L.M. (eds) (1989), *Acquiring Culture: Cross cultural studies in child development* (Routledge: London).
James, A. and Prout, A. (eds) (1990), *Constructing and Reconstructing Childhood: Contemporary issues in the sociological study of childhood* (Falmer: London).
Jameson, F. (1984), 'Post-modernism, or the cultural logic of late capitalism', *New Left Review* **146**, pp. 79–146.
Jenkins, S. (1975), 'Child welfare as a class system' in Schorr, A.L. (ed.) *Children and Decent People* (Allen & Unwin: London).
Jenks, C. (ed.) (1982), *The Sociology of Childhood: Essential readings* (Batsford: London).
Jensen, A. (1969), 'How much can we boost IQ and scholastic performance?' *Harvard Education Review*, **39**, pp. 1-123.
Jobling, M. (1978), 'Child Abuse: The historical and social concept' in Carver, V. (ed.) *Child Abuse: A Study Text* (Open University Press: Milton Keynes).
Jones, D.N., Pickett, J., Oates, M.R. and Barbor, P.R.H. (1982), *Understanding Child Abuse* (Hodder & Stoughton: Sevenoaks, Kent).
Jordanova, L. (1989), 'Children in history: Concepts of nature and society' in Scarre, G. (ed.) *Children, Parents and Politics* (Cambridge University Press: Cambridge).
Kamin, L.J. (1974), *The Science and Politics of IQ* (Erlbaum: Potomac, Md).
Kanter, R.M. (1972), *Commitment and Community: Communes and utopias in sociological perspective* (Harvard University Press: Cambridge, Mass).
Katz, H.A., Greenberg, M.H. and Warrick, P.S. (1977), *Introductory Psychology through Science Fiction* (Chicago: Rand McNally).
Keller, M. (1986), *The Untutored Eye: Childhood in the films of Cocteau, Cornell and Brakhage* (Fairleigh Dickinson University Press: Cranbury, NJ).
Kellmer Pringle, M. (1908), *A Fairer Future for Children* (Macmillan: London).
Kempe, C.H., Silverman, F., Steele, B., Droegmueller, W. and Silver, H. (1962), 'The battered child syndrome', *Journal of the American Medical Association*, **181** pp. 17–24.
Kempe, R.S. and Kempe, C.H. (1978), *Child Abuse* (Fontana: London).
Kessen, W. (ed.) (1975), *Childhood in China* (Yale University Press: New Haven).
Kessen, W. (1990), *The Rise and Fall of Developmentalism* (Clark University Press: Worcester, MA).
Kett, J.P. (1977), *Rites of Passage: Adolescence in America 1790 to the present* (Basic Books: New York).
Kincade, K. (1973), *A Walden Two Experiment* (Morrow: New York).
King, M. (ed.) (1981), *Childhood, Welfare and Justice* (Batsford: London).
King, M. and Piper, C. (1990), *How the Law Thinks About Children* (Gower: Aldershot).
Kingsley, C. (1853), *The Water Babies* (Macmillan: London).
Kipling, R. (1899), *Stalky and Co.* (Penguin: Harmondsworth).
Kitzinger, C. (1987), *The Social Construction of Lesbianism* (Sage: London).
Kitzinger, C. (1988), *Humiliation*, paper presented to the British Psychological Society London Conference, December.
Kitzinger, C. (1989), 'Liberal humanism as an ideology of social control: The regulation of lesbian identities' in Shotter, J. and Gergen, K. (eds) *Texts of Identity* (Sage: London).
Kitzinger, J. (1989), 'Feminist self-help' in Stainton Rogers, W., Hevey, D. and Ash, E. (eds) *Child Abuse and Neglect: Facing the challenge* (Batsford: London).

Kitzinger, J. (1990),'Who are you kidding? Children, power and the struggle against sexual abuse', in James, A. and Prout, A. (eds) *Constructing and Reconstructing Childhood: Contemporary issues in the sociological study of childhood* (Falmer: London).

Knorr-Cetina, K.D. (1981), *The Manufacture of Knowledge: An essay on the constructivist and contextual nature of science* (Pergamon: Oxford).

Kohl, H. (1971), *36 Children* (Penguin: Harmondsworth).

Kohlberg, L. (1969), 'Stage and sequence: The cognitive developmental approach to socialisation' in Goslin, D.A. (ed.) *Handbook of Socialization Theory and Research* (Rand McNally: Chicago).

Kohlberg, L. (1976), 'Moral stages and moralisation: The cognitive-developmental approach' in Lickona, T. (ed.) *Moral Development and Behaviour* (Holt, Rinehart & Winston: New York).

Kopelman, L.M. and Moskop, J.C. (eds) (1989), *Children and Health Care: Moral and social issues* (Kluwer: Dordrecht).

Kuhn, T.S. (1970), *The Structure of Scientific Revolutions* (2nd ed) (University of Chicago Press: Chicago).

Lacan, J. (1977), (trans. Sheridan, A.) *Ecrits* (orig. pub. 1966) (Tavistock: London).

Lefanu, S. (1988), *In the Chinks of the World Machine: Feminism and science fiction* (London: Women's Press).

Le Guin, U. (1975), *The Dispossessed* (Panther: St Albans).

Lessing, D. (1976), *The Memoirs of a Survivor* (Picador: London).

Lewis, C. (1986), *Becoming a Father* (Open University Press: Milton Keynes).

Lewis, J. (1980), *The Politics of Motherhood* (Croom Helm: London).

Lifton, B. J. (1988), *The King of the Children* (Pan: London).

Lilar, S. (Tr. Griffin, J.) (1967), *Aspects of Love in Western Society* (Panther: London).

Lively, W.J. and Bromley D.B. (1973), *Person Perception in Childhood and Adolescence* (Wiley: London).

Lomax, E.M.R. (with Kagan, J. and Rosenkrantz, B.G.) (1978), *Science and Patterns of Child Care* (Freeman: San Francisco).

Lowell, J. (1929), *Child of the Deep* (Heinemann: London).

Lynch J. (1990), *The Secret Diary of Laura Palmer* (Penguin: London).

Lyotard, J.-F. (1984), *The Postmodern Condition* (Manchester University Press: Manchester).

Mackenzie, R.F. (1967), *The Sins of the Children* (Collins: London).

Magid, K. and McKelvey, C.A. (1988), *High Risk: Children without a conscience* (Bantam: Toronto).

Manton, J. (1976), *Reformatory Schools: Mary Carpenter and the children of the streets* (Heinemann: London).

Martin, E. (1989), *The Woman in the Body: A cultural analysis of reproduction* (Open University Press: Milton Keynes).

Massey, V. (1978), *One Child's War* (Ariel: London).

Masson, J. (1990a) *Against Therapy* (Fontana/Collins: London).

Masson, J. (1990b), *The Children Act 1989: Text and commentary* (Sweet and Maxwell: London).

Mays, J.B. (1969), *The Young Pretenders* (Sphere: London).

McCann, P. (1977), *Popular Education and Socialisation in the Nineteeth Century* (Methuen: London).

McKenna, W. and Kessler, S. (1985), 'Asking taboo questions and doing taboo deeds' in Gergen, K.J. and Davis K.E. (eds) *The Social Construction of the Person* (Springer-Verlag: New York).

McKeon, M. (1988), *The Origins of the English Novel* (Radius: London).
Mead, M. and Wolfenstein, M. (eds) (1963), *Childhood in Contemporary Cultures* (University of Chicago Press: Chicago).
Mead, M. (1977), *Coming of Age in Samoa* (Penguin: Harmondsworth). (Orig. pub. 1928.)
Mead, M. (1972), *Culture and Commitment* (Panther: St Albans).
Meyer, J.W. (1986), 'Myths of socialization and of personality' in Heller, T.C. *et al., Reconstructing Individualism* (Stanford University Press: Stanford).
Miller, A. (trans. Hannum, H. and Hannum, H.) (1985), *Thou Shalt Not Be Aware: Society's betrayal of the child* (Pluto: London).
Miller, H. (1961), *The Crucible* (Cresset: London).
Monroe, P. (1906), *A Text-book in the History of Education* (Macmillan: London).
Moorehead, C. (ed.) (1989), *Betrayal: Child exploitation in today's world* (Barrie and Jenkins: London).
Morison, S.E. (1972), *The Oxford History of the American People: Vol. 1 Prehistory to 1789* (Mentor: New York).
Morris, D. (1991), 'Looking at the world through a baby's eyes' *The Sunday Times Magazine*, 18–28, 10 November.
Morss, J. and Linzey, T. (eds) (1991), *Growing Up* (Longman Paul: New Zealand).
Morss, J.R. (1990), *The Biologising of Childhood* (Lawrence Erlbaum: Hove).
Moscovici, S. (1984), 'The phenomenon of social representations' in Farr, R.M. and Moscovici, S. (eds) *Social Representations* (Cambridge University Press: Cambridge).
Mount, F. (1982), *The Subversive Family: An alternative history of love and marriage* (Unwin: London).
Mrazek, P. and Kempe, H. (eds) (1981), *Sexually Abused Children and their Families* (Pergamon: Oxford).
Mulkay, M. (1989), 'Textual fragments on science, social science and literature' in Rousseau, G. and Privateer, P. (eds.), *Literature and Science: New Essays in Interdisciplinary Theories and Practices* (Cambridge University Press: Cambridge).
Mulkay, M. (1991), *Sociology of Science* (Open University Press: Milton Keynes).
Mullan, B. (1987), *Are Mothers Really Necessary?* (Boxtree: London).
Muller, P. (trans. Masson, A.) (1969), *The Tasks of Childhood* (Weidenfeld & Nicolson: London).
Murphy, G. (1929), *An Historical Introduction to Modern Psychology* (Kegan Paul: London).
Musgrave, P.W. (1987), *Socialising Contexts: The subject in society* (Allen & Unwin: Sydney).
Musgrove, F. (1964), *Youth and the Social Order* (Routledge & Kegan Paul: New York).
Nabokov, V. (1968), *Speak Memory: An autobiography revisited* (Pyramid: New York).
Nabokov, V. (1980), *Lolita* (Penguin: Harmondsworth).
Nash, J. (1970), *Developmental Psychology: A psychobiological approach* (Prentice Hall: Englewood-Cliffs, NJ).
Neville, R. (1971), *Playpower* (Paladin: London).
Newell, P. (1989), *Children are People Too* (Bedford Square: London).
O'Neil, O. and Ruddick, W. (eds) (1979), *Having Children: Philosophical and legal reflections on parenthood* (Oxford University Press: New York).

Ogbu, J.U. (1981), 'Origins of human competence: A cultural-ethological perspective', *Child Development*, **52**, pp. 413–29.

Opie, I. and Opie, P. (1959), *The Lore and Language of Schoolchildren* (Oxford University Press: London).

Orwell, G. (1989), *1984* (Penguin: London). (Orig. pub. 1949).

Packard, V. (1957), *The Hidden Persuaders* (McKay: New York).

Panchin, A. (1970), *Rite of Passage* (Sphere: London).

Parker, I. (1989), *The Crisis in Modern Social Psychology – and How to End It* (Routledge: London).

Parker, I. and Shotter, J. (eds) (1990), *Deconstructing Social Psychology* (Routledge: London).

Parton, N. (1991), *Governing the Family: Child care, child protection and the state* (Macmillan: Basingstoke).

Patrick, J. (1973), *A Glasgow Gang Observed* (Eyre Methuen: London).

Pearsall, R. (1971), *The Worm in the Bud: The world of Victorian sexuality* (Penguin: Harmondsworth).

Pekow, C. (1990), 'Bruno Bettelheim: changes of crimes and punishments' *The Guardian*, 31 August.

Perrault, C. (attrib.) (1969), *Contes du temps passée* 1697. Quoted by Ariès, P. (trans. M. Brooks) 'At the point of origin' in Brooks, P. (ed.) *The Child's Part* (Beacon Press: Boston).

Petronius, G. (trans. Lindsay, J.) (1960), *The Satyricon* (Paul Elek: London).

Peukert, D.J.K. (trans. R. Deveson) (1989), *Inside Nazi Germany: Conformity, opposition and racism in everyday life* (Penguin: London).

Phillips, J.L. (1975), *The Origins of Intellect: Piaget's theory* (second edition) (Freeman: San Francisco).

Phillips, R. (ed.) (1974), *Aspects of Alice* (Penguin: Harmondsworth).

Piaget, J. (trans. Peircy, M. and Berlyne, D.E.) (1950), *The Psychology of Intelligence* (Routledge & Kegan Paul: London).

Pickard, P.M. (1961), *I Could a Tale Unfold* (Tavistock: London).

Pickard, P.M. (1965), *The Activity of Children* (Longman: London).

Piercy, M. (1979), *Woman on the Edge of Time* (Women's Press: London).

Pinchbeck, I. and Hewitt, M. (1969 & 1973), *Children in English Society* (2 vols) (Routledge: London).

Plumb, J.H.P. (1975), 'The new world of children in eighteenth-century England' *Past and Present* **67**, pp. 64-93.

Pollock, L.A. (1983), *Forgotten Children: Parent-child relations from 1500 to 1900* (Cambridge University Press: Cambridge).

Postman, N. and Weingartner, C. (1971), *Teaching as a Subversive Activity* (Penguin: Harmondsworth).

Rabain, J. (1979), *L'enfant du lignage. Du sevrage a la classe d'age* (Payot: Paris).

Ransome, A. (1930), *Swallows and Amazons* (Jonathan Cape: London).

Rapaport, R., Rapaport, R.N. and Strelitz, Z. (1978), *Fathers, Mothers and Others* (Routledge & Kegan Paul: London).

Reich, W. (1983), *Children of the Future* (Farrar, Straus, Giroux: New York).

Reich, W. (1942), *The Function of the Orgasm* (revised version of 1927 original) (Orgone Institute Press: New York).

Reigal, K. (1979), *Foundations of a Dialectical Psychology* (Academic Press: New York).

Reimer, E. (1971), *School is Dead* (Penguin: Harmondsworth).

Rhinehart, L. (1972), *The Dice Man* (Panther: St Albans).

Rhodes, E.H. (1979), *An Army of Children* (Granada, St Albans).

Richards, M. and Light P. (eds) (1986), *Children of Social Worlds* (Polity: Cambridge).

Richards, M. (1986), 'Introduction' in Richards, M. and Light P. (eds) *Children of Social Worlds* (Polity: Cambridge).

Richards, M.P.M. (ed.) (1974), *The Integration of a Child into a Social World* (Cambridge University Press: Cambridge).

Richardson, S. and Bacon, H. (1991), 'A framework of belief' in Richardson, S. and Bacon, H. (eds) *Child Sexual Abuse: Whose problem?* (Venture Press: Birmingham).

Richmond, M.E. and Hall, F.S. (1925), *Child Marriages* (Russell Sage Foundation: New York).

Riley, D. (1983), *War in the Nursery* (Virago: London).

Robert, M. (1969), 'The Grimm Brothers' in Brooks, P. (ed.) *The Child's Part* (Beacon: Boston).

Roche, J. (1989), 'Children's rights and the welfare of the child' in Stainton Rogers, W., Hevey, D. and Ash, E. (eds) *Child Abuse and Neglect: Facing the challenge* (Batsford: London).

Rogers, R. and Rogers, W. (1978), *Men and Women* (Nelson: Sunbury-on-Thames).

Rogers, R.S. [= Stainton Rogers, R.] (1969), *A Consolidated Report on the 'Draw-a-Classroom Test': A study of the drawing behaviour of children in Toronto public schools.* (Toronto Board of Education: Toronto).

Rogers, R.S. (ed.) (1974a), *Sex Education: Rationale and reaction* (Cambridge University Press: Cambridge).

Rogers, R.S. (1974b), 'A normative approach to attitudes and cognitive consistency', unpublished doctoral dissertation, University of London.

Rorty, A.O. (1987), 'Persons as Rhetorical Categories', *Social Research* 54(1), pp. 55-72.

Rorty, R. (1986), 'Freud and moral reflection' in Smith, J.H. and Harrigan, W. (eds) *Pragmatism's Freud: The moral disposition of psychoanalysis* (Johns Hopkins University Press, Baltimore).

Rorty, R. (1989), *Contingency, irony and solidarity* (Cambridge University Press: Cambridge).

Rose, J. (1984), *The Case of Peter Pan: The impossibility of children's fiction* (Macmillan: London).

Rose, J. (1987), *For the Sake of the Children* (Hodder & Stoughton: London).

Rose, N. (1985), *The Psychological Complex* (Routledge: London).

Rose, N. (1990), *Governing the Soul: The shaping of the private self* (Routledge: London).

Rose, S., Lewontin, R.C. and Kamin, L.J. (1984), *Not in our Genes: Biology, ideology and human nature* (Penguin: Harmondsworth).

Rosen, R.D. (1978), *Psychobabble: Fast talk and quick cure in the era of feeling* (Wildwood House: London).

Rosenthal, R. and Jacobson, L. (1968), *Pygmalion in the Classroom* (Holt, Rinehart & Winston: New York).

Rousseau J.J. (1955), *Emile* (trans. B. Foxley) (Dutton: New York). (1st edn 1762).

Rustin, M. and Rustin, M. (1987), *Narratives of Love and Loss: Studies in modern children's fiction* (Verso: London).

Sants J. (ed.) (1980), *Developmental Psychology and Society* (Macmillan: London).

Saraga, E. and Macleod, M. (1991), 'A feminist reading of recent literature on child sexual abuse' in Carter, P., Jeffs, T. and Smith, M.K. (eds), *Social Work and Social Welfare Yearbook, 3* (Open University Press: Buckingham).

Sarbin, T. (ed.) (1986), *Narrative Psychology: The storied nature of human conduct* (Praeger: New York).
Saussure, F. de (1974), *Course in General Linguistics* (Fontana: London).
Scarre, G. (ed.) (1989), *Children, Parents and Politics* (Cambridge University Press: Cambridge).
Schechter, M.D. and Roberge, L. (1976), 'Sexual exploitation' in Helfler, R.E. and Kempe, C.H. (eds) *Child Abuse and Neglect: The family and the community* (Ballinger: Cambridge, Mass.).
Scheper-Hughes, N. (1984), 'Infant mortality and infant care: cultural and economic constraints on nuturing in northeast Brazil', *Social Science and Medicine* **19** (5), pp. 535–46.
Scheper-Hughes, N. (1987), *Child Survival: Anthropological perspectives on the treatment of children* (D. Reidel: Dordrecht).
Schiebe, K. (1986), 'Self-narratives and adventures' in Sarbin, T. (ed.) *Narrative Psychology: The storied nature of human conduct* (Praeger: New York).
Schorr, A.L. (ed.) (1975), *Children and Decent People* (Allen & Unwin: London).
Schorsch, A. (1979), *Images of Childhood: An illustrated social history* (Mayflower: New York).
Scott, J.P. (1968), *Early Experience and the Organisation of Behavior* (Brooks/Cole: Belmont, California).
Searle, C. (1975), *Classrooms of Resistance* (Writers and Readers: London).
Sedgwick, P. (1982), *Psychopolitics* (Pluto: London).
Sellar, W.C. and Yeatman, R.J. (1960), *1066, And All That* (Penguin: Harmondsworth). (Orig. 1930.)
Sereny, G. (1986), *The Hidden Children* (Pan: London).
Shaffer, D.R. (1985), *Developmental Psychology: Theory, research and applications* (Brooks/Cole: Monterey).
Shahar, S. (1990), *Childhood in the Middle Ages* (Routledge: London).
Sharah, M. (1984), *Fury on Earth: A biography of Wilhelm Reich* (Hutchinson: London).
Shorter, E. (1976), *The Making of the Modern Family* (Collins: London).
Shotter, J. (1982), 'Models of childhood in British developmental psychology', paper given at the BPS Developmental Psychology Conference, Durham.
Shotter, J. (1984), *Social Accountability and Selfhood* (Blackwell: Oxford).
Shotter, J. and Gergen, K.J. (eds) (1889), *Texts of Identity* (Sage: London).
Shusterman, R. (1988), 'Postmodern aestheticism: A new moral philosophy?' in Featherstone, M. (ed.) *Theory, Culture and Society* (volume 5 (2,3) 'Special Issue on Postmodernism') (Sage: London).
Skinner, B.F. (1971), *Beyond Freedom and Dignity* (Knopf: New York).
Skinner, B.F. (1979), *The Shaping of a Behaviorist* (Knopf: New York).
Skinner, B.F. (1948), *Walden Two* (Macmillan: New York).
Smith, P. and Blake, B. (1965), *Portrait of a Young Girl* (Hutchinson: London).
Smoller, J.W. (1985), 'The etiology and treatment of childhood', *Journal of Polymorphous Perversity* [sic] (Wry-Bred Press: New York).
Sommer, B.B. (1978), *Puberty and Adolescence* (Oxford University Press: New York).
Soriano, M. (1969), 'From tales of warning to formulettes' in Brooks, P. (ed.) *The Child's Part* (Beacon Press: Boston).
Spencer, J.R. and Flin, R. (1990), *The Evidence of Children: The law and the psychology* (Blackstone: London).
Spindler, G. and Spindler, L. (1989), 'There are no dropouts among the Arunta and Hutterites' in Trueba, H.T., Spindler, G. and Spindler, L. (eds), *What Do Anthropologists Have to Say about Dropouts?* (Falmer: New York).

Spock, B. (1963), *Baby and Child Care* (Pocket Books of Canada: Montreal).
Staffordshire County Council (1991), *The Pindown Experience and the Protection of Children: the report of the Staffordshire child care inquiry.*
Stainton Rogers, R. (1989), 'The social construction of childhood' in Stainton Rogers, W., Hevey, D. and Ash, E. (eds) *Child Abuse and Neglect: Facing the challenge* (Batsford: London).
Stainton Rogers, R. (1991), 'Now you see it, now you don't' in Elliot, M. (ed.) *Bullying: A practical guide to coping for schools* (Longman: Harlow).
Stainton Rogers, R. and Stainton Rogers, W. (1986), *Human Growth and Development* (Open University/Caledonian Scheme: Milton Keynes).
Stainton Rogers, W. (1988), 'Taken into care', Unit 16 in *Social Problems and Social Welfare* (The Open University: Milton Keynes).
Stainton Rogers, W. (1991), *Explaining Health and Illness* (Harvester Wheatsheaf: Hemel Hempstead).
Stainton Rogers, W. and Stainton Rogers, R. (1989), *'Taking the child abuse debate apart'* in Stainton Rogers, W., Hevey, D. and Ash, E. (eds) *Child Abuse and Neglect: Facing the challenge* (Batsford: London).
Stainton Rogers, W., Hevey, D. and Ash, E. (eds) (1989), *Child Abuse and Neglect: Facing the challenge* (Batsford: London).
Stannard, D.E. (1980), *Shrinking History: On Freud and the Failure of Psychohistory* (Oxford University Press: New York).
Stevens, O. (1982), *Children Talking Politics: Political Learning in Childhood* (Martin Robertson: Oxford).
Strickland, L.H., Aboud, F.E. and Gergen, K.J. (eds) (1976), *Social Psychology in Transition* (Plenum: New York).
Sully, J. (1895), *Studies in Childhood* (Longmans, Green: London).
Summit, R. (1983), 'The child sexual abuse accommodation syndrome' *Child Abuse and Neglect*, **7**, pp. 177–93.
Suransky, V.P. (1982), *The Erosion of Childhood* (University of Chicago Press: Chicago).
Süskind, P. (trans. Woods J.E.) (1987), *Perfume: The Story of a Murderer* (Penguin: Harmondsworth).
Swift, G. (1984), *Waterland* (Picador: London).
Tanner, J.M. (1978), *Fetus into Man: Physical growth from conception to maturity* (Harvard University Press: Cambridge, MA).
Tanner, K. (1987), 'The life history of adoption: A social-psychological perspective'. Unpublished masters dissertation, University of Reading.
Taylor, H.F. (1980), *The IQ Game* (Harvester: Brighton).
Terman, L.M. (1916), *The Measurement of Intelligence* (Houghton Mifflin: Boston).
Terman, L.M. and Oden, M.H. (1947), *The Gifted Child Grows Up* (Stanford University Press: Stanford).
Thomas A. and Chess S. (1980), *The Dynamics of Psychological Development* (Brunner/Mazel: New York).
Thomas, E.M. (1985), *Comparing Theories of Child Development* (second edition) (Wadsworth: Belmont, CA).
Thurber, J. (1953), 'The Macbeth Murder Mystery' in Thurber, J., *The Thurber Carnival* (abridgement of 1945 text) (Penguin: Harmondsworth).
Tomalin, C. (ed.) (1981), *Parents and Children* (Oxford University Press: Oxford).
Townsend, P. (1980), *The Smallest Pawns in the Game* (Granada: London).
Townsend, S. (1983), *The Secret Diary of Adrian Mole Aged 13¾* (Methuen: London).

Trail, H.D. and Mann J.S. (1904), *Social England* (6 vols) (illustrated edition) (Cassell: London).

Trevarthen, C. (1989), 'Universal co-operative motives: How infants begin to know the language and culture of their parents' in Jahoda, G. and Lewis, L.M. (eds) *Acquiring Culture: Cross Cultural Studies in Child Development* (Routledge: London).

Trueba, H.T., Spindle, G. and Spindle, L. (eds) (1989), *What Do Anthropologists Have to Say about Dropouts?* (Falmer: New York).

Turing, A. (1950), 'Computing Machinery and Intelligence' *Mind*, LIX, p. 236.

Turnbull, C.M. (1976), *The Forest People* (Picador: London).

Turner, J. (1989), *Home is Where the Hurt Is* (Thorsons: Wellingborough).

Twain, M. (1959 [1884]) *The Adventures of Huckleberry Finn* (Signet: New York).

Twain, M. (1975 [1876]), *The Adventures of Tom Sawyer* (Purnell: London).

Twain, M. (1983), *The Prince and the Pauper* (Penguin: Harmondsworth).

Vattimo, G. (1988), (trans. J.R. Snyder) *The End of Modernity* (Polity: Cambridge).

Vidal, F. (1987), 'Jean Piaget and the liberal protestant tradition' in Ash, M.G. and Woodward, W.R. *Psychology in Twentieth-Century Thought and Society* (Cambridge University Press: Cambridge).

Vittachi, A. (1989), *Stolen Childhood* (Polity: Cambridge).

Vizard, E. (1985), 'The historical and cultural context of child abuse' in Maher, P. (ed.) *Child Abuse: The Educational Perspective* (Blackwell: Oxford).

Vizard, E. and Tranter, M. (1988), '4: Recognition and Assessment of Child Sexual Abuse; 5: Helping Young Children to Describe Experiences of Sexual Abuse – General Issues; 6: Ditto – A Guide to Practice' in Bentovim, A. *et al.*, (eds) *Child Sexual Abuse within the Family* (Wright: London).

Wagner, D. A. and Stevenson, H.W. (eds) (1982), *Cultural Perspectives on Child Development* (Freeman: San Francisco).

Walkerdine, V. (1984), 'Developmental psychology and the child-centred pedagogy: the insertion of Piaget into early education.' in Henriques, J., Hollway, W., Urwin, C., Venn, C. and Walkerdine, V., *Changing the Subject: Psychology, Social Regulation and Subjectivity* (Methuen, London).

Walkerdine, V. (1986a), 'Post-structuralist theory and everyday social practices: The family and the school.' in Wilkinson, S. (ed.) *Feminist Social Psychology: Developing theory and practice* (Open University Press, Milton Keynes).

Walkerdine, V. (1986b), 'Video Replay: families, films and fantasies' in Burgin, V., Donald, J. and Kaplin, C. (eds) *Formations of Fantasy* (Methuen: London).

Walkerdine, V. (1987), 'No laughing matter: Girl's comics and the preparation for adolescent sexuality' in Broughton J.M. (ed.) *Critical Theories of Psychological Development* (Plenum: New York).

Walkerdine, V. (1990), *Schoolgirl Fictions* (Verso, London).

Wall, W.D. (1948), *The Adolescent Child* (Methuen: London).

Waller, W. (1936), 'Social problems and the mores' *American Sociological Review*, **1**, pp. 922-33.

Walling, W.H. (ed.) (1909), *Sexology* (Puritan: Philadelphia, PA).

Walvin, J. (1982), *A Child's World* (Penguin: Harmondsworth).

Ward, T. and Ward, C. (1991), *Images of Childhood in Old Postcards* (Alan Sutton: Stroud).

Warner, M. (1989), *Into the Dangerous World* (Chatto & Windus: London).

Wason, P. (1977), 'The theory of formal operations – A critique' in Geber, B.A. (ed.) *Piaget and Knowing: Studies in Genetic Epistomology* (Routledge & Kegan Paul: London).

Watson, G. (1980), 'An investigation into the sex education of mildly educationally subnormal children', unpublished doctoral dissertation, University of Reading.

Watson, G. (1989), 'The abuse of disabled children and young people' in Stainton Rogers, W., Hevey, D. and Ash, E. (eds) *Child Abuse and Neglect: Facing the challenge* (Batsford: London).

Watson, J.B. (1925), *Behaviorism* (Norton: New York).

Wells, J. (1982), *A Herstory of Prostitution in Western Europe* (Shameless Hussy: Berkeley).

Wells, H.G. (1927), 'The Time Machine' in Wells, H.G., *The Short Stories of H.G. Wells* (Ernest Benn: London).

West, D.J. (1967), *The Young Offender* (Penguin: Harmondsworth).

Whorton, J. (1982), *Crusaders for Fitness: The History of American Health Reformers* (Princeton University Press: Princeton, NJ).

Wicks, B. (1988), *No Time To Wave Goodbye* (Bloomsbury: London).

Williams, F. (in press 1992), 'Somewhere over the rainbow: universality and diversity in social policy' in Manning, N. and Page, R. (eds) *Social Policy Review* (Social Policy Association).

Williams, R. (1965), *The Long Revolution* (Pelican: Harmondsworth).

Williamson, J. (1987), *Consuming Passions* (Marion Boyar: London).

Willy, A. [sic], Vander, L., Fisher, O. and others (Trans. and Mod. Haire, N.) *The Encyclopaedia of Sex Practice* (Encyclopaedia Press: London). (Undated: orig. 1933.)

Wilson, E.O. (1975), *Sociobiology: The New Synthesis* (Harvard University Press: Cambridge, Mass.).

Winn, M. (1984), *Children without Childhood* (Penguin: Harmondsworth).

Winterson, J. (1987), *Oranges Are Not the Only Fruit* (Pandora: London)

Wise, A. (1972), *The Naughty Girls* (W.H. Allen: London).

Wittgenstein, L. (1953), *Philosophical Investigations* (Blackwell: Oxford).

Woodhead, M. (1990),'Psychology and the cultural construction of children's needs' in James, A. and Prout, A. (eds) *Constructing and Reconstructing Childhood* (Falmer: London).

Woolgar, S. (ed.) (1988a), *Knowledge and Reflexivity: New Frontiers in the Sociology of Knowledge* (Sage: London).

Woolgar, S. (1988b), *Science: The Very Idea* (Ellis Horwood: Chichester).

Wuthnow, R., Hunter, J.D., Bergesen, A., and Kurzwell, E. (1984), *Cultural Analysis* (Routledge & Kegan Paul: Boston, Mass).

Wyatt, G. and Higgs, M. (1991), 'The medical diagnosis of child sexual abuse: The paediatrician's dilemma' in Richardson, S. and Bacon, H. (eds) *Child Sexual Abuse: Whose Problem?* (Venture Press: Birmingham).

Wyre, R. (1989), 'Gracewell Clinic' in Stainton Rogers, W., Hevey, D. and Ash, E. (eds) *Child Abuse and Neglect: Facing the challenge* (Batsford: London).

Yablonsky, L. and Haskell, M. (1988), *Juvenile Delinquency* (fourth edition) (Harper and Row: Cambridge, PA).

Young, A.F. and Ashton E.T. (1956), *British Social Work in the Nineteenth Century* (Routledge and Kegan Paul: London).

Index

abandonment, 65, 67, 68
abortion, 66, 68, 111, 190
abuse, *see* child abuse
accounting, 60, 64, 76, 86
  language, 90
accounts, 15, 16, 18
  children's oral, 35
  of child development, 87
Adam and Eve, 27
adolescence, 88, 147–53
  as alien, 151
  as savage, 149
  as storm and strife, 149
  gender and, 148
  growth spurt, 43
adoption, 68, 112, 113
adult–child sexual contact
  assault vs abuse, 179
  varying constructions,
    164–6
adultery, 67
adults
  adultism, 95
'age of consent', 4, 143, 161
  homosexual, 143
  varying, 109, 143
'age of majority', 142
affection (parent–child), 65–6, *see also*
  bonding
ageism, 83
agrarian metaphors, 45, 160
AID, 2
AIDS, 112
Albert B. (little Albert), 97
alchemy, 38, 40, 106
alembic, the, 37

alembic myth, 37–42, 47, 48, 50, 51,
  101, 149, 194
  as a moral analytic, 40
Alice (Liddell), 181
America, *see* United States
American Psychiatric Association, 48
Amish, 79, 129
'anarchy', 68, 91, 128, 157–60
Andres, Abbot of, 67
Anglo-centrism, 11
animality, 27
Annares, 128, 157
anthropology, 51
apes, *see* monkeys
Aphrodite, 114
apprenticeship, 60, 61, 110
  cultural, 113
archive (cultural), 8, 19, 101, 193
Aristotelian, 27, 95
art, children's, 17, 36
Artful Dodger, 26, 154
Arunta, 129
assault, sexual, 22
authenticity, 117
author
  children as, 34
  function, 20, 31
autobiography, 19, 21
  as myth, 35
  children's, 35
  automobile, 114
baby, 3, 111
  box, 99
Bacon, H., 191
Bangkok, 6, 158
bank clerk (as ego), 91

Barnardo (Dr), 24, 37, 72
  'Act', 76
  legend challenged, 73, 74
'battered child', 75
Baudelaire, 93
BCFC (Beryl Curt Fan Club), 103
beating, 22
Beatles, the, 34
Beck Case, 195
Beckett, S., 93
Beckford, J. 75
Beggar Maid, The, 182
behavioural genetics, 44
behaviourism, 97–100
Bettelheim, B., 128
Beyond Freedom and Dignity, 100
bi-culturality, 128
binary divides, 13, 15, 25, 37, 47, 89,
    148, *see also* fact, fiction;
    naturalness, precocity; nature,
    nurture; personal, social; psyche,
    soma; ontology, epistomology;
    repression, liberation (sexual);
    subjectivity, objectivity
Binet, A., 87, 94, 100
Biographical Sketch of an Infant, A,
    87
biography, 87, *see also* autobiography:
    baby, 87
biological
  and social disciplines as immiscible,
    46
  bases of behaviour, 43
  biology, 43
  clock, 112
bio-social compounding
  as a myth, 115, 128
  as dominant discourse, 40
  deconstruction of, 46
bio-social science, 38, *see also* human
    science
bio-sociology, 106–7
birth control, 110, 111, 113, 120, 147
birth
  by natal-chine, 4
  defects, 67
  risks of, 118
Blacknall, M., 63
Blake, W., 27
Blyton, E., 20
boarding schools, 60, 81, 164

body
  deconstructed, 43, *see also*
    embodiment
  mind dualism, 43
Boer War, 115, 196
Boke of Chyldren, The, 86
bonds, parent–child, 60
Bowlby, J., 86
Boy Scouts, 149
boys, *see* children
Boys' Brigade, 149
Boy's Own Paper, The, 148
brainwashing, 174
Brave New World, 97
Brazil, 66, 196
breast, budding of, 142
Britain/British, 28, 71, 72, 73, 77, 87,
    128, 133, 151, 152, 176
  forces, 144
Bromley,D.B., 36
bullying, 119, 135
'bundling', 110
bureaucratic cultures, 142
Burney, F., 87

cake making (as a metaphor in loose
    interactionism), 49–50
Caldwell, B., 137
Camino Real, 187
'Carrots', 72
care in the community, 108
care-givers, 125–6
Carlile, K., 75
Carpenter, M., 153
Carroll, L., 31, 181
Carter, A., 33
'Catch 22', 181
causality
  as socially constructed, 47
  biological and social, 48
  strict, 48
celibacy, 107
Centre for the Child, 82
CCETSW, 80
Changing Childhood, 12
charity, 71, 81
chemistry, 29, *see also* cake making
  as a masculine metaphor, 49
  as a metaphor for development, 38
child, 15, 16, 51, 57, 59, 71, 88
  as a word, 56, 164

as childish, 36
as the subject of developmentalism, 37
-knowledge, 61, 71
-management, 71
mistreatment, 74, 191, *see also* child abuse
pre-school, 126
proto-, 56
taxonomy, 78
Child of the Deep, 21–4, 166
child abuse, 21, 22, 23, 29, 34, 72, 73, 78, 94, 157
cycle of, 173
disclosure, 170
discourses of, 164–76
discovered, 175
emotional, 21, 22, 29
perpetrators, 171
physical, 21, 22, 29
pursuit as abusive, 174
pursuit by professionals, 72, 73
ritual, 11, 21–3, 88
sexual, 21, 22, 29, 34, 75, 76, 88, 89, 163–81
child care workers, 73, 80
child concern, 68, 70–83
as discovery, 74
child emancipation, 80
child marriages, 63, 64
child prostitution, 6, 145, 164
child as client, 164
child protection, 75, 81, 90, 159, 187, 191, 192
child psychology, 80, *see also* developmental psychology
childhood, 5, 15, 16, 26, 51, 54, 57, 59, 106
as a game, 118
as a social construction, 54, 55, 64, 160
changing constitution of, 64, 66, 68
critical polytextual treatment, 160–1
end of, 33, 64, 141–61
experience, 94
heroic journey to adulthood, 34
historic, 54–69
invention of, 54, 65–9, 85
romantic, 21, 23, 27
sexuality, 62, 63, 109, 145, 160, 162–87

sexuality as childhood's end, 186
stages of, 65
Childhood in China, 137–9
'child love', 177
children/young people, 15, 16, 59, 61, 106
advocates, 82
as commodities, 68
destitute, 74, 196–7
girl–children, 33
new, 119–22
ombudsmen, 82;
and sex, 175–187
their drawings, *see* art, children's
their evidence, 35, 73
wanting to have children, 111
with learning disabilities, 100
working, 144
Children of the Dream, 128
Children Act 1908, 76; 1989, 68, 77, 111, 147, 177
Children's Crusade, 32, 158
children's exclusion
from enfranchisement, 145
from sexuality, 145
from utilisation of wealth, 145
children's homes, 78
Children's Legal Centre, 82
children's rights and entitlements, 71, 81–2, 192
children's shelters, 76
Children Without Childhood, 159
'child saving', 24, 72
child study movement, 88
child welfare, 71, 73, 191
'child within', 6, 174
its storying, 175
China (People's Republic of), 74, 136–9, 149, 174
Christianity, 27, 68, 92, 107, 113, 164
circumcision, 189
Clarke, I. F., 25
class, 58
Cleveland crisis, 75–6
clitorectomy, 114
clothing, children's, 59
CND, 155
co-education, 63
cognition, 102
cognitive–developmentalism, 87–8, 94–6

creation of child as cognitive alien, 143
cohabitation, 111
coition, *see* copulation
Colwell, M., 75
Coming of Age in Samoa, 105
commonsense knowledge, 15, 25, 59, 101
    as a warrant for developmentalism, 39
communes, 99
Company of Wolves, The, 186
competency, 4, 127, 147
    as location dependent, 129
    elective, 144
conception, 91, 111
'concern', 14
    about concern, 188–97
    as a postmodern ethic, 189
    fatigue, 179
    for the child, 185–7
    modernist concern criticised, 190
conscience, 98
consent, child's to sex, 177, *see also* age of consent
conservatism, 79, 110
conspiracy theory, 116, 122
conspiracy theory tale, 72
    of schooling, 132
constructionist, 64, *see also* social constructionist
contraception, *see* birth control
control–release tension, 165
Cooper, F., 148
copulation, 114, 115
Coram, T., 54
corporal punishment, 22, 68, 193, *see also* beating
cosmology, *see* world-view
crap detection, 134
'cretin', 100
critical polytextualism, 7, 12, 13, 14, 18, 24, 51, 54, 66, 83, 118, 120, 124, 126, 127, 132, 133, 149, 160, 161, 187, 188–97
cross-cultural confusions, 127
    studies of education criticised, 137–40, *see also* anthropology
cross-dressing, 22
cross-textuality, 155, *see also* intertextuality

Crucible, The, 179
cruelty, 66, 178, 188, *see also* child abuse
cultural
    analysis, 155
    archive, *see* archive
    determinism, 116, 119
    imperialism of USA, 149
    myth, 94
    regulation, 116
    sedimentation, 39
    tectonics, 156, *see also* tectonics
cultural competence, 89
    partiality of, 129, *see also*, competence
cultural medium, 40
    deconstruction of, 42, 44
cultural melodramatisation, 39
    of parenthood, 118
cultural wisdom, 34
    children and the craft of, 36
    transmission of, 34
culture
    children and, 107
    oral, 121
    pluralistic, 132
    thematic decomposition of the term, 41
culture-of-subjectivity, 187
Custody of Children Act 1891, 76, 77
Cutting, M., 196
'cycles of deprivation', 21

Daimon, 29
Darwin, C., 87, 151, 152
Day They Came to Arrest the Book, The, 141
Debbie (Little), 99
deconstruction, 10, 11, 12, 15, 31, 42, 65, 83, 100, 106, 130, 188
    radicalising, 59, 186, *see also* reconstruction
defloration, 114
delinquency, 30, 128, 149, 153–7, 195
    its discoursing, 156
    moral panic about, 155
depowerment, 33
Dennis the Menace, 30
dependency, 194–5
deschooling, 87, 133
desexualisation, 33

desparecidos, 196
DeTag,4
development
  as process, 53
  cognitive, 102
  deconstructed, 50, 51, *see also*
    developmentalism
developmental psychology, *see*
  psychology
developmentalism, 7, 14, 15, 37, 91,
    103, 137, 143
  as hegemony, 41
  as narratives, 52, 59
  as predicated upon image of the
    adult, 95
  as self-constructive, 50, 53
  deconstruction of, 42, 50, 52,
    85–104,126–7
developmentalists, 87, 150
  'American', 137
deviance, 48
dialogic, 13
  dialectics, 95
  false dialectics, 166
diaries, 35, 60
diaspora, 73
Dice Man, The, 92
Dickens, C., 25, 26, 153
Digby, K., 63
dilemmatics, 9
disability, 67
discourse, 11, 31, 57
  and materiality, 124
  child-abuse, 62, 165
  child-emancipatory, 81
  child rights, 81, 192
  cultural, 89
  family, 117
  humanistic, 100, 160
  on sexuality, 163
  permitting, 33
  pro-natal, 103
  right-wing, 59
  singularising, 104
discursive
  archive, 193
  flux, 20
Disney, W., 20
Dispossessed, The, 157
Disraeli, B., 152
divorce, 77

dogs,as a model for children, 43
doubt, 191
  in critical polytextualism, 191
Down's syndrome, 67
drawings, children's, *see art*, children's
dream babies, 16
dualisms, *see* binary divides
'dwarfism' (sic), 17
Dylan, B., 157
dyslexia, 11, 12
dystopia, 97, 99

earth mother, 116
ecology, cultural, 106
economics as child abuse, 196–7
education, 51
  adult, 131
  as a 'right', 130
ego-psychology, 92
Einstein, A., 76
Eloi, The, 25
emblematics, 20, 32
embodiment, 17, 43, 125, 127, 142
  first, 43
  and gender, 127
emotions, 162
enculturalisation, *see* socialisation
English Children in the Olden Time,
    62–4
Enlightenment, 54, 87, *see also* post-
    Enlightenment
entitlements, children's, 194
environment, 2, 26
  deconstruction of, 44–6
  deconstruction of 'good', 46, *see*
    also biosocial myth, heredity
episteme, 102
epistemology, 10, 15
  and power, 61
  continuity, 39
  social, 19
Equal Rights Law of 2030 (sic), 3
erotica, 62, *see also* pornography
essentialism, criticised, 36, 99
ethics, 13, 14, 18, 32
  of child protection, 178
  under postmodernism, 188–9
ethnocentrism, 71, 95, 127
ethnography, 14
ethology, 86
eugenics, 100, 105

Euripides, 66
Europe, 59, 65, 69, 85, 149, 197
Even the Rat was White, 97
Everly, K., 110
Exorcist, The, 29
extra-terrestrials, 180

'facts', 6, *see also* binary divides
faculty psychology, 101
fairy tales, 25, 92, 190
family, 116
    as site of reproduction, 107–9
    as subversive, 108
    authoritarian, 91
    dynamics, 121
    'ersatz', 79
    planning, *see also* birth control,
        112–13
    reconstituted, 121
famine, 67, 71
fanny, 176
fashion
    in developmentalism, 154
    in discourses of child concern, 75
Faust, 29, 40
Faust, B., 162, 184
feelings, *see* emotions
feminism, 10, 31, 54, 72, 175
    analytics, perspectives, theories, 75,
        104, 117, 132, 187, 189, 190
fertility motivation, 124
fiction, 25, 61, *see also* binary divides,
    history of fiction
fluoridation, 122
foeticide, 66
folk material, *see* commonsense
    knowledge
Foster, J., 185
Foucault, M., 10, 20, 162, 163, 184
foundationals, 127
Francis Xavier, St, 98
free market, 140
free-schooling, 134
Freud, A., 93
Freud, S., 13, 88–93, 101, 108, 174, 181
Freudian theory, 86, 88, 165, *see also*
    psychoanalysis
Froebel, 152

Gandhi, Mahatma, 29
Garden of Eden, 92

gaze, 11, 20, 24, 30, 43, 44, 47, 48, 58,
    59, 60, 71, 74, 75, 84, 90, 99, 101,
    103, 109, 126, 132, 189, 190, 194
    adult, 35
    child dependency, 194
    ethical, 21
    historical visual, 59
    international, 82
    medical, 21, 122
    moral, 83
    on sexuality and the child, 166
    philanthropic, 54, 80
    professionalised, 71, 80
    puritan, 86
    reformatory, 80
gender, 59, 60
    divides, 30, 48, 111, 142
genes, 26
    selfish, 106
genetic epistomology, 94
genetics, 26
    deconstruction of, 44
genocide, 79
girls, *see* children
Gillick judgment, 146
Giton, 62
'globalisation of childhood',
    85
globalisation of child mistreatment,
    197
gnomics, 38, 39, 59, 71, 120
gods
    Hermes and Aphrodite, 114
    lares and *penates*, 85, 104
'golden age', 129, 178
Golding, W., 158
Gould, S. J., 59, 100
Gramsci, A., 11
Grand Narrative, 102
    developmental, decay of, 104
    modernisitic criticised, 190
    scientific, decay of, 103
Grand Theory, 9
Grange Hill, 30
Great Expectations, 26
Green politics, 103
Grimm, Brothers, 33, 34
groping prose, 176
g-string, 114
Guineapig, The, 26
    gym-slip mother', 2

HAL, 26
Hansel and Gretel, 34
harm warrant, and sexual abuse, 163–6
Haskell, M., 157
Havero, M., 147
head lice, 122
hegemony, 41, 51, 72, 103
    Catholic, 186
Henry VII, 59
heridity, 2, *see also* biosocial myth, environment
Hermaphroditus, 114
hermeneutics, 89
Hentoff, N. 141
*her*story, 54
heterosexuality, 91, 143
Hiawatha's Photographing, 181
Higgs, M., 168
history, *see* social history
history of childhood, 54, 56
    as civilising process, 66
Hitler, A., 93, 105
HIV, 4, 110, 134, 160
Hobbes, 86
Holmes, O.W., 148
holocaust, 128
homosexuality, 110, 112, 114, 134, 143
    as developmentally theorised, 48
    reconstituted by the APA, 48
honeymoon, 114
hormones, 150
horrors, 29, 196
Huckleberry Finn, vii, 141
'human nature', 86
human sciences, 13
humanism, 7
Hutterites, *see* Amish
hymen, 114
hyperactivity, 138
hyper-real, 35
hypothetical constructs, nature and nurture as, 39, 44

Ibañez, T., 7, 9, 102
iconoclasm, 58
iconography, 57
    of the child, 181–4
id, 90
identity, 20, 21, 78
    elective construction of, 33

-politics, 78
-story, 124
ideology, 19, 83, 95
If, 135
IQ, 1, 15, 16, 17, 45, 47, 48, 100, 105
images, *see* iconography, representations
immigrants, 79
immunisation, 122
impotence, 113
incest, 64, 164
India, 74
indoctrination, 136
infanticide, 66
infantiolatry, 103
infertility, 113
information processing approach, 101–2
inheritance (of property), 67
innocence, 27, 28, 30
    female, 113
Innocents, The, 186
institutional care, 73
Intafada, 196
intelligence, Piagetian, 94–6
intelligence, psychometric, *see* IQ
interactionalism, loose, 47–8
intertextuality, 13, 28, 73
    over children and sex, 166–74
ironism, 14, *see also* liberal-ironist
Israel, 82, 128
Ives, R., 109

Jacobson, L., 47
Japan, 5, 74
Jenkins, S., 80
Jesus, 6, 26
    baby, 72
Jews, 128, 142
Juliet, 109
Jung, C. G., 29
juvenile delinquency, *see* delinquency
Juvenile Delinquents, their Condition and Treatment, 153
juvenile courts, 153
Juvies, The, 155

Kafka, F., 93
Kagan, J., 137
Kent, C., 26
Kenwood, H., 163

Kessler, S. 176
kibbutzim, 128, 158
kidnap, 71
Kingsley, C., 26
Kitchener of Kartoum, Lord, 196
Kitzinger, C., 10, 11, 59, 82, 188
Kitzinger, J., 186
knowingness, 27
knowledge
    architects of, 10
    creation, 8
    mongering, 96
    /power synarchy, 85
    sameness in, 133
'knowledging', 7, 15, 18, 19, 51, 108,
    see also 'storying'
Korezak, J., 72

language, 10
    acquisition, 126
    and thought, 57
    game, 41, 46, 64, 88, 90, 96, 101,
    116, 176
law, and the child, 73, 76, 146, see also
    Children Act
Lean, D., 108
learning
    as a loose interactional concept, 48
    and behaviourism, 96–100
    disabilities, 100
Lefanu, S., 5
Le Guin, U., 5, 128
lesbianism, 4, 112
Lessing, D., 5, 158
leuchorrhea, 169
liberal democracies, 151
liberalism/liberal-humanism, 59, 95,
    100, 127, 152, 165, 188
liberal-ironist, 13, 188
liberal utopia, 13
libido, 107
life-games, 117
life-story tracking, 124–7
    as alternative to determinism, 124–
    5
'little adult', 65
Little Red Riding Hood, 33
'living in sin', 111
living together, 111, 160
location, 32, 61, 124
    biographic, 90

sexual, 33
Locke, J., 80, 86, 101
Lolita, 20, 188
Longfellow, 181
long-term memory, 102
Lord of the Flies, 158
love, romantic, 110
Love Child, 30
Luckmann, T., 10, 11, 43, 116, 191

Macbeth Murder Mystery, The, 60
magic, 185
'mal de mere' syndrome, 119
Mann, J.S., 28
Mao Tse-Tung, 137
march of civilisation tale, 59, 72
Mariolatry, 31, 35
market forces, 9
marriage, popular, 109, see also living
    together
Marxism, 10, 90, 117, 132
    Marxism–Leninism, 140
masonry of the mature, 146
Masson, Jeffrey, 89, 92, 93
masturbation, 89, 114, 115, 164
    and insanity, 164
    variously discoursed, 165
material frame, 40
    deconstruction of, 42
maternal deprivation, 96
Matthew, St, 45
maturation, 36
Mead, M., 79, 105, 142, 149
meanings, 18
medicine, 51
Mediterranean, 142
Mein Kampf, 160, see also Hitler, A.
melodramatic 'hot spots', 195
Memoirs of a Survivor, The, 158
memory, short-term, 102
men
    as the dangerous sex, 31
    as mankind, 55, 58
    and sex, 33
    new, see new men
menstruation taboo, 115
mental age, 100, see also IQ
meta-gaze, 192
meta-narrative, 9, 120
    feminist, 104
metaphor, 38, 57, 58

root, 13
  science as, 38
meta-story, 64
metatheory, 91
Middle Ages, 27, 58, 67, 68
  their psychology, 101
Miller, Alice, 93, 94, 171, 175
Miller, Arthur, 179
mill girls, 131
minimum wage, 144
misogyny, 171
mods, 139
modernism/modernity, 7, 9, 10, 15, 51,
  102, 103, 120, 140, 162, 165, 166
molecular theory, 39, *see also*
  chemistry
molestation 22, *see also* child abuse,
  sexual
moments, of critical polytextualism,
  11
monkeys, 17, 50, 165
  sex-crazed (as id), 91
Montessori, 80
moral crusade, 190
moral education, 34
moral panic, 174
morals, *see* ethics
More, T., 60
Morlocks, 25
Morss, J.R . . . 38, 41, 42, 51, 104, 151
mothers, *see 'mal de mere'* syndrome
Mount, F., 58, 59, 108, 116
Mozart, 93
Mubti, 142
Mulkay, M., 10, 19, 20
multi-culturality, 128
Muria, 158
Musgrave, P.W., 148, 151
myths, 25, 65
  of the family, 116

Nabokov, V., 20, 188
Naples, 157
narrative, 13, 21, 60, 75, 90
  as analytic, 52
  as root metaphor, 13
  counter-, 106, 110
  mechanisms, new, 179
  singularisation, 76
naturalness, 148
nature, 25

nativist, 105
nature–nurture, 1, 37, 49, 51, 89,
  101, 127
non-commensurability of
  knowledges of, 37
  problematic, 88
naughty, 30
  boys, 30
  girls, 30
Naughty Girls, The, 30
NAYPIC, 82
neglect, 66, 178, *see also* child abuse
needs, children's, 80, 82
Neighbours, 6, 118
Nema, 1–7, 30
neo-Marxism, 11, *see also* Marxism
neonate, 125, *see also* baby
Newcastle Report, 152
new children, 120–3
New England Primer, The, 86
new men, 50, 115
new right, 194
nineteenth century and reform, 151
nomic order, 71
North America, 59, 74, 92, 96, *see also*
  United States
  as the foundational norm, 149, 153
Nostradamus, 89
novels, 61, *see also* fiction
NSPCC, 76, 188
nuclear war, 70
nudity, children's, 182–3
nurture, 25

oblation, 67, 107
observation, 17, 18
Odoratus Sexualis, 29
Oedipus Rex, 25, 118, 164
'olders', 5
Oliver Twist, 26, 153, 158
Onan, 106
  onanism, 172
ontology, 15
operants, 98
operant subjectivity, 98
oral culture, children's, 34
Oranges Are Not the Only Fruit, 27
orphanage, 80
orphanhood, 78
orthodontics, 122
Orwell, G., 97

Oxfam, 72

Pacific, the, 21
  Rim, 197
paedology, 73
paedophiles, 31, 164, 179, 185
Pannychis, 62
parables, 61
  as instruction, 33
parental
  affection, 65–6
  custody,care and control, 77
  responsibilities, 68
  rights, 68, 77, 79, 115
parenthood/parentings/parents
  abusive, 117
  angst, 159
  before birth, 123
  'good enough', 80
  priming young people for, 110
  surrogate, 113
passing, as adult, 35
past, non-singularity of, 133
patriarchy, 117, 164, 186, 190, *see also*
  feminism
Pavlov, 98
peer group, 4
Pekow, C., 73
Perfume, 29
perinatal mortality, 125
persons/personhood, 84
  as gained through sexuality, 161
Peter Pan, 27
Petronius, 61–2
petting, 149
Phares, T., 86
pheremones, 29
philanthropy, 73
Phillipines, 197
photography, 87, 182
Piaget, J., 94–6
Picard, P.M., 150
pindown, 194–5
place[ment], 120, *see also* location
plausibility, 14
  structures, 116
play (for sex play *see* sex)
PLU, 45
policing of youth, 149
politics, 23
  and children, 32

and child concern, 197
  Green, 103
polytextualism, *see* critical
  polytextualism
popular marriage, *see* marriage,
  popular
popular understandings, *see*
  commonsense knowledge
pornography, 62, 184
positivism, 64
post-Enlightenment project, 7
Postman, N., 134
postmodernism/postmodernity, 9–11,
  20, 24, 31, 35, 60, 78, 106, 121,
  152, 188
post-structuralism, 7, 60, 96
potty training, 19
poverty, 66
power
  and children, 192
  and knowledge, 8, 75
  challenging, 82
precocity, 148
  sexual, 176
prefects, 135
pregnancy, 4, 118, 122, 129, 160
  for adoption, 124
pre-schoolers, 135
Prevention of Cruelty to Children Act
  1889, 76
primogeniture, 67
Prince and the Pauper, 25
prodigies, 35, 145, *see also*
  'unchildren'
progress, 55, 59, *see also* development
  in critical polytextualism, 193
pro-natalism, 104
protectionism, beyond, 185
proto-children, 56
'psy-complex', 19, 51
psyche, 37
psychiatry, 51, 71
psychoanalysis, 6, 23, 88–94
psychobabble, 97
psycho-chemistry, 38
psychodynamics, 23, 88–94
  hydraulic metaphor, 101
psychohistory, 66
psychologist(s), 8
  developmental, 18, 71
psychology, 37, 51

developmental, 6, 27, 37, 108, 109
ego, 92
faculty, 101
North Americanisation of, 96
Psychology of Adolescence, 154
psycho-social crisis, 148
psychotherapy, 88
puberty, 142
  iconography, 184
  rites and rituals, 142
public relations, 75
Public Schools, 133, 136, 148
  Winchester, 136
pupilage, 64, 142
puritanism, 27, 86
Pygmalion in the Classroom, 47

Quartilla, 62
'quick-fix', rejected, 195

racism, 100
radicalism, 80, 92
rape, 178, 179
reading, 6, 20, 24, 33
readings
  alternating, 132   alternative, 65,
  191
'real', the, 18
  and realism, 40
recall, 102
recapitulation, 88
recoding, 59
reconstruction, 83, 166
reflexivity, 11, 61, 126
Reform Schools, 152
*Reformatory Schools for Children of
  the Perishing and Dangerous
  Classes and for Juvenile
  Offenders,* 153
reification, 12, 186
relationship, social rules governing,
  112
relativism, 13
relativity effect, 76
Renaissance canon law, 109
representation
  of children, 20, 33, 58, 59, 65, 181–7
  of the family, 117
re-presentation, 18
representational labour, 8
repression, 91, 92

repression/liberation, and discoursing
  sexuality, 163
reproduction, 107–10
residential care, 78
retrieval process, 102
Richards, M.P.M., 48–50
right-wing discourse, 59
  historians, 58
rights
  children, 82, 84
  children's sexual, 99
Rights of Man, The, 160
risk, 118
rite of passage, 112, 114
ritual abuse, *see* child abuse, sexual
road movies, 23
rockers, 139
Rogers, R.S., 34, 36, 165, *see* also
  Stainton Rogers, R.
Rolling Stones, 139
Romans, 58, 61, 65, 67, 109, 164
Romeo, 109
Romulus and Remus, 26
Rorty, R., 10, 11, 13, 188, 189
Rose, N.,19, 37, 90
Rose, S., 42, 49, 59, 100, 101
Rosen, R.D., 93, 175
Rousseau, J.J., 25, 27, 80, 86, 95, 148

Sacre du Printemps, 27
St Augustine of Hippo, 27
St Joan, 5
St Trinian's, 30
St Paul, 89
Salem, 28
Samoa, 142, 149
San Francisco, 21
Sapir–Whorf hypothesis, 57
Satanism, 28
SATs, 16
Scheherazade, 115
school
  as power–structure, 135
  phobia, 12
  refusing, 123
schools
  boarding, 60, *see also* Public
    Schools
  exploitative and exploited, 134
  homogenising and heterogenising,
    132

monastic, 107
politics of, 133
reactive and subversive, 135
reproductive and innovatory, 133
schooling, 35, 129–40
schooling-working tension, 131
Schorsch, A., 57, 58, 60, 65
science, 8, 39
challenged, 102
march of, 87
rhetoric of, 93
science fiction, 5, 147
ideology of scientism, 37
Scotland, 142, 143
Scott, J. P., 42-5
Secret Diary of Adrian Mole Aged 13, 35
Secret Diary of Laura Palmer, 35
seduction theory, 88, 94
seedbed metaphor
deconstruction of, 46, *see also* agrarian metaphor
segmentation, 121
'selfish teens', 109
self-tracking, 126
semiotics, 11
sex, 22, 28
anal, 115
education, 176
non-penetrative, 107, 110, 113
play, 31
Sex Education: The Erroneous Zone, 176
sexology, 98, 113
sexual
abuse *see* child abuse; *see also* childhood sexuality
assault, 179
development (precocious), 6, 176
egalitarianism, 122
opportunities, 114
relationships, 2
release, 28
sexually transmitted diseases, 122
vocabulary, 176
sexualisation, 31
as sexual socialisation, 113
sexuality, 33
Shakers, 107
Shakespeare, 20, 109, 136
children in, 63

Shotter, J., 6, 11, 13, 14
Shunamitism, 29
signification, 18, 27, 176
sinfulness, 27
Skinner, B.F., 25, 97, 98
slavery, 197
social anthropology, 21
social being, 123
social 'chartism', 80
social class, 109, 141
dissensus, 136
social construction, 11, 12, 116
of knowledge, 96
links to radical behaviourism, 99
social evolution, 37, 59
social history, 18, 21, 60, 61-4
as *her*story, 54
social hygienism, 152
socialisation, 7, 26, 37, 38, 113, 127, 129
agents of 123
as a myth, 26
as a story, 39
natural experiments in, 128
primary, 125
process, 51
secondary, 130
unwarranted faith in, 140
social policy, 77, 195
social sedimentation, 6, 29
social tectonics, 121
social workers, 90
socio-biology, 106
sociology, 51
of childhood, 103
of knowledge, 11
of the family, 124
specialness of sex, 175-81
children and enjoyment, 178
thought experiment upon, 180
Stainton Rogers, R., 52, 114, 135, 165
Stainton Rogers, W., 52, 54, 135, 167, 175, 178, 181
Stalin, 105
Stalky and Co, 148
Stanford-Binet test, 100
Stephen of Cloyes, 32
step-parents, 79
sterilisation, 145
'Stitches', 21

story, 6, 7, 26, 115, 122, 157, *see also* narrative
-making, 13
peddling, 19
-telling, 13
'storying', 19, *see also* 'knowledging'
multiply storied, 75
storied into being, 34
Stravinsky, I., 27
Strelitz, Z., 123
structuralism, 32, 95, 99
structural-functionalism, 81, 109
student dorm, 114
subjectivity, 35
Summerhill, 134
Summer of '42, 186
Summit, R., 173
super-ego, 90
Superman, 26
surrogate parenthood, 113
Svenson, A., 22, 23
Swallows and Amazons, 27
Sweden, 133
Sylvie and Bruno, 182
symbolic-interactionism, 103

taboo, over child sex, 177
Taine, 87
Tales of Fifteen, 148
'Tales of Warning', 33
Tardieu, 89
Tarzan, 26
tectonics, 83, 121, 156, 179, 192, 195
teenagers, 35, *see also* adolescents
teleology, 190
Temple, C., 148
Terman, L., 100, 149
text, 6, 20, 24, 31, 60, 65
and texts, 59
of identity, 118
textual disputation, 86
textuality, 13, 187
Thatcherism, 77, 133
Third World, 71, 196
thought experiment, 30
Thurber, J., 60
Teidemann, Do, 87
Time Machine, The, 25
time travel, 5
'Todd', 6
Tomalin, C., 59, 60, 86

Tom Brown's Schooldays, 30, 148
Tom Sawyer, 23, 141
total environments, 100
institutions as, 135
Townsend, P., 144, 196, 197
toys, 56, 63
traditionalism, 78-9
traits, 16, 17, 46
transdisciplinarity, 14
transformation, 42, 45-7
translation, 60
Trantor, M., 168, 169, 170, 172
trophy wife, 112
truancy, 134
trust bandits, 191
truth, 38
its mandates and regimes, 38, 65, 173
Twain, M.,vii, 13, 25, 29, 141
Twain (otherwise Clements), S., 35
Twin Oaks, 99
Twin Peaks, 35
twins, 67
Two Worlds of Childhood: USA and USSR, 139-40

'unchildren', 32, 35
United Kingdom, *see* Britain
United Nations, 72
United States, 28, 86, 87, 88, 96, 98, 99, 100, 127, 128, 139, 140, 143, 148, 153, 197
USSR, 97, 139-40
utopianism, 99, 134, 190

Venice, 58, 59
Victorian era, 6, 28, 63, 163
virginity, 110, 113
virgins and whores, 184
visceral clutch, 162, 177
Vizard, E., 168, 169, 170, 172
voice, 60
and intertextuality, 166
voices, 59, 71, 78, 80
voicing, 60
vulvovaginitis, 169

Walden Two, 25, 99
Walkerdine, V., 27, 50, 135, 184, 185
Wall, The, 135
Walling, W.H., 152, 166-74

discourse reflected and refracted, 173-4
wanker, 117, 196
wanted children, 121
warrants
  of female immunity, 32, 93
  of feminist uniqueness, 189
  of science, 102
  over the child and sex, 166
Water Babies, The, 26
Waterland, vii
Weingartner, C., 134
welfare, 108
  state, 77
  welfarism, 133
Welfarist Protectionism, 80
Wells, H.G., 25
Wild Boy of Aveyron, 26
Wilmott, Earl of Rochester, 65
Winn, M., 144, 159, 160, 172
Winterson, J., 27
witchcraft, 28
  trials, 28
Wittgenstein, L., 10, 41
Woodstock, 165
Wollstoncraft, M., 87
wolves, 33

Woman at the Edge of Time, 31
women 54
  and children, 31, 54
Wordsworth, W., 27
working
  ideas, 41
  tales, 117
Worrell, M., 175
World Wars, 105
  One, and children, 144
  Two, and children, 158
world-view, 59, 84, 90, 136

x-rays, 43

young, the, 123, 134
  as raw material of schooling, 134
  understandings of, 38
young people/persons, *see*
  adolescents, children, the young,
  youth
Young Pioneers, 139
youth, 34
  culture, 110

Zeitgeist, 8, 172
Zero de Conduit, 135